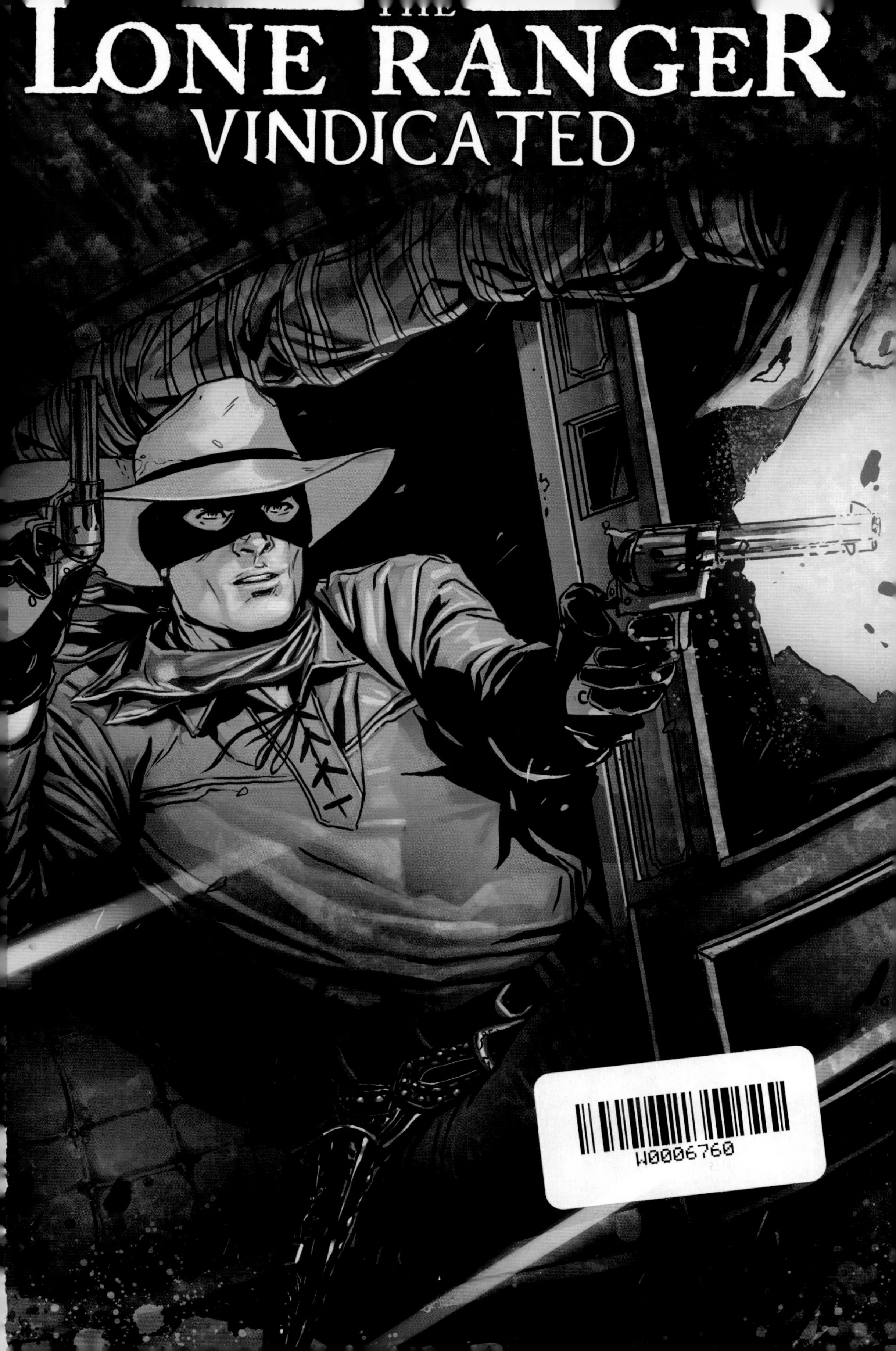
THE
LONE RANGER
VINDICATED

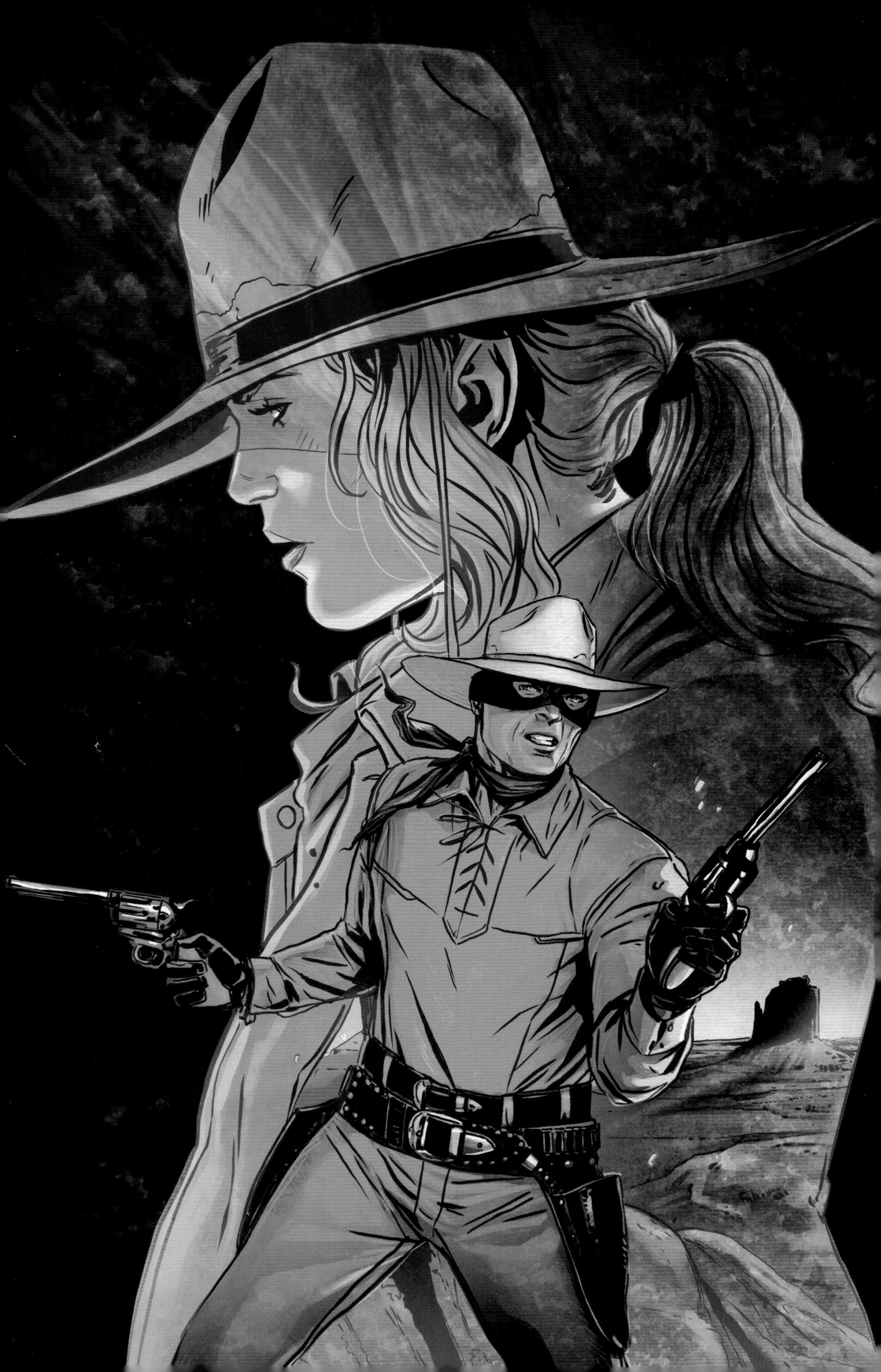

THE LONE RANGER
VINDICATED

WRITTEN BY
JUSTIN GRAY

ART BY
REY VILLEGAS

COLORS BY
MORGAN HICKMAN

LETTERS BY
SIMON BOWLAND

COLLECTION COVER BY
JOHN CASSADAY

COLLECTION COVER COLORS BY
IVAN NUNES

COLLECTION DESIGN BY
KATIE HIDALGO

SPECIAL THANKS TO SCOTT SHILLET, COLIN MCLAUGHLIN, AND DAMIEN TROMEL

THIS VOLUME COLLECTS ISSUES 1-4 OF THE LONE RANGER: VINDICATED BY DYNAMITE ENTERTAINMENT.

ck Barrucci, CEO / Publisher
an Collado, President / COO

e Rybandt, Senior Editor
nnah Elder, Associate Editor

son Ullmeyer, Design Director
tie Hidalgo, Graphic Designer
eoff Harkins, Graphic Designer
ris Caniano, Digital Associate
chel Kilbury, Digital Assistant

ch Young, Director Business Development
ith Davidsen, Marketing Manager
vin Pearl, Sales Associate

Online at www.DYNAMITE.com
On Twitter @dynamitecomics
On Facebook /Dynamitecomics
On YouTube /Dynamitecomics

ISBN-10: 1-60690-699-2   ISBN-13: 978-1-60690-699-6   First Printing   10 9 8 7 6 5 4 3 2

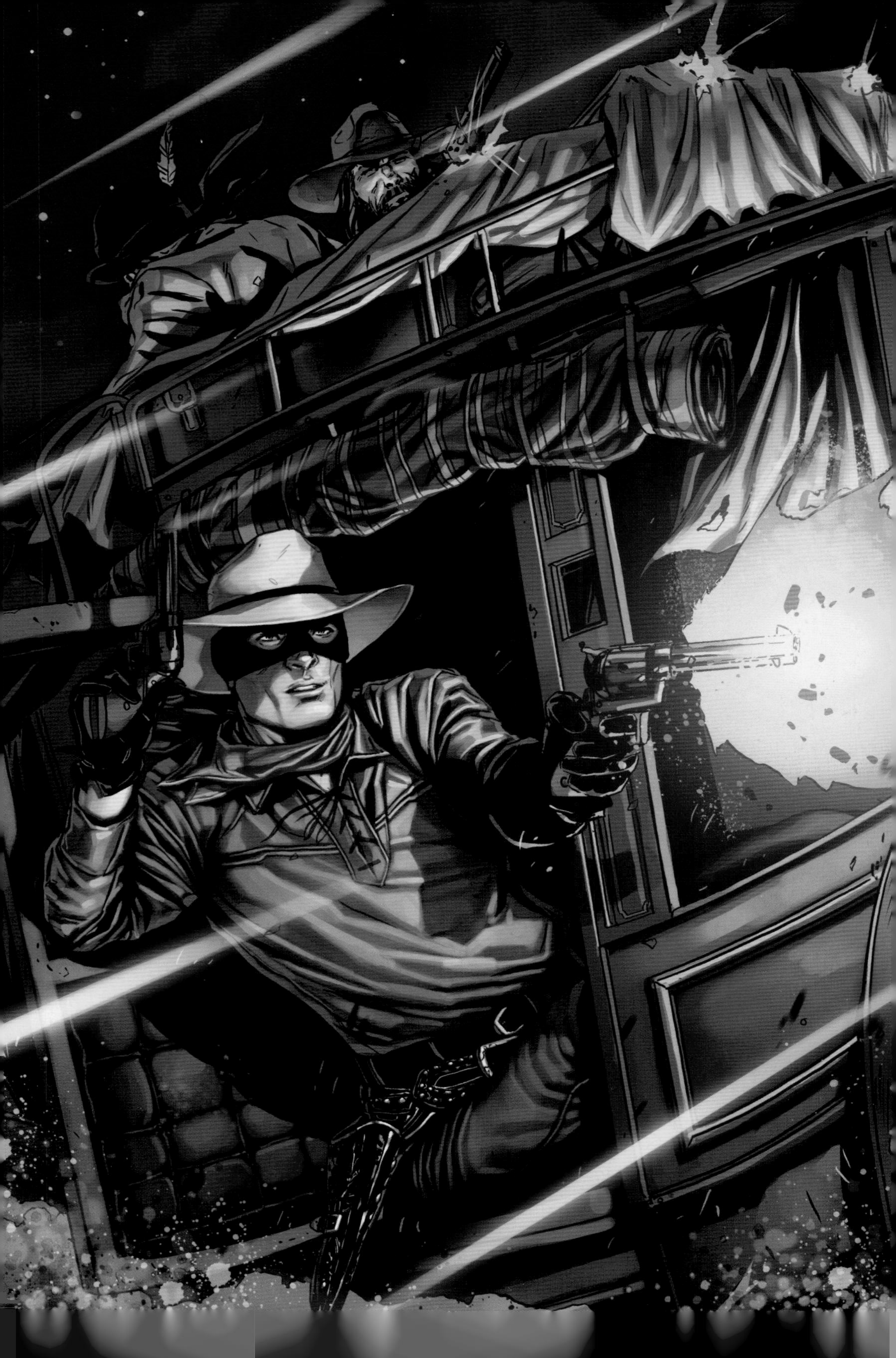

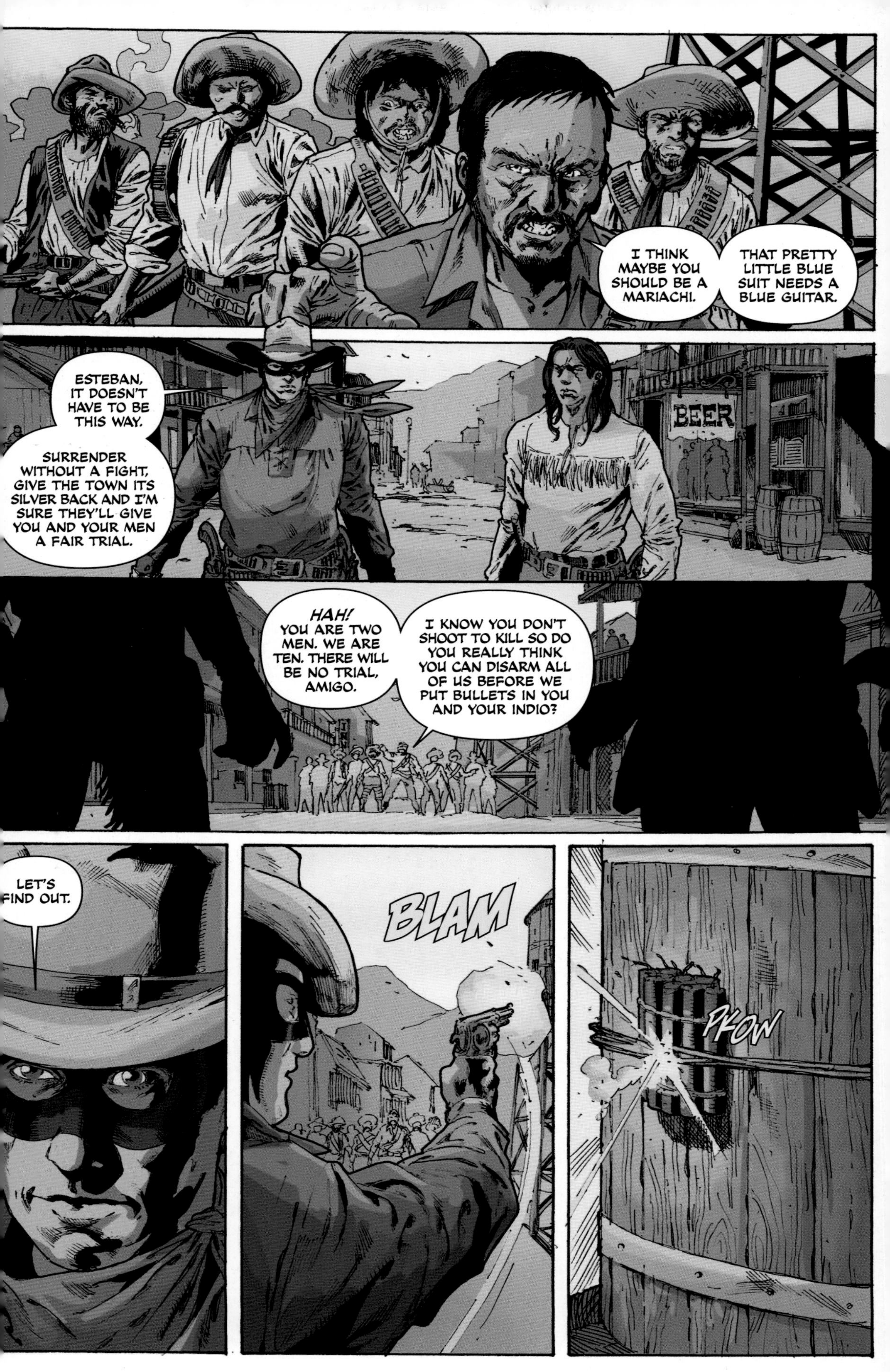

I THINK MAYBE YOU SHOULD BE A MARIACHI.
THAT PRETTY LITTLE BLUE SUIT NEEDS A BLUE GUITAR.
ESTEBAN, IT DOESN'T HAVE TO BE THIS WAY.
SURRENDER WITHOUT A FIGHT, GIVE THE TOWN ITS SILVER BACK AND I'M SURE THEY'LL GIVE YOU AND YOUR MEN A FAIR TRIAL.
BEER
HAH! YOU ARE TWO MEN. WE ARE TEN. THERE WILL BE NO TRIAL, AMIGO.
I KNOW YOU DON'T SHOOT TO KILL SO DO YOU REALLY THINK YOU CAN DISARM ALL OF US BEFORE WE PUT BULLETS IN YOU AND YOUR INDIO?
LET'S FIND OUT.
BLAM
PKOW

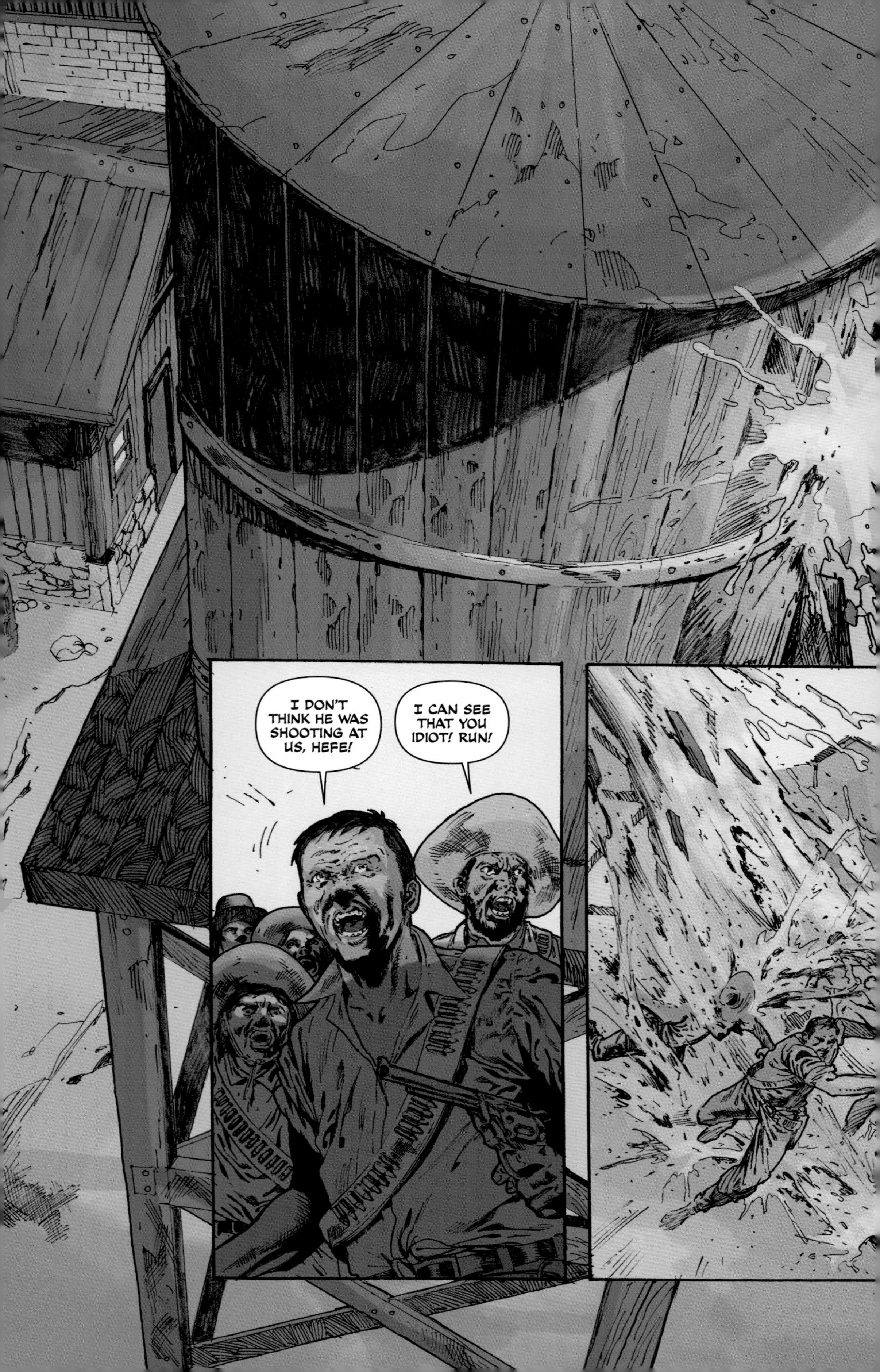
I DON'T THINK HE WAS SHOOTING AT US, HEFE!
I CAN SEE THAT YOU IDIOT! RUN!

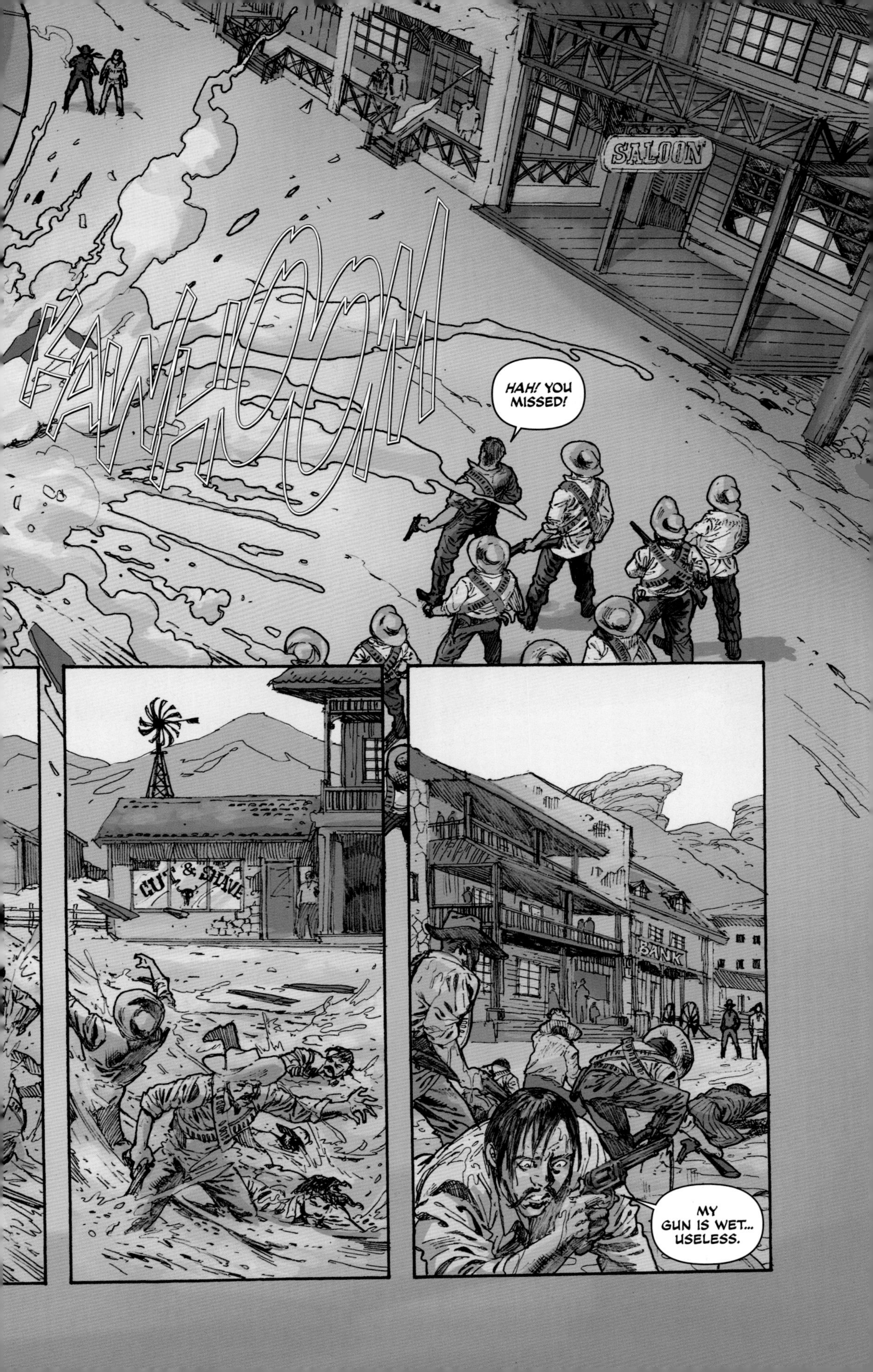
SALOON
KAWHOOM
HAH! YOU MISSED!
CUT & SHAVE
BANK
MY GUN IS WET... USELESS.

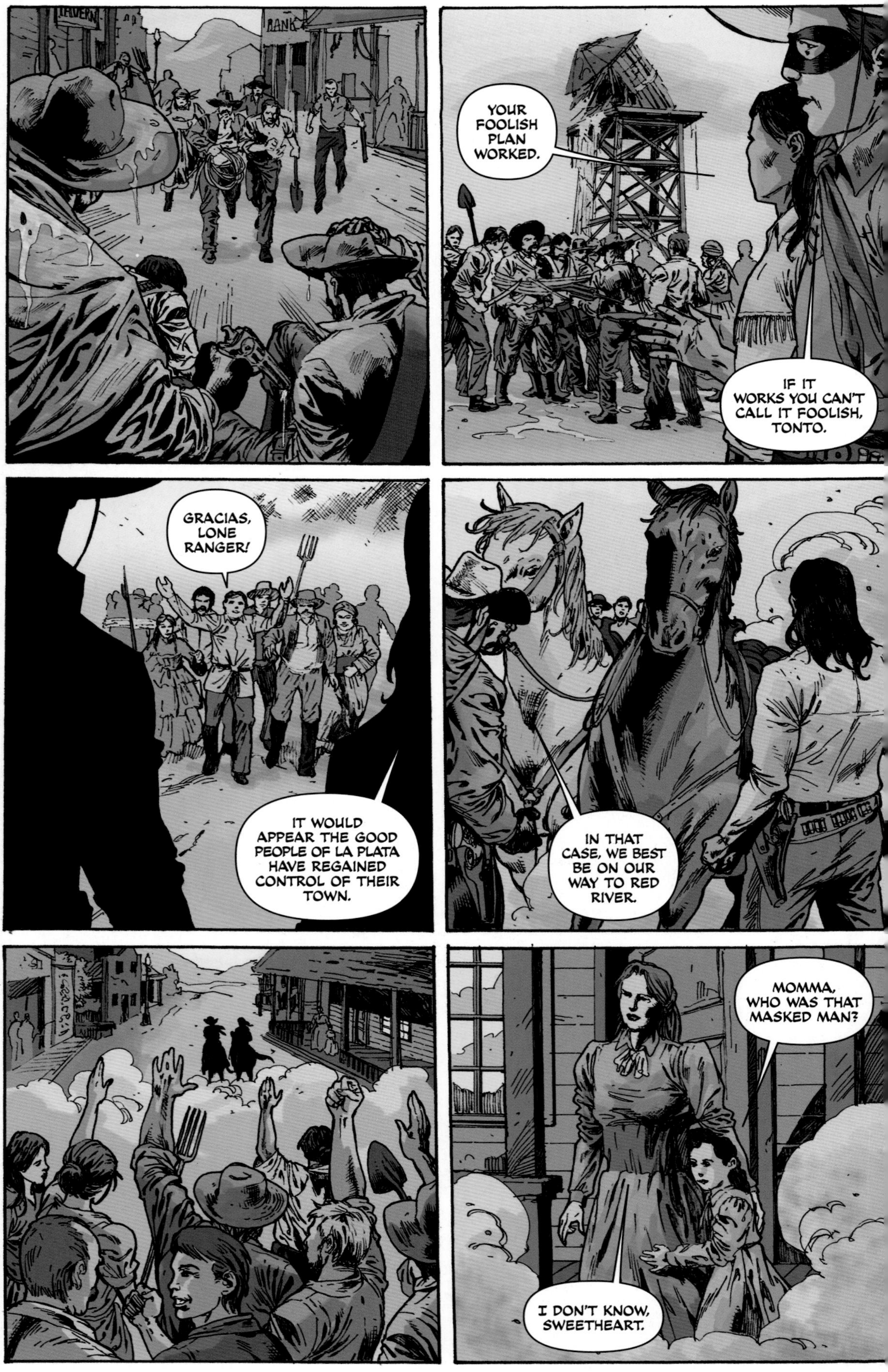
TAVERN
BANK
YOUR FOOLISH PLAN WORKED.
IF IT WORKS YOU CAN'T CALL IT FOOLISH, TONTO.
GRACIAS, LONE RANGER!
IT WOULD APPEAR THE GOOD PEOPLE OF LA PLATA HAVE REGAINED CONTROL OF THEIR TOWN.
IN THAT CASE, WE BEST BE ON OUR WAY TO RED RIVER.
MOMMA, WHO WAS THAT MASKED MAN?
I DON'T KNOW, SWEETHEART.

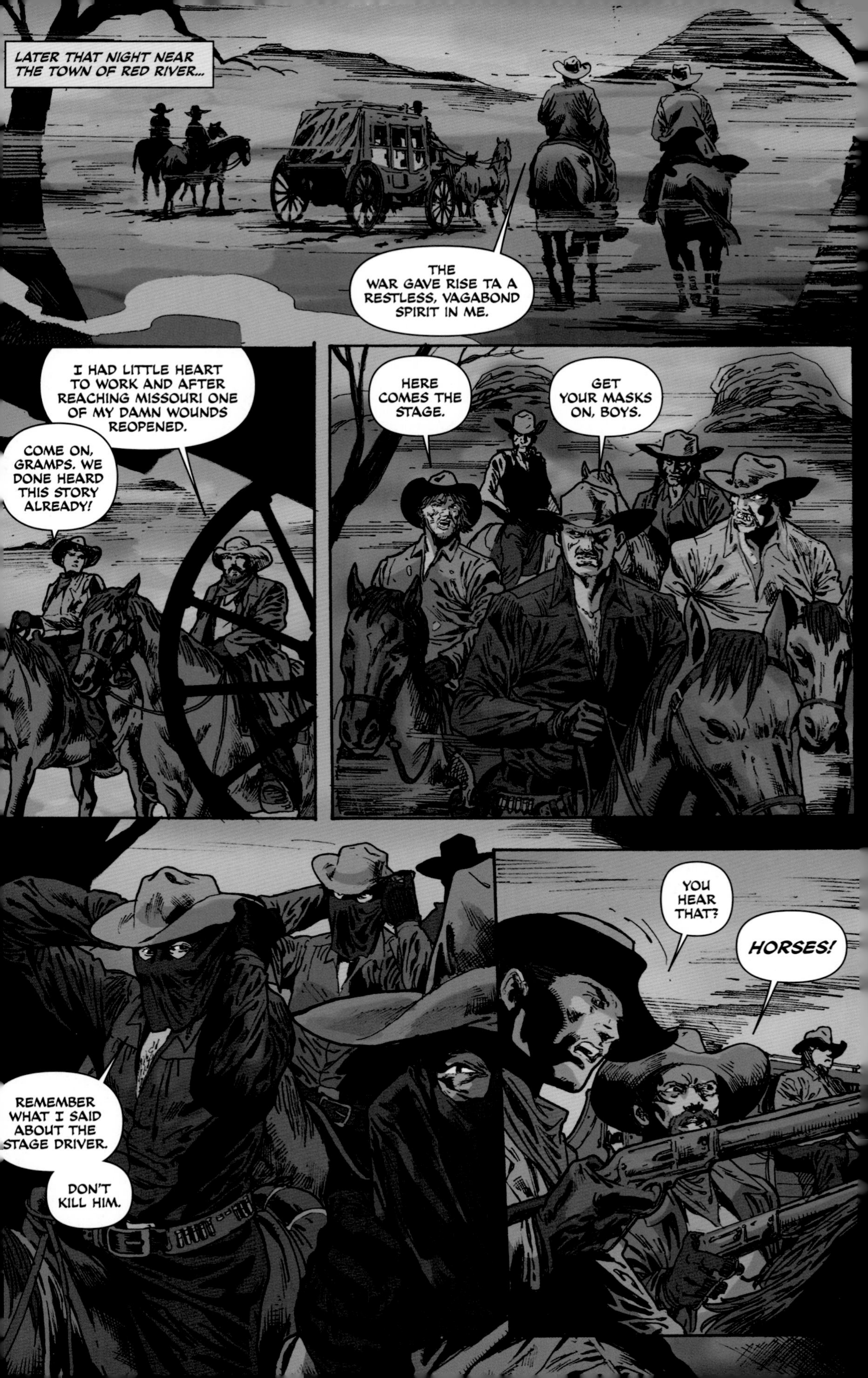
LATER THAT NIGHT NEAR THE TOWN OF RED RIVER...
THE WAR GAVE RISE TA A RESTLESS, VAGABOND SPIRIT IN ME.
I HAD LITTLE HEART TO WORK AND AFTER REACHING MISSOURI ONE OF MY DAMN WOUNDS REOPENED.
COME ON, GRAMPS. WE DONE HEARD THIS STORY ALREADY!
HERE COMES THE STAGE.
GET YOUR MASKS ON, BOYS.
REMEMBER WHAT I SAID ABOUT THE STAGE DRIVER.
DON'T KILL HIM.
YOU HEAR THAT?
HORSES!

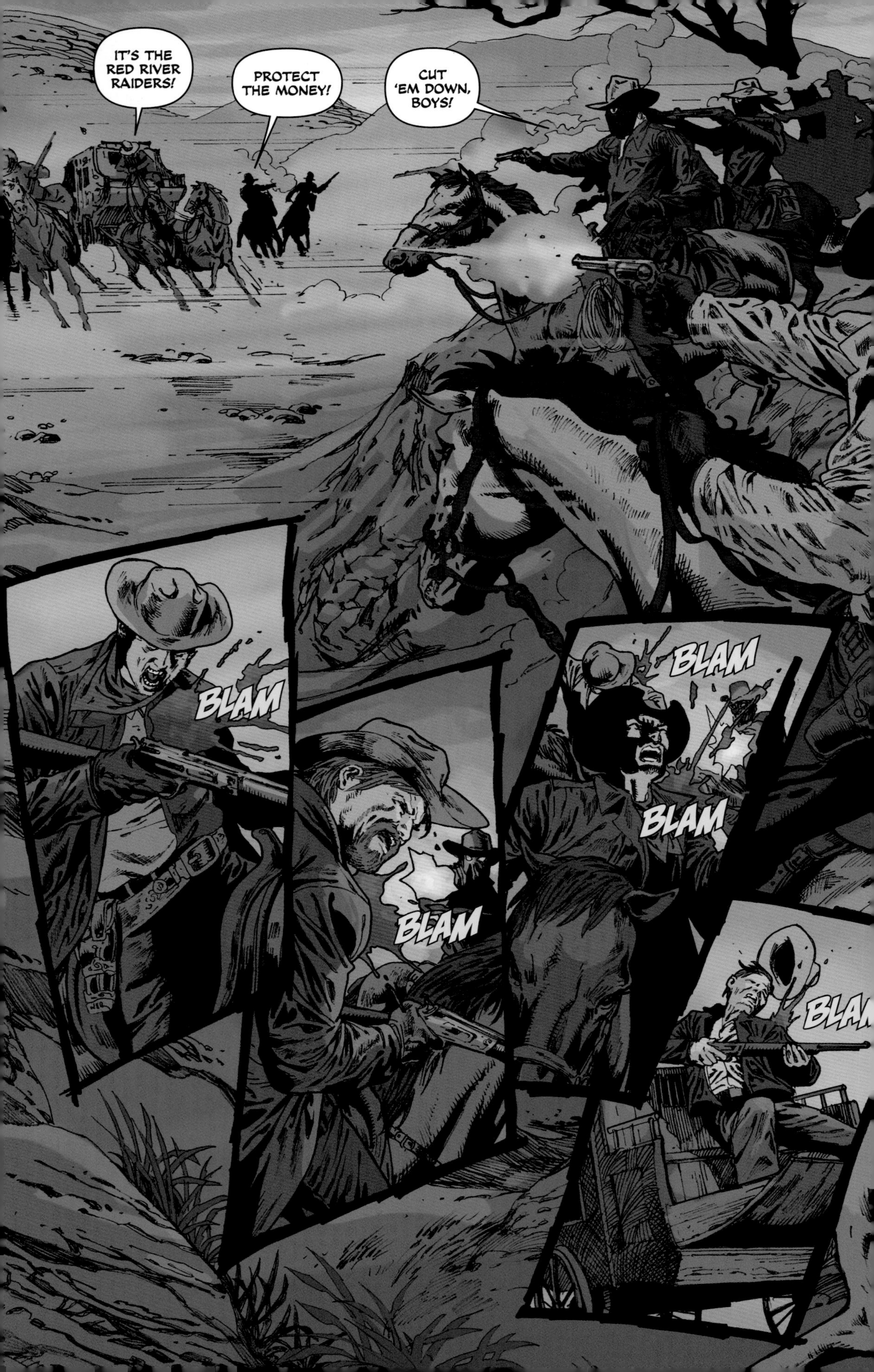
IT'S THE RED RIVER RAIDERS!
PROTECT THE MONEY!
CUT 'EM DOWN, BOYS!
BLAM
BLAM
BLAM
BLAM
BLAM

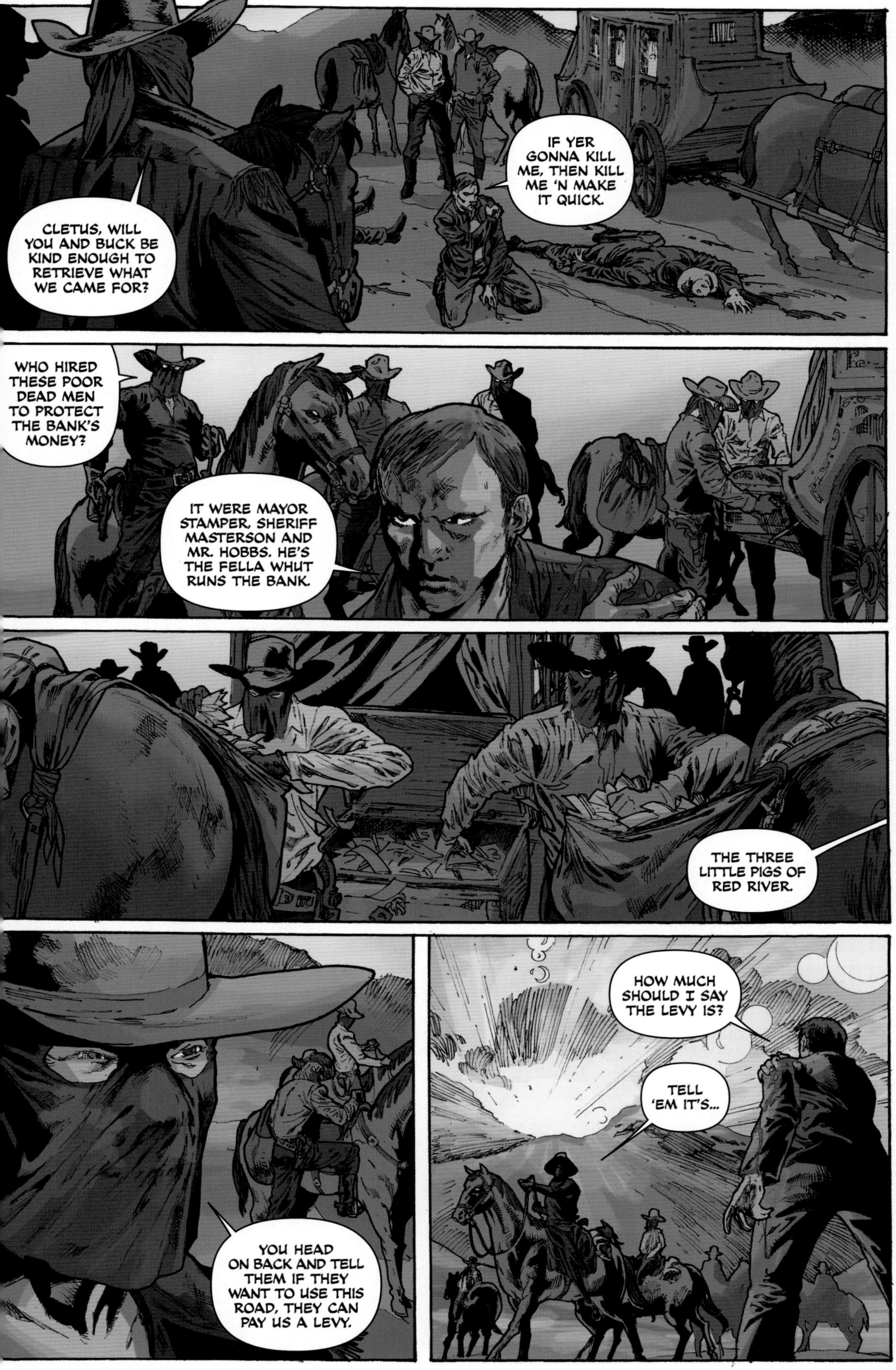

IF YER GONNA KILL ME, THEN KILL ME 'N MAKE IT QUICK.
CLETUS, WILL YOU AND BUCK BE KIND ENOUGH TO RETRIEVE WHAT WE CAME FOR?
WHO HIRED THESE POOR DEAD MEN TO PROTECT THE BANK'S MONEY?
IT WERE MAYOR STAMPER, SHERIFF MASTERSON AND MR. HOBBS. HE'S THE FELLA WHUT RUNS THE BANK.
THE THREE LITTLE PIGS OF RED RIVER.
YOU HEAD ON BACK AND TELL THEM IF THEY WANT TO USE THIS ROAD, THEY CAN PAY US A LEVY.
HOW MUCH SHOULD I SAY THE LEVY IS?
TELL 'EM IT'S...

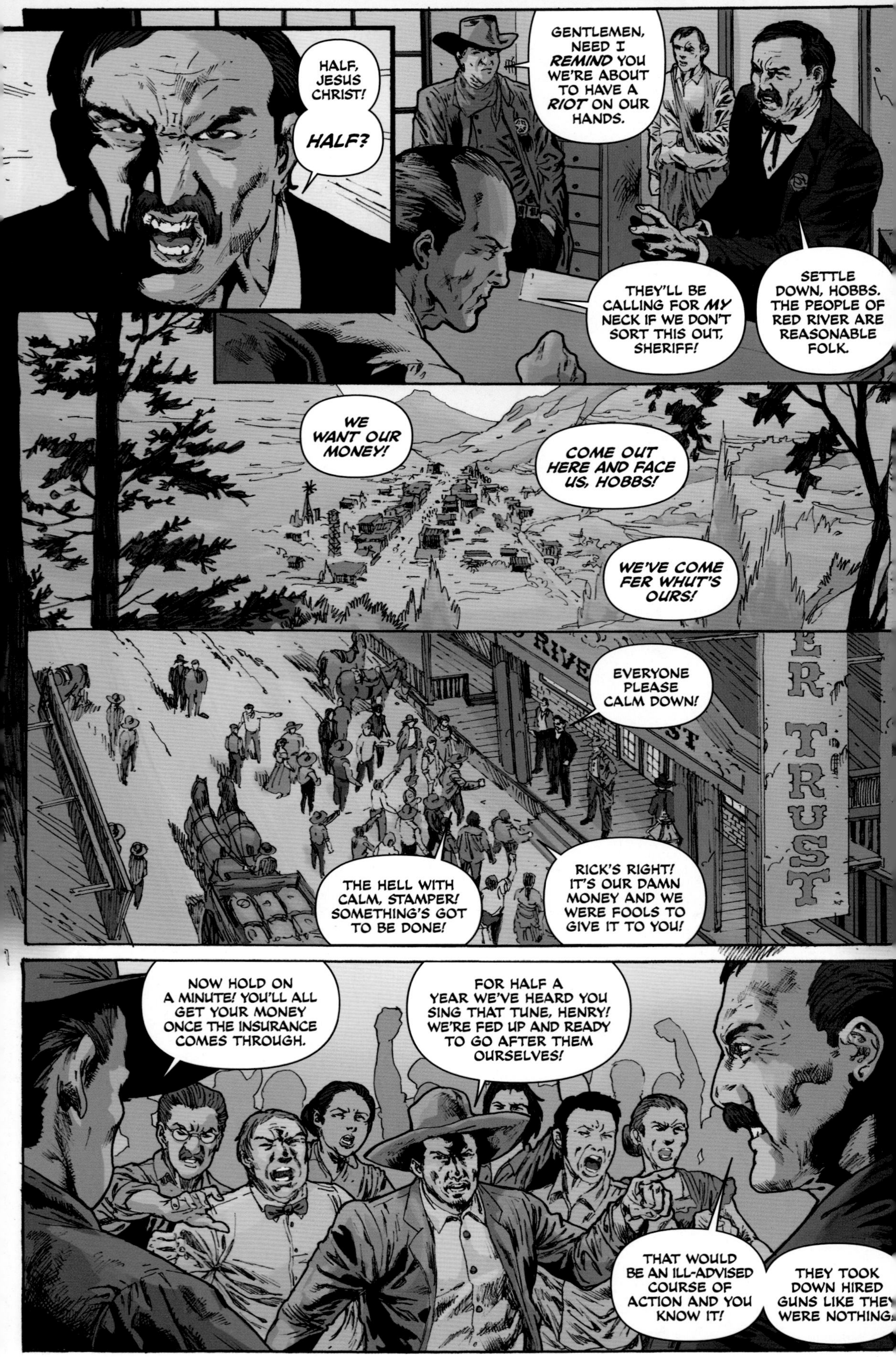
HALF, JESUS CHRIST!
HALF?
GENTLEMEN, NEED I REMIND YOU WE'RE ABOUT TO HAVE A RIOT ON OUR HANDS.
THEY'LL BE CALLING FOR MY NECK IF WE DON'T SORT THIS OUT, SHERIFF!
SETTLE DOWN, HOBBS. THE PEOPLE OF RED RIVER ARE REASONABLE FOLK.
WE WANT OUR MONEY!
COME OUT HERE AND FACE US, HOBBS!
WE'VE COME FER WHUT'S OURS!
RIVE
ER TRUST
EVERYONE PLEASE CALM DOWN!
THE HELL WITH CALM, STAMPER! SOMETHING'S GOT TO BE DONE!
RICK'S RIGHT! IT'S OUR DAMN MONEY AND WE WERE FOOLS TO GIVE IT TO YOU!
NOW HOLD ON A MINUTE! YOU'LL ALL GET YOUR MONEY ONCE THE INSURANCE COMES THROUGH.
FOR HALF A YEAR WE'VE HEARD YOU SING THAT TUNE, HENRY! WE'RE FED UP AND READY TO GO AFTER THEM OURSELVES!
THAT WOULD BE AN ILL-ADVISED COURSE OF ACTION AND YOU KNOW IT!
THEY TOOK DOWN HIRED GUNS LIKE THEY WERE NOTHING.

HIRED GUNS *WE* PAID FOR!

NOW, BEFORE Y'ALL GO OFF HALF-COCKED LOOKING FOR A FIGHT, JUST GIVE US A LITTLE MORE TIME AND WE'LL HAVE IT SORTED.

YOU'LL GET WHAT'S OWED.

YOU BET WE WILL, SHERIFF! I'VE ALREADY SENT WORD TO THE MEN I THINK CAN TRULY HELP US IN OUR HOUR OF NEED.

MEN WHO GET RESULTS. MEN THAT DON'T TAKE HARD EARNED MONEY FROM FOLKS BECAUSE THEY BELIEVE IN JUSTICE OVER PERSONAL GAIN.

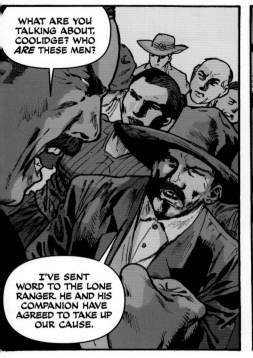

WHAT ARE YOU TALKING ABOUT, COOLIDGE? WHO *ARE* THESE MEN?

I'VE SENT WORD TO THE LONE RANGER HE AND HIS COMPANION HAVE AGREED TO TAKE UP OUR CAUSE.

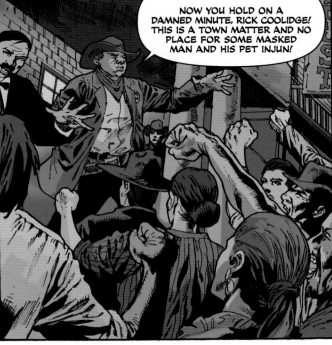

NOW YOU HOLD ON A DAMNED MINUTE, RICK COOLIDGE! THIS IS A TOWN MATTER AND NO PLACE FOR SOME MASKED MAN AND HIS PET INJUN!

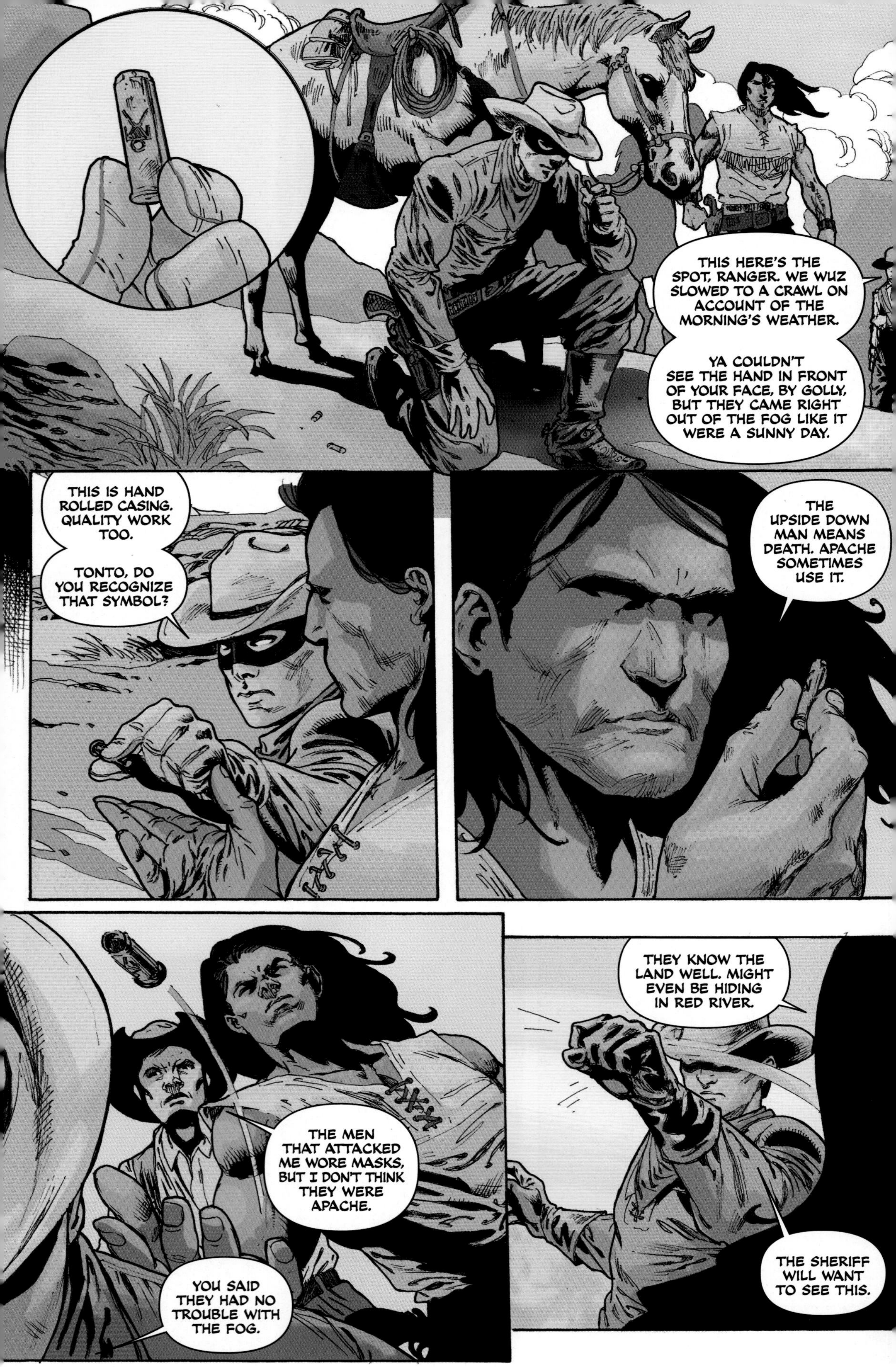
THIS HERE'S THE SPOT, RANGER. WE WUZ SLOWED TO A CRAWL ON ACCOUNT OF THE MORNING'S WEATHER.
YA COULDN'T SEE THE HAND IN FRONT OF YOUR FACE, BY GOLLY, BUT THEY CAME RIGHT OUT OF THE FOG LIKE IT WERE A SUNNY DAY.
THIS IS HAND ROLLED CASING. QUALITY WORK TOO.
TONTO, DO YOU RECOGNIZE THAT SYMBOL?
THE UPSIDE DOWN MAN MEANS DEATH. APACHE SOMETIMES USE IT.
THE MEN THAT ATTACKED ME WORE MASKS, BUT I DON'T THINK THEY WERE APACHE.
YOU SAID THEY HAD NO TROUBLE WITH THE FOG.
THEY KNOW THE LAND WELL. MIGHT EVEN BE HIDING IN RED RIVER.
THE SHERIFF WILL WANT TO SEE THIS.

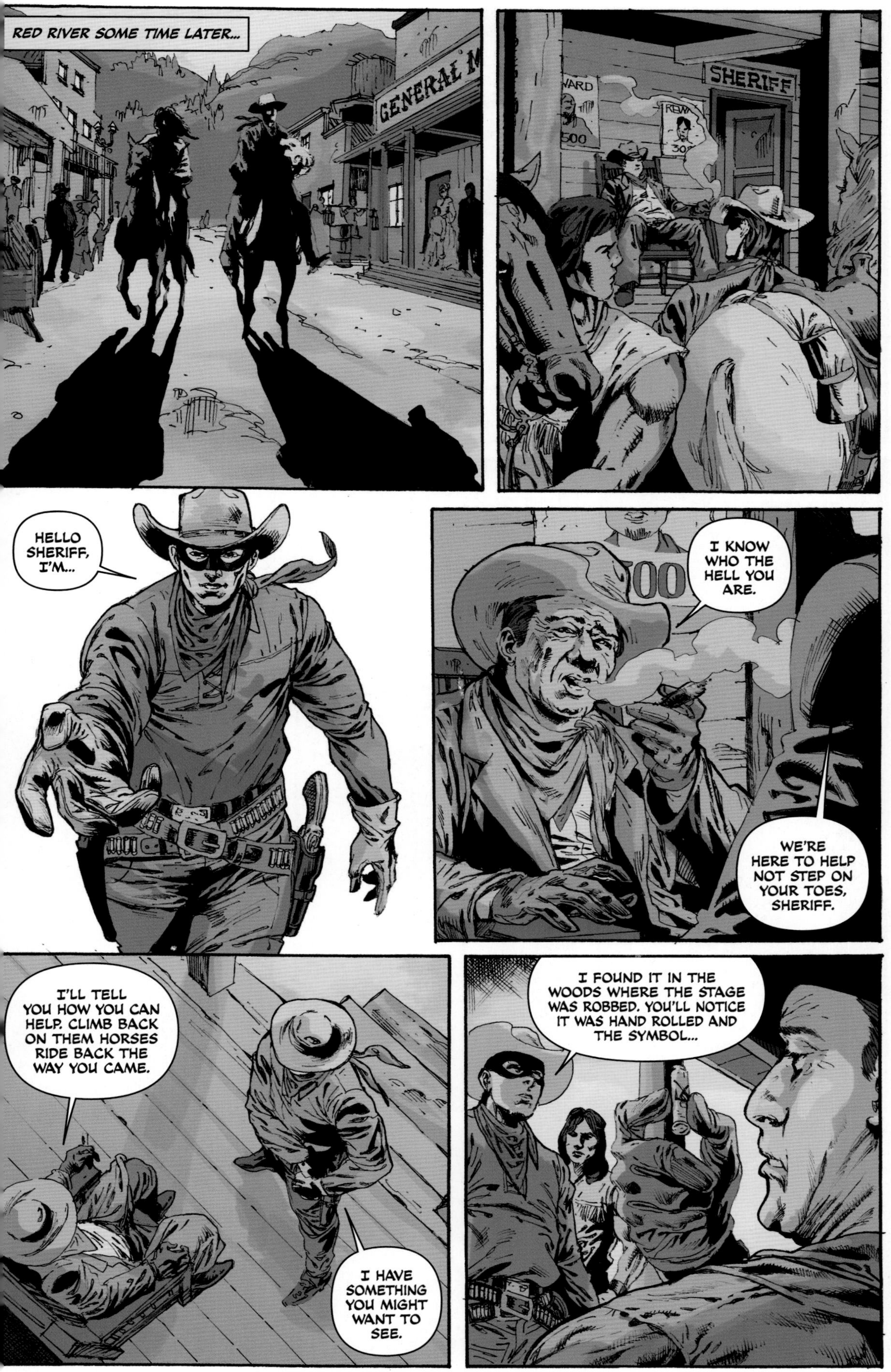
RED RIVER SOME TIME LATER...
GENERAL M
SHERIFF
HELLO SHERIFF, I'M...
I KNOW WHO THE HELL YOU ARE.
WE'RE HERE TO HELP NOT STEP ON YOUR TOES, SHERIFF.
I'LL TELL YOU HOW YOU CAN HELP. CLIMB BACK ON THEM HORSES RIDE BACK THE WAY YOU CAME.
I HAVE SOMETHING YOU MIGHT WANT TO SEE.
I FOUND IT IN THE WOODS WHERE THE STAGE WAS ROBBED. YOU'LL NOTICE IT WAS HAND ROLLED AND THE SYMBOL...

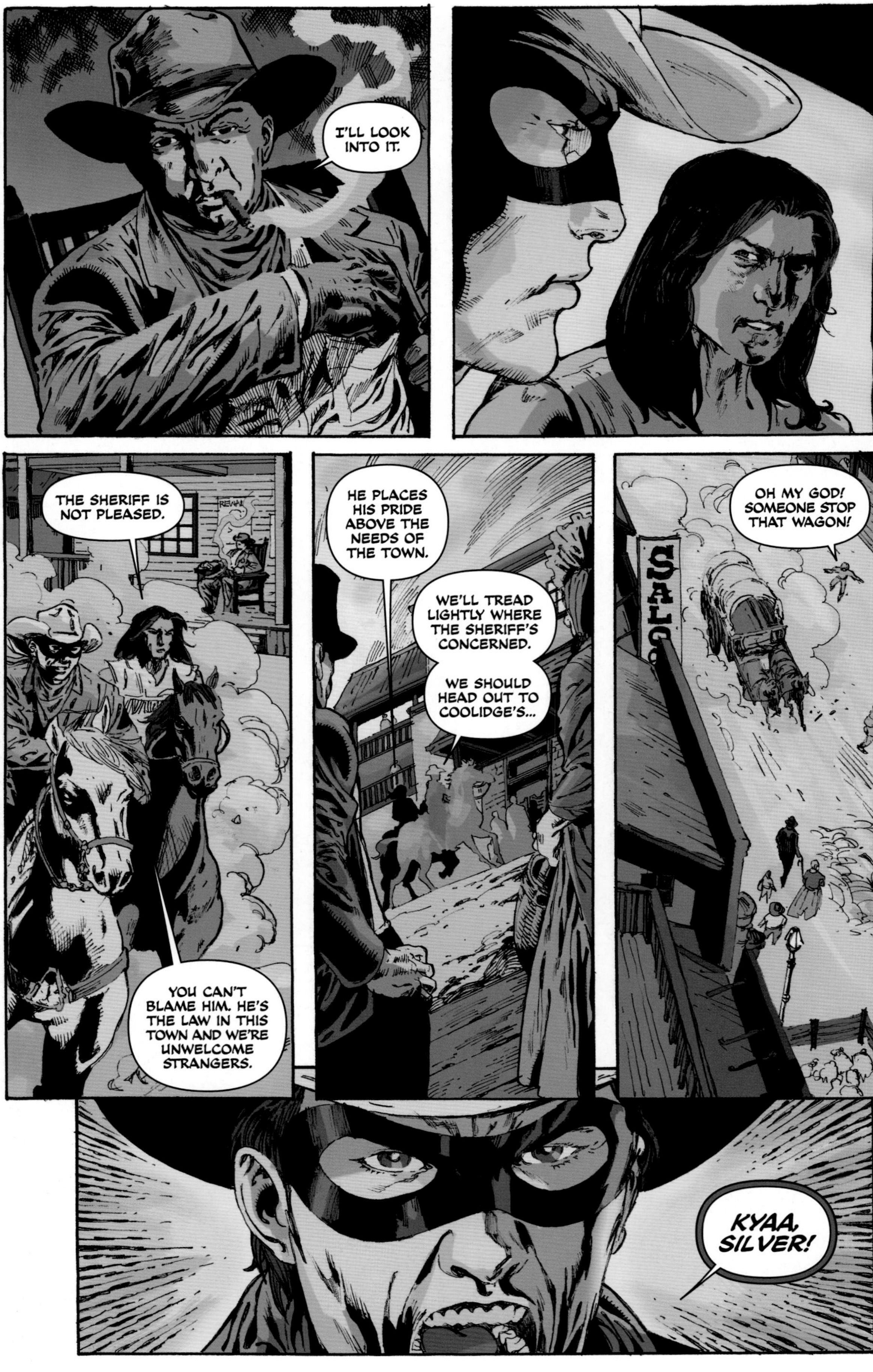
I'LL LOOK INTO IT.
THE SHERIFF IS NOT PLEASED.
YOU CAN'T BLAME HIM. HE'S THE LAW IN THIS TOWN AND WE'RE UNWELCOME STRANGERS.
HE PLACES HIS PRIDE ABOVE THE NEEDS OF THE TOWN.
WE'LL TREAD LIGHTLY WHERE THE SHERIFF'S CONCERNED.
WE SHOULD HEAD OUT TO COOLIDGE'S...
OH MY GOD! SOMEONE STOP THAT WAGON!
KYAA, SILVER!

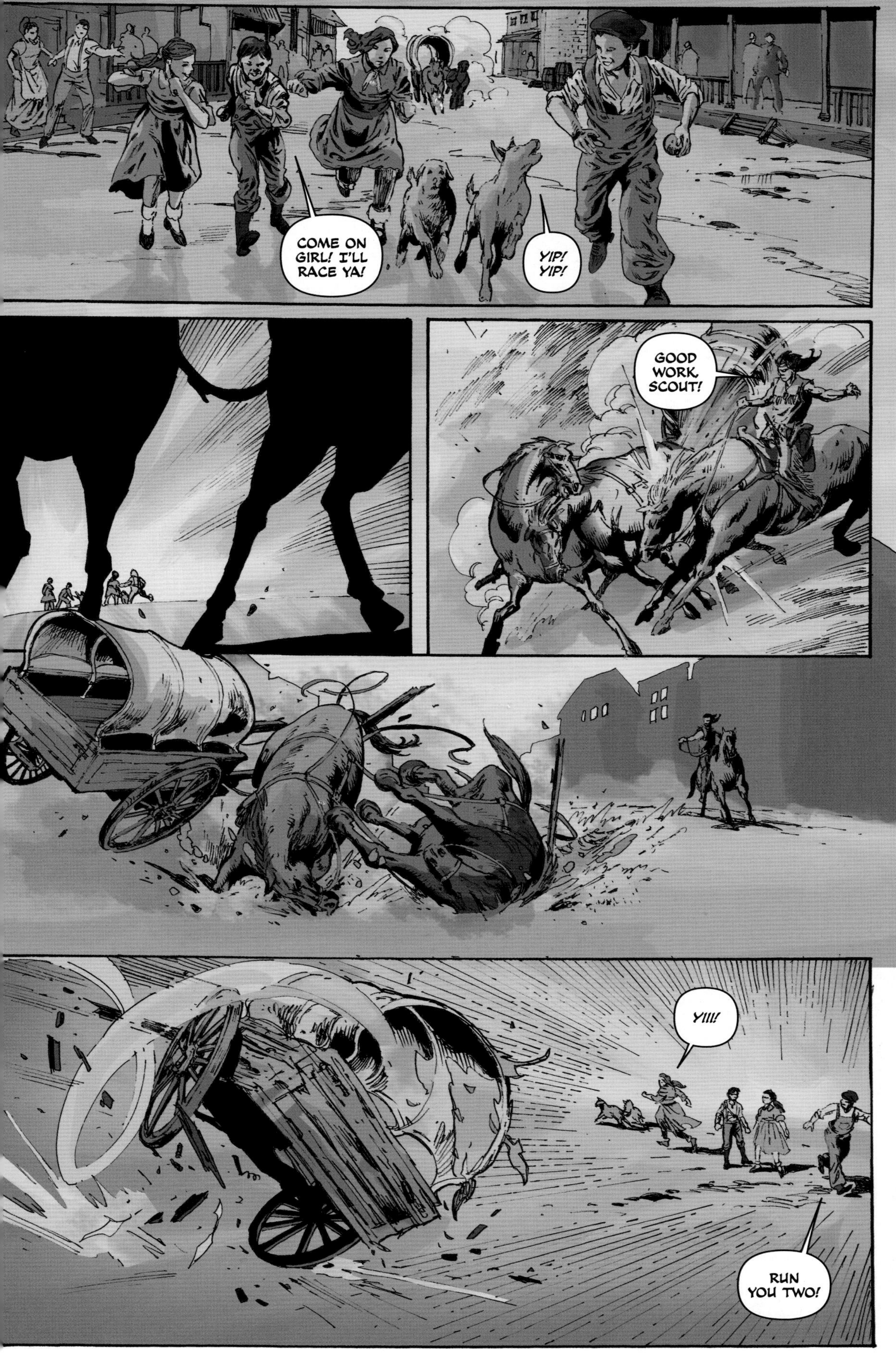
COME ON GIRL! I'LL RACE YA!
YIP! YIP!
GOOD WORK, SCOUT!
YIII!
RUN YOU TWO!

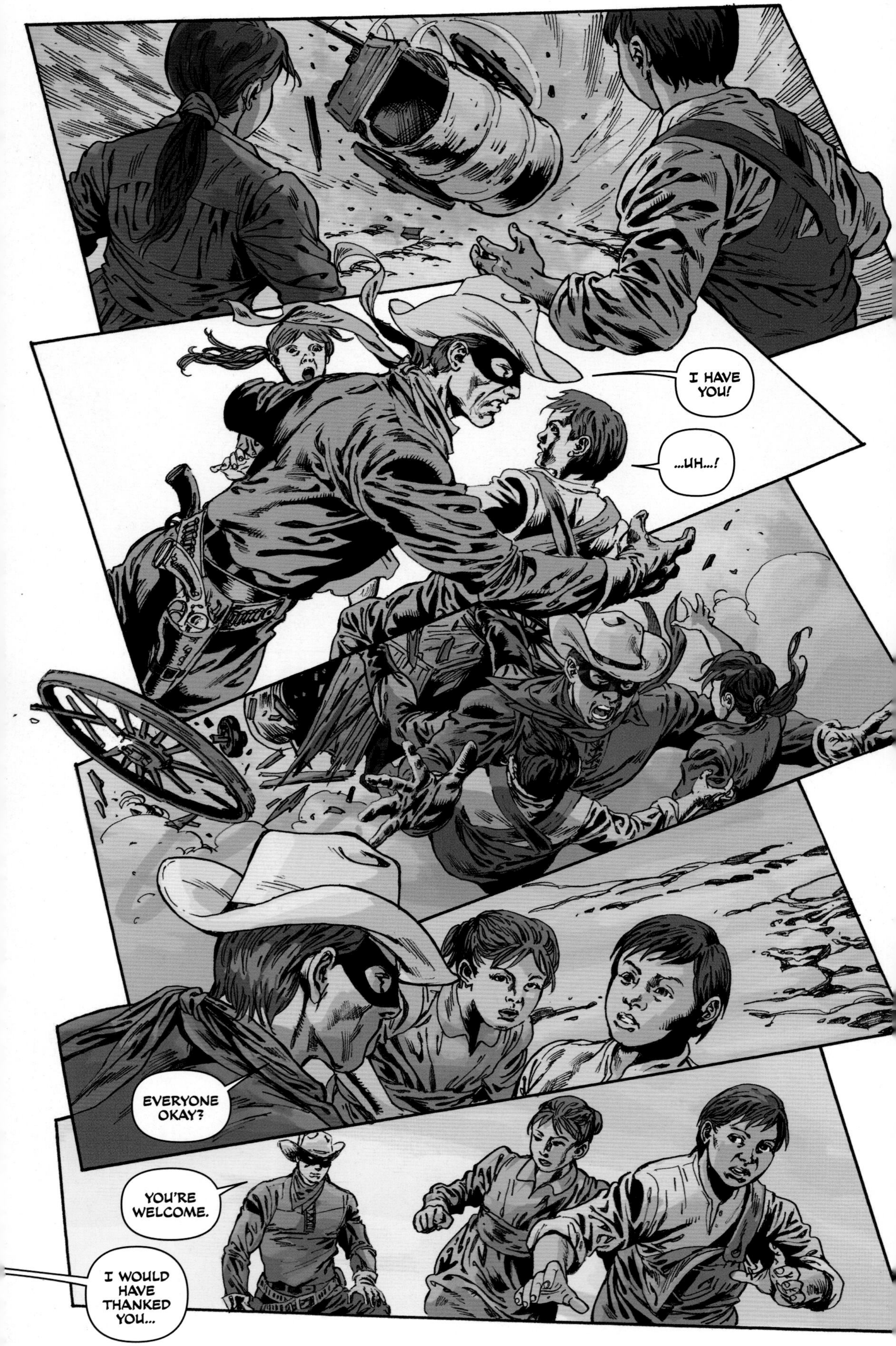
I HAVE YOU!
...UH...!
EVERYONE OKAY?
YOU'RE WELCOME.
I WOULD HAVE THANKED YOU...

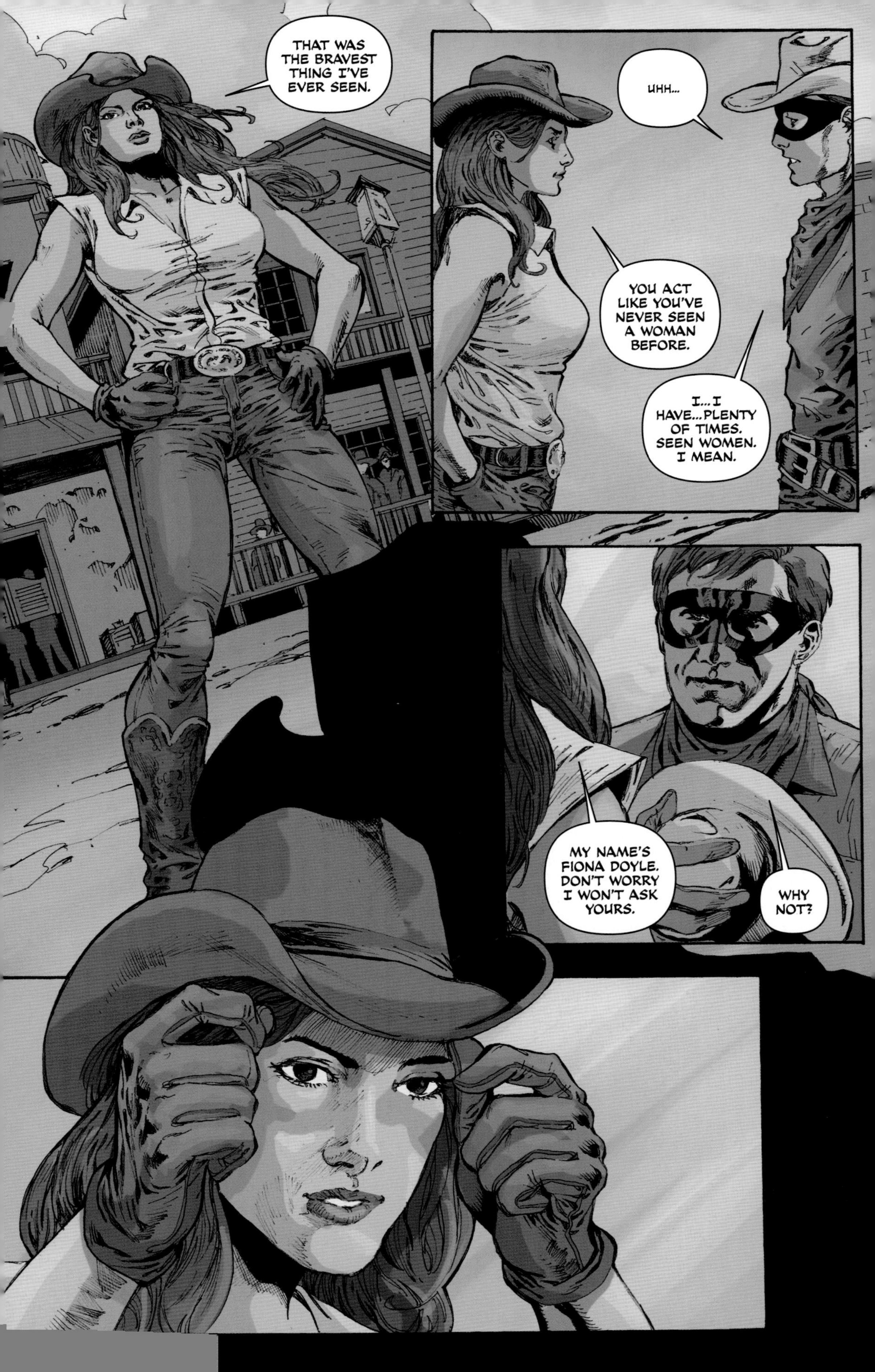
THAT WAS THE BRAVEST THING I'VE EVER SEEN.
UHH...
YOU ACT LIKE YOU'VE NEVER SEEN A WOMAN BEFORE.
I...I HAVE...PLENTY OF TIMES. SEEN WOMEN. I MEAN.
MY NAME'S FIONA DOYLE. DON'T WORRY I WON'T ASK YOURS.
WHY NOT?

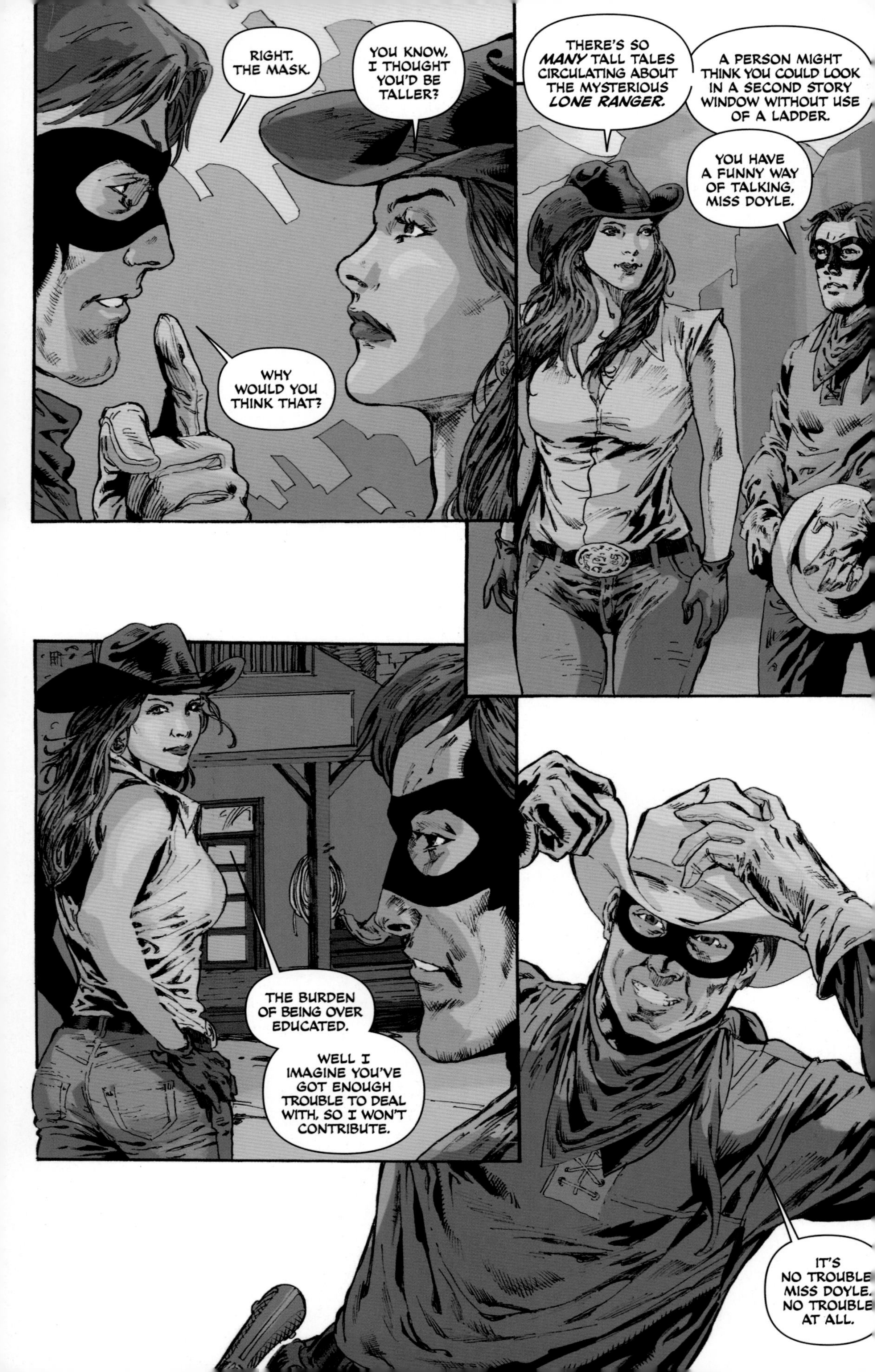
RIGHT. THE MASK.
YOU KNOW, I THOUGHT YOU'D BE TALLER?
WHY WOULD YOU THINK THAT?
THERE'S SO MANY TALL TALES CIRCULATING ABOUT THE MYSTERIOUS LONE RANGER.
A PERSON MIGHT THINK YOU COULD LOOK IN A SECOND STORY WINDOW WITHOUT USE OF A LADDER.
YOU HAVE A FUNNY WAY OF TALKING, MISS DOYLE.
THE BURDEN OF BEING OVER EDUCATED.
WELL I IMAGINE YOU'VE GOT ENOUGH TROUBLE TO DEAL WITH, SO I WON'T CONTRIBUTE.
IT'S NO TROUBLE MISS DOYLE. NO TROUBLE AT ALL.

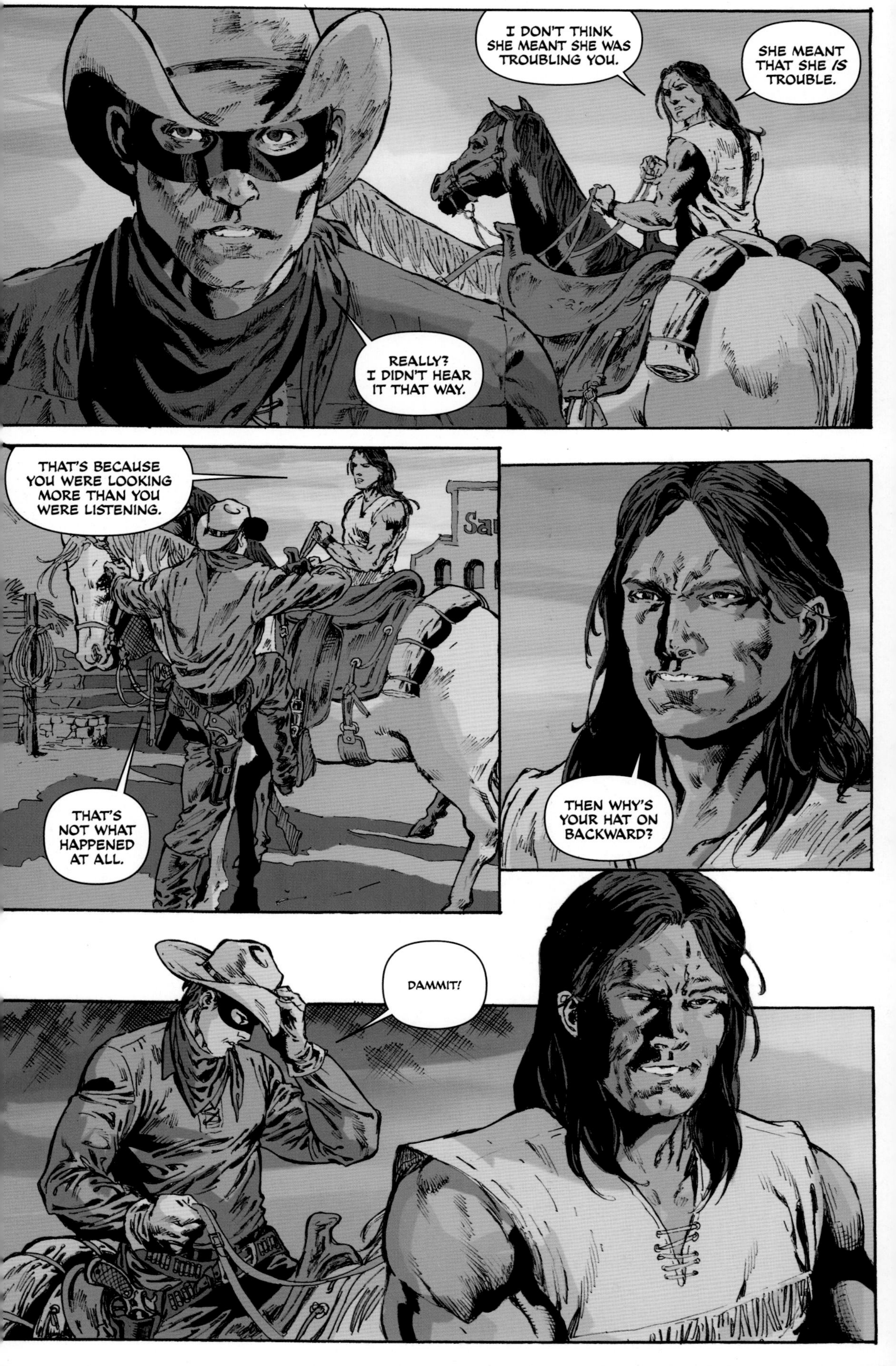
I DON'T THINK SHE MEANT SHE WAS TROUBLING YOU.
SHE MEANT THAT SHE IS TROUBLE.
REALLY? I DIDN'T HEAR IT THAT WAY.
THAT'S BECAUSE YOU WERE LOOKING MORE THAN YOU WERE LISTENING.
THAT'S NOT WHAT HAPPENED AT ALL.
THEN WHY'S YOUR HAT ON BACKWARD?
DAMMIT!

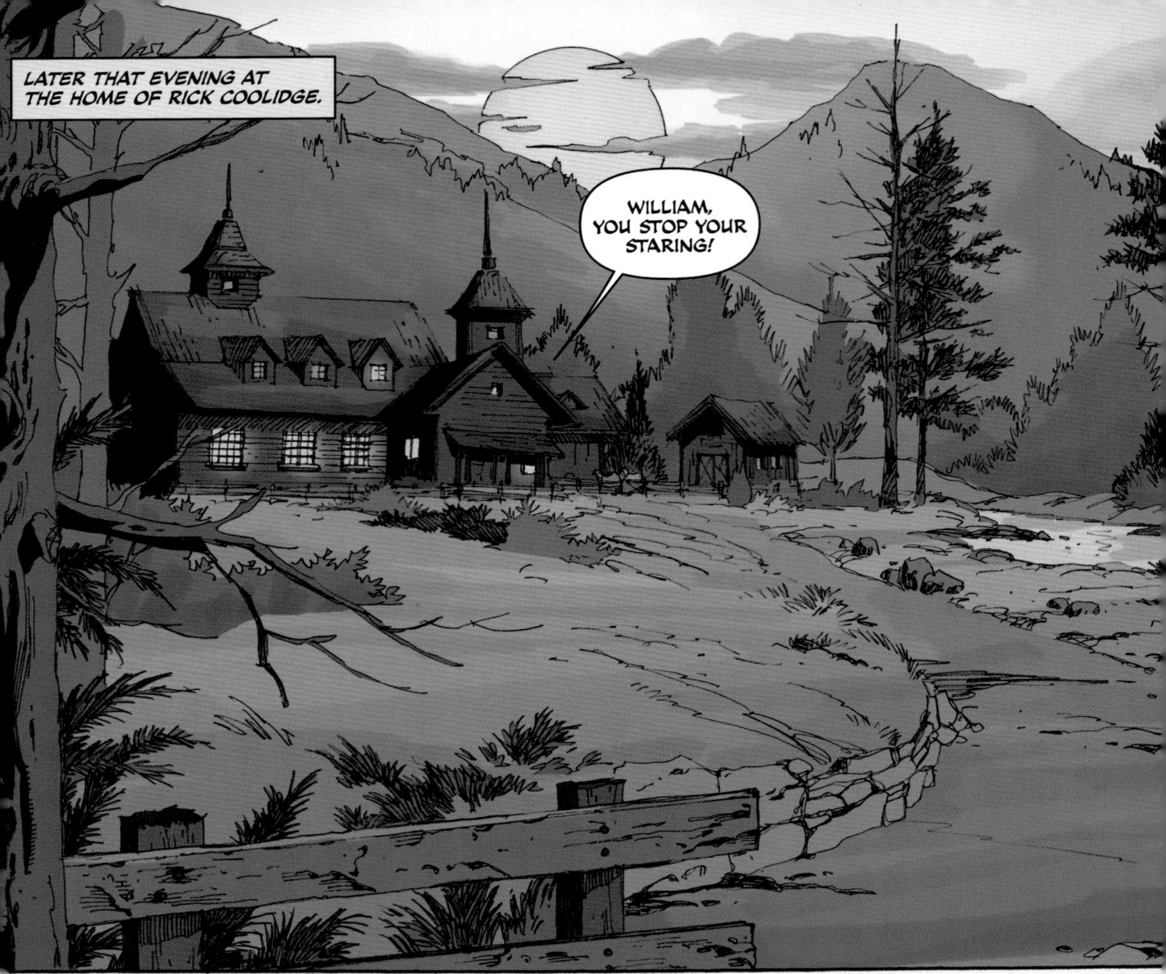
LATER THAT EVENING AT THE HOME OF RICK COOLIDGE.
WILLIAM, YOU STOP YOUR STARING!

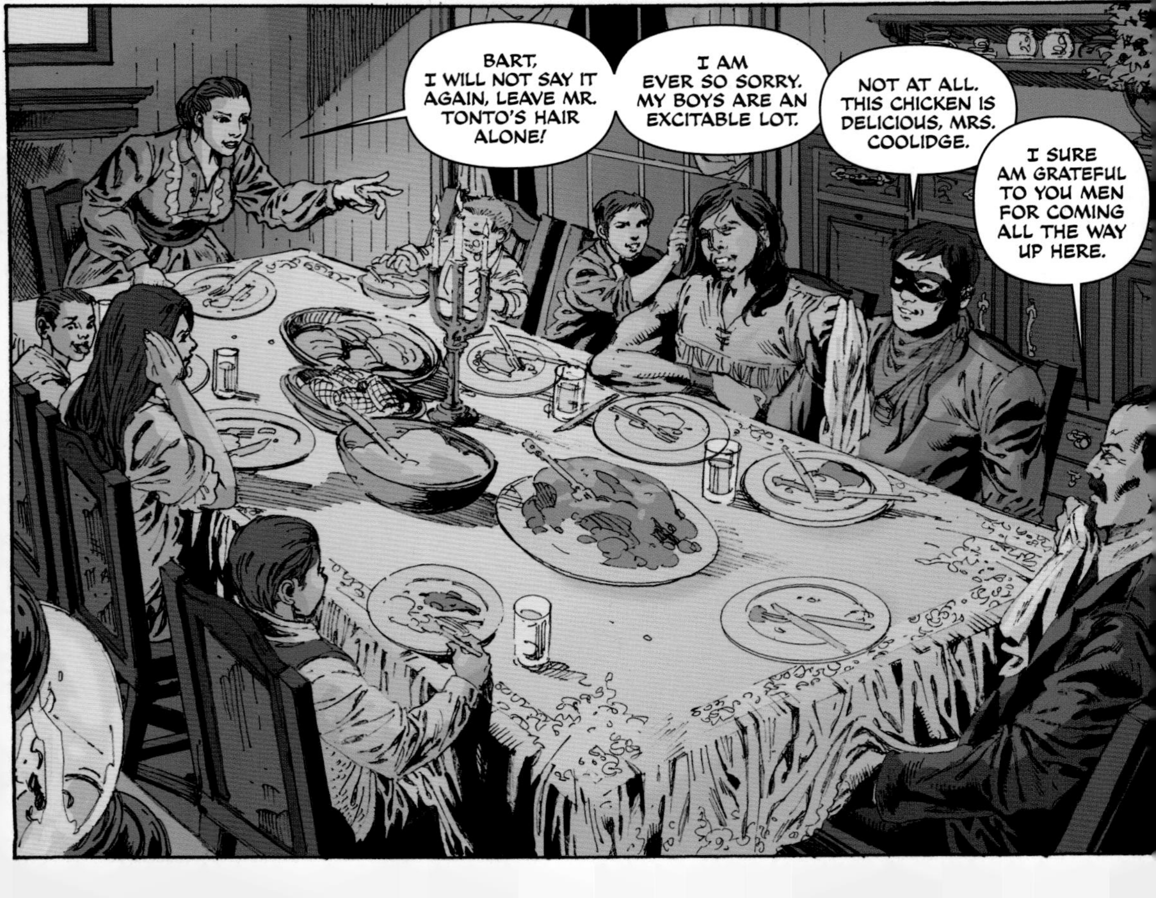
BART, I WILL NOT SAY IT AGAIN, LEAVE MR. TONTO'S HAIR ALONE!
I AM EVER SO SORRY. MY BOYS ARE AN EXCITABLE LOT.
NOT AT ALL. THIS CHICKEN IS DELICIOUS, MRS. COOLIDGE.
I SURE AM GRATEFUL TO YOU MEN FOR COMING ALL THE WAY UP HERE.

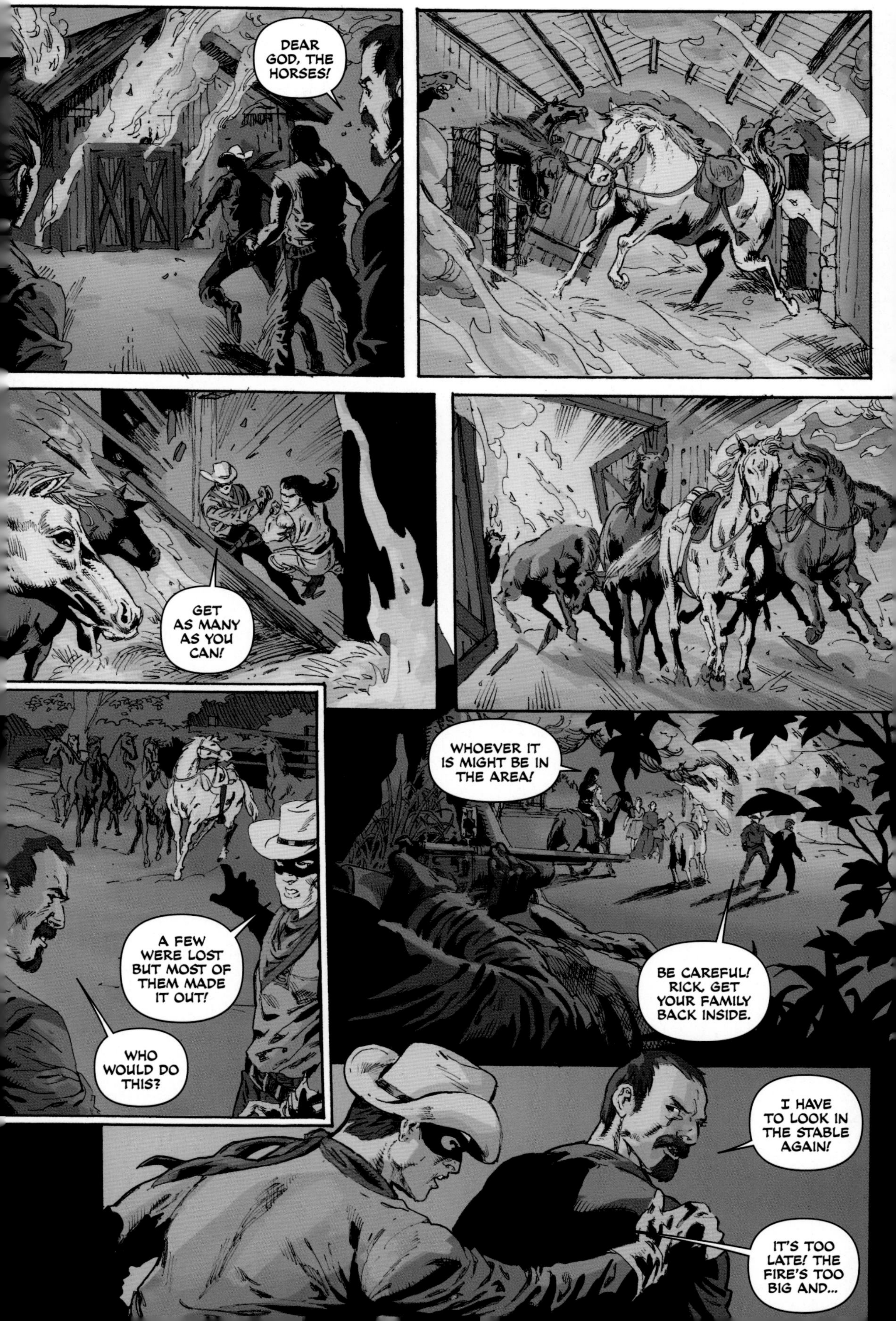
DEAR GOD, THE HORSES!
GET AS MANY AS YOU CAN!
A FEW WERE LOST BUT MOST OF THEM MADE IT OUT!
WHO WOULD DO THIS?
WHOEVER IT IS MIGHT BE IN THE AREA!
BE CAREFUL! RICK, GET YOUR FAMILY BACK INSIDE.
I HAVE TO LOOK IN THE STABLE AGAIN!
IT'S TOO LATE! THE FIRE'S TOO BIG AND...

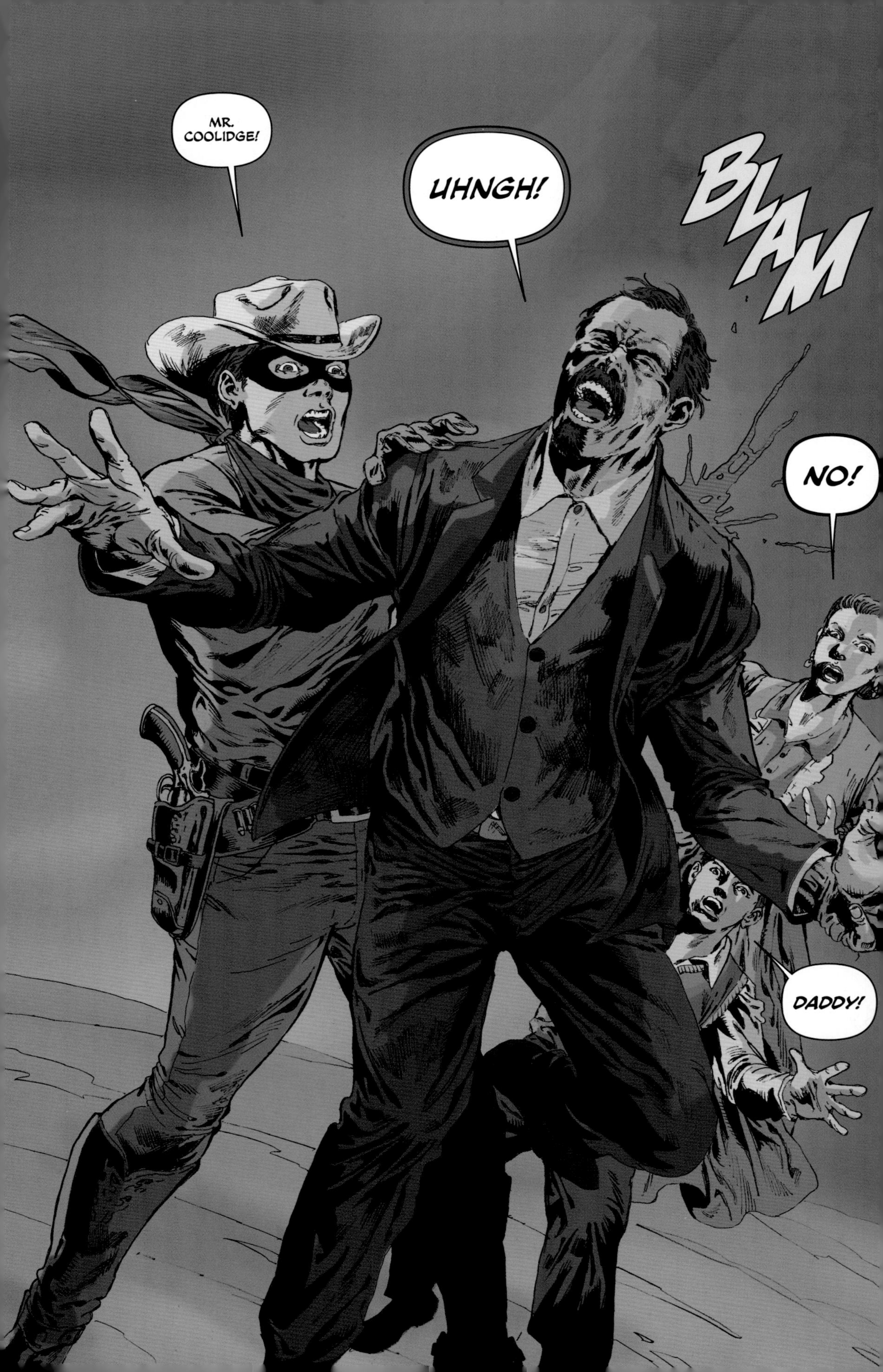
MR. COOLIDGE!
UHNGH!
BLAM
NO!
DADDY!

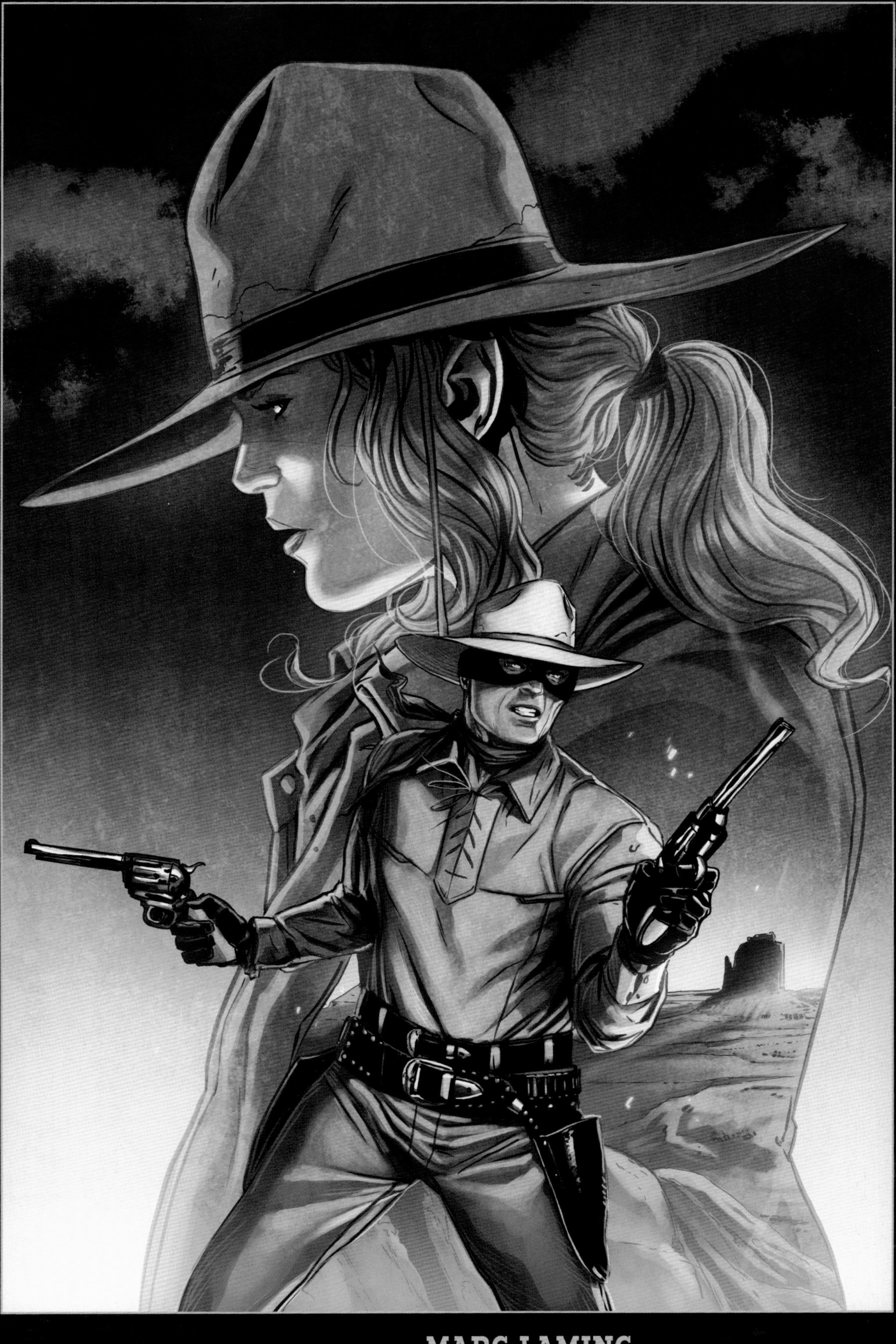

issue #2 cover by **MARC LAMING**
colors by **ELMER SANTOS**

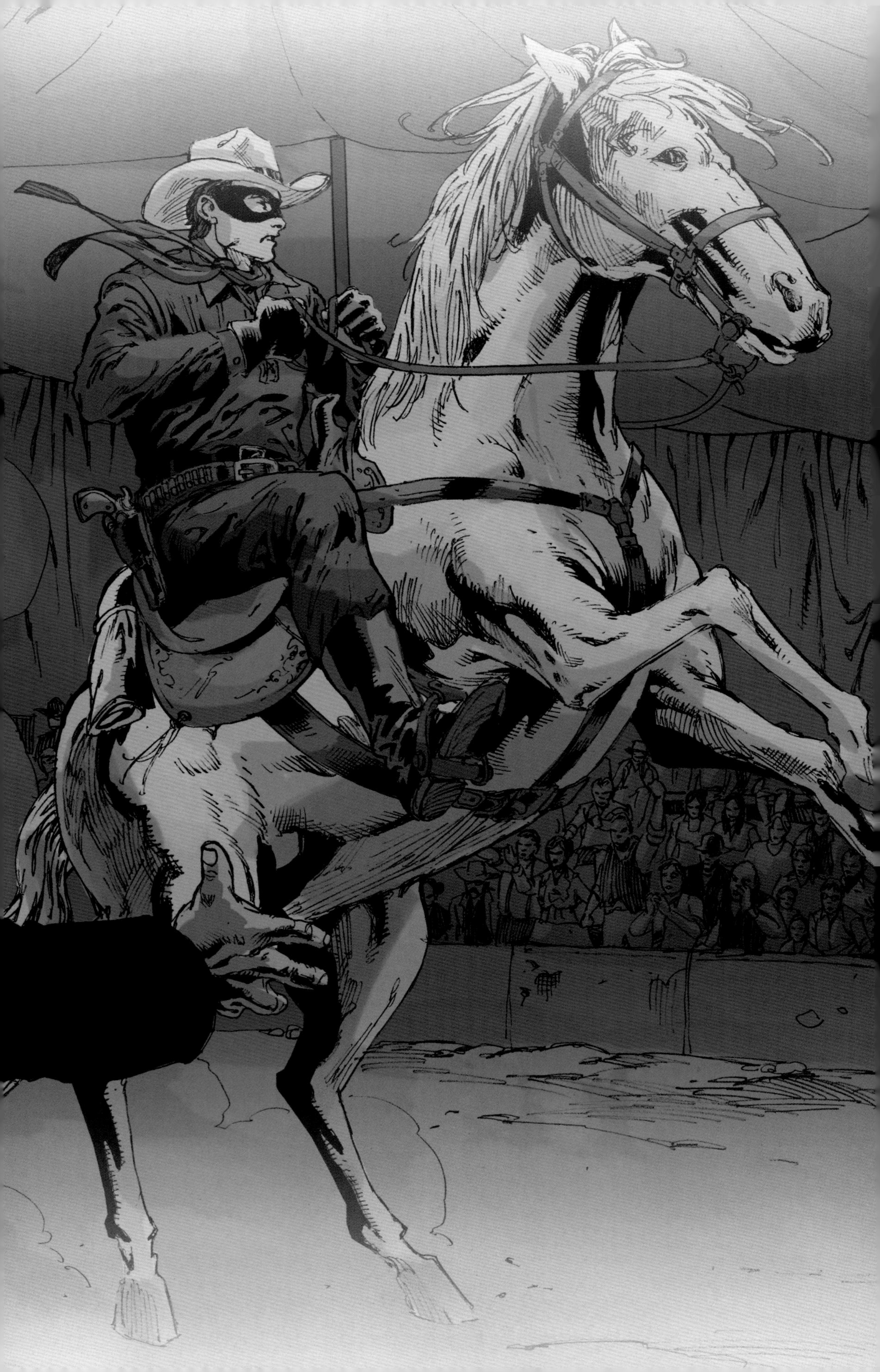

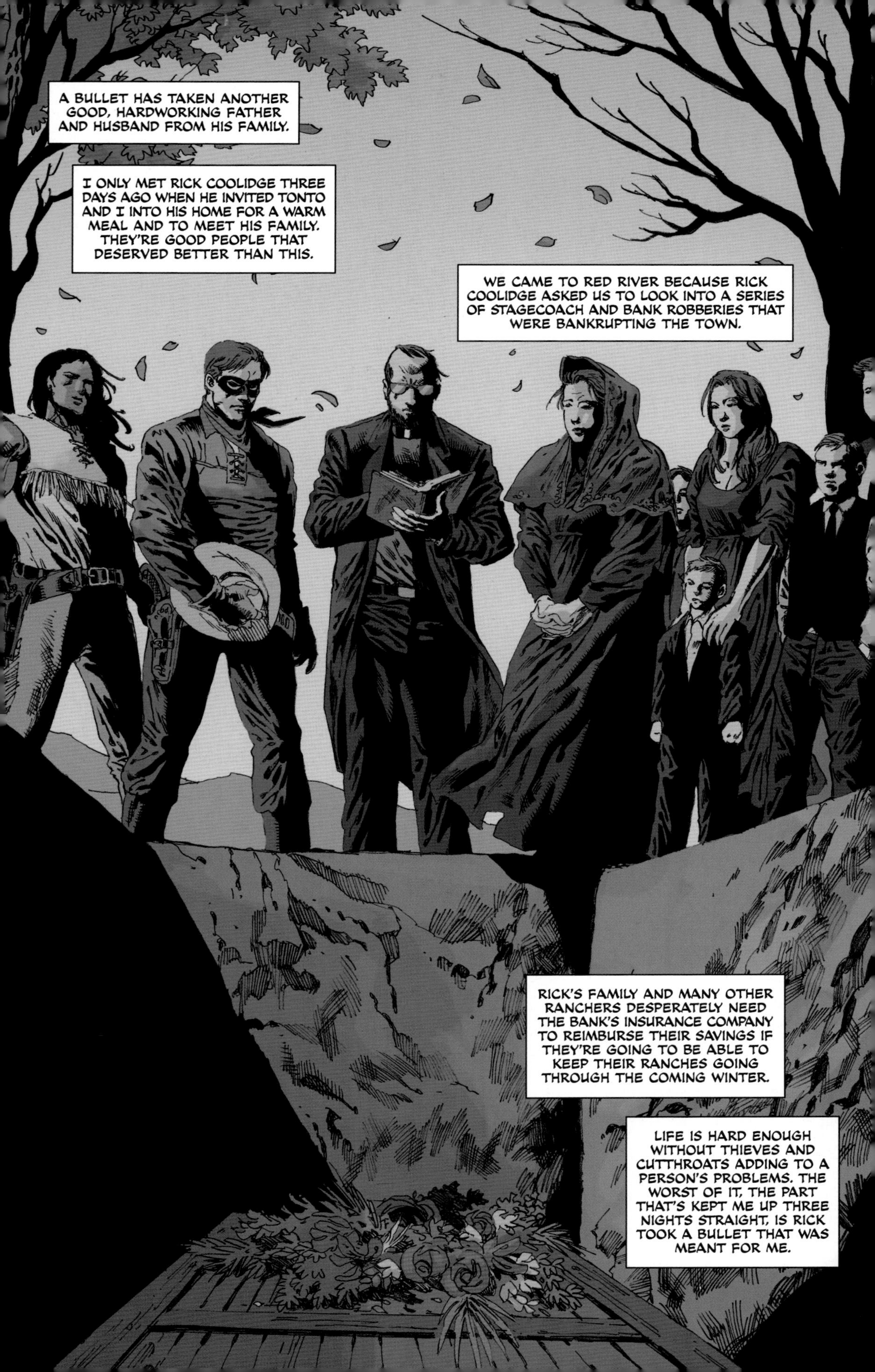
A BULLET HAS TAKEN ANOTHER GOOD, HARDWORKING FATHER AND HUSBAND FROM HIS FAMILY.
I ONLY MET RICK COOLIDGE THREE DAYS AGO WHEN HE INVITED TONTO AND I INTO HIS HOME FOR A WARM MEAL AND TO MEET HIS FAMILY. THEY'RE GOOD PEOPLE THAT DESERVED BETTER THAN THIS.
WE CAME TO RED RIVER BECAUSE RICK COOLIDGE ASKED US TO LOOK INTO A SERIES OF STAGECOACH AND BANK ROBBERIES THAT WERE BANKRUPTING THE TOWN.
RICK'S FAMILY AND MANY OTHER RANCHERS DESPERATELY NEED THE BANK'S INSURANCE COMPANY TO REIMBURSE THEIR SAVINGS IF THEY'RE GOING TO BE ABLE TO KEEP THEIR RANCHES GOING THROUGH THE COMING WINTER.
LIFE IS HARD ENOUGH WITHOUT THIEVES AND CUTTHROATS ADDING TO A PERSON'S PROBLEMS. THE WORST OF IT, THE PART THAT'S KEPT ME UP THREE NIGHTS STRAIGHT, IS RICK TOOK A BULLET THAT WAS MEANT FOR ME.

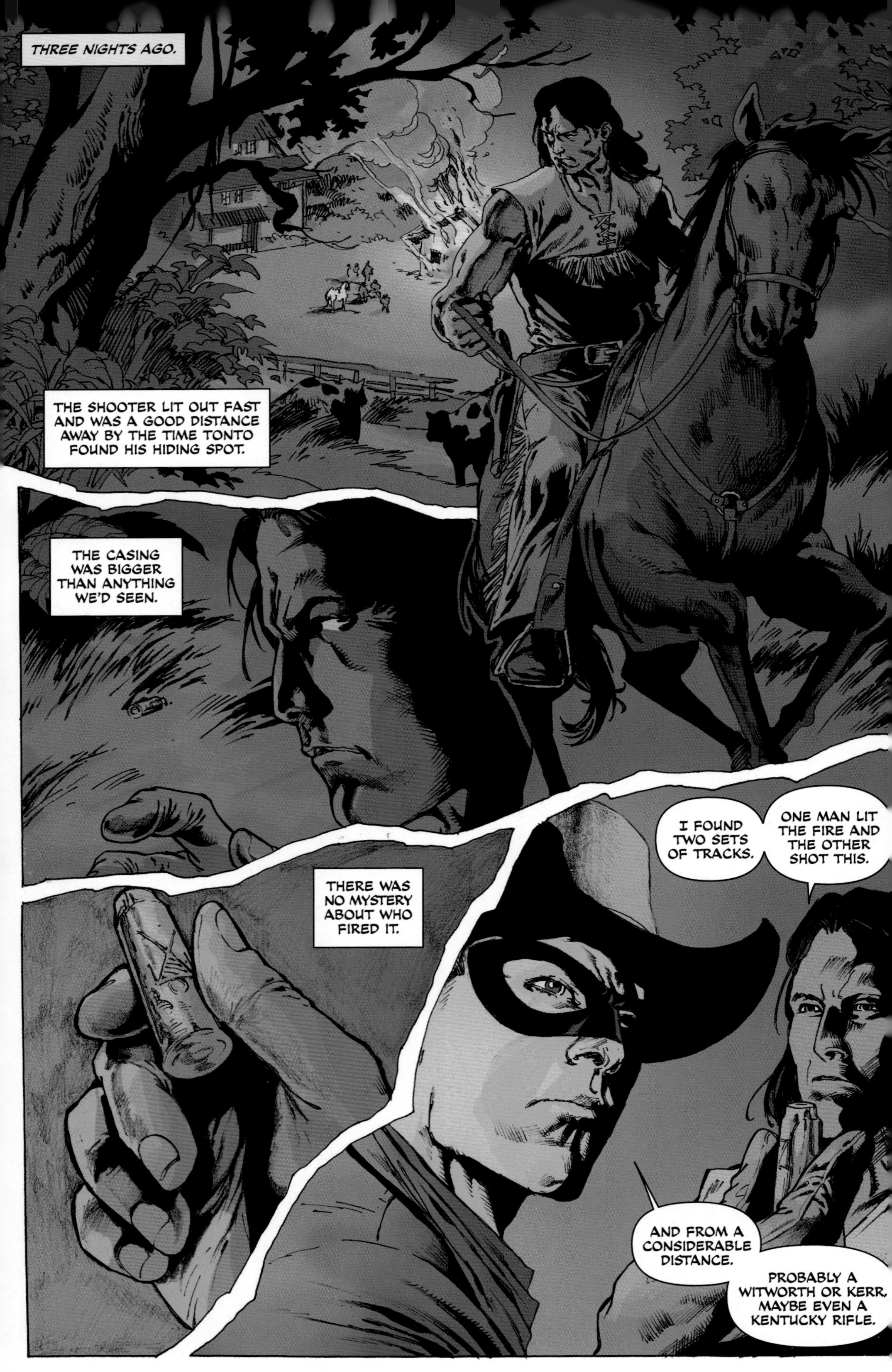
THREE NIGHTS AGO.
THE SHOOTER LIT OUT FAST AND WAS A GOOD DISTANCE AWAY BY THE TIME TONTO FOUND HIS HIDING SPOT.
THE CASING WAS BIGGER THAN ANYTHING WE'D SEEN.
THERE WAS NO MYSTERY ABOUT WHO FIRED IT.
I FOUND TWO SETS OF TRACKS.
ONE MAN LIT THE FIRE AND THE OTHER SHOT THIS.
AND FROM A CONSIDERABLE DISTANCE.
PROBABLY A WITWORTH OR KERR, MAYBE EVEN A KENTUCKY RIFLE.

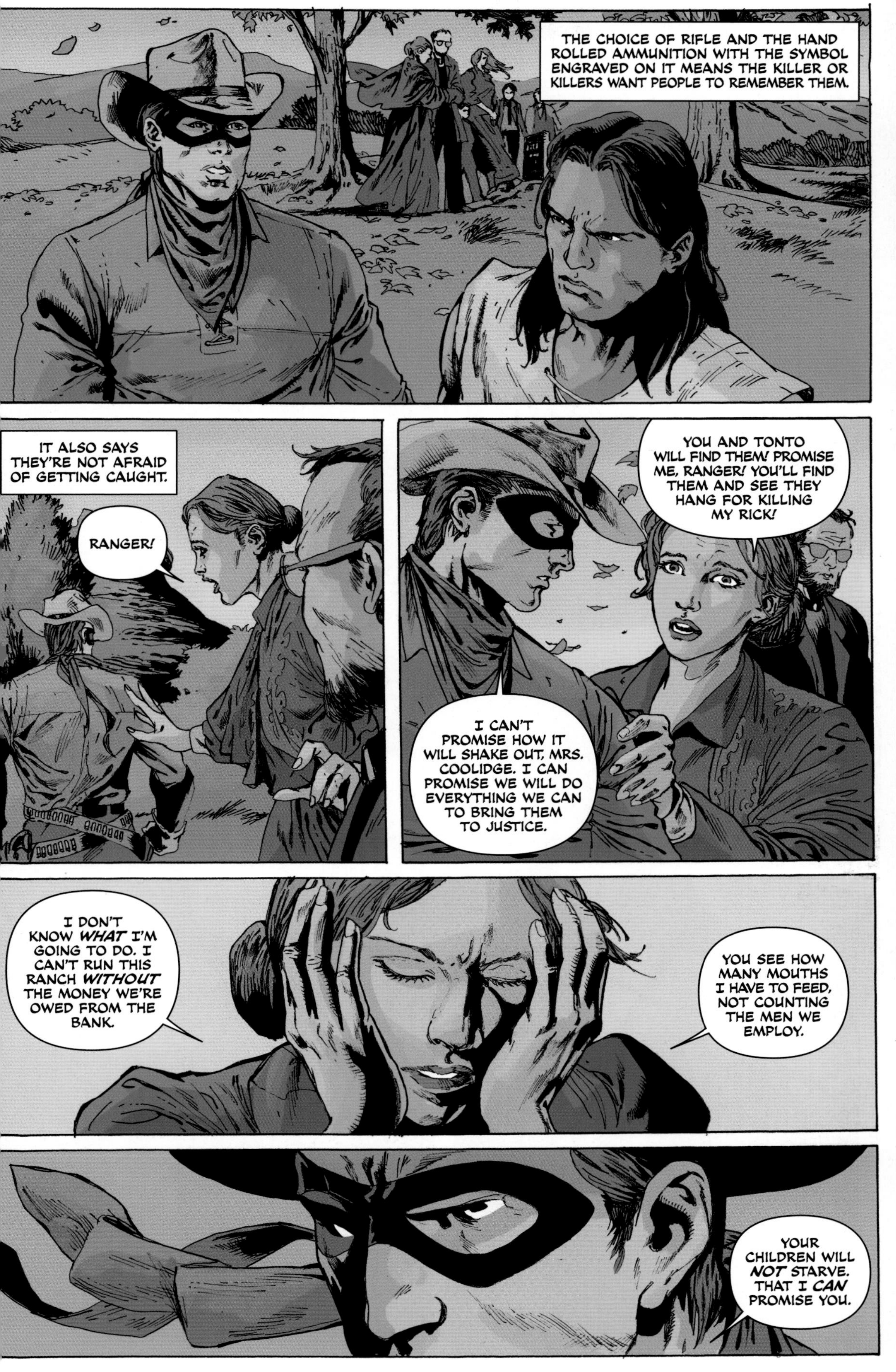
THE CHOICE OF RIFLE AND THE HAND ROLLED AMMUNITION WITH THE SYMBOL ENGRAVED ON IT MEANS THE KILLER OR KILLERS WANT PEOPLE TO REMEMBER THEM.
IT ALSO SAYS THEY'RE NOT AFRAID OF GETTING CAUGHT.
RANGER!
YOU AND TONTO WILL FIND THEM! PROMISE ME, RANGER! YOU'LL FIND THEM AND SEE THEY HANG FOR KILLING MY RICK!
I CAN'T PROMISE HOW IT WILL SHAKE OUT, MRS. COOLIDGE. I CAN PROMISE WE WILL DO EVERYTHING WE CAN TO BRING THEM TO JUSTICE.
I DON'T KNOW *WHAT* I'M GOING TO DO. I CAN'T RUN THIS RANCH *WITHOUT* THE MONEY WE'RE OWED FROM THE BANK.
YOU SEE HOW MANY MOUTHS I HAVE TO FEED, NOT COUNTING THE MEN WE EMPLOY.
YOUR CHILDREN WILL *NOT* STARVE. THAT I *CAN* PROMISE YOU.

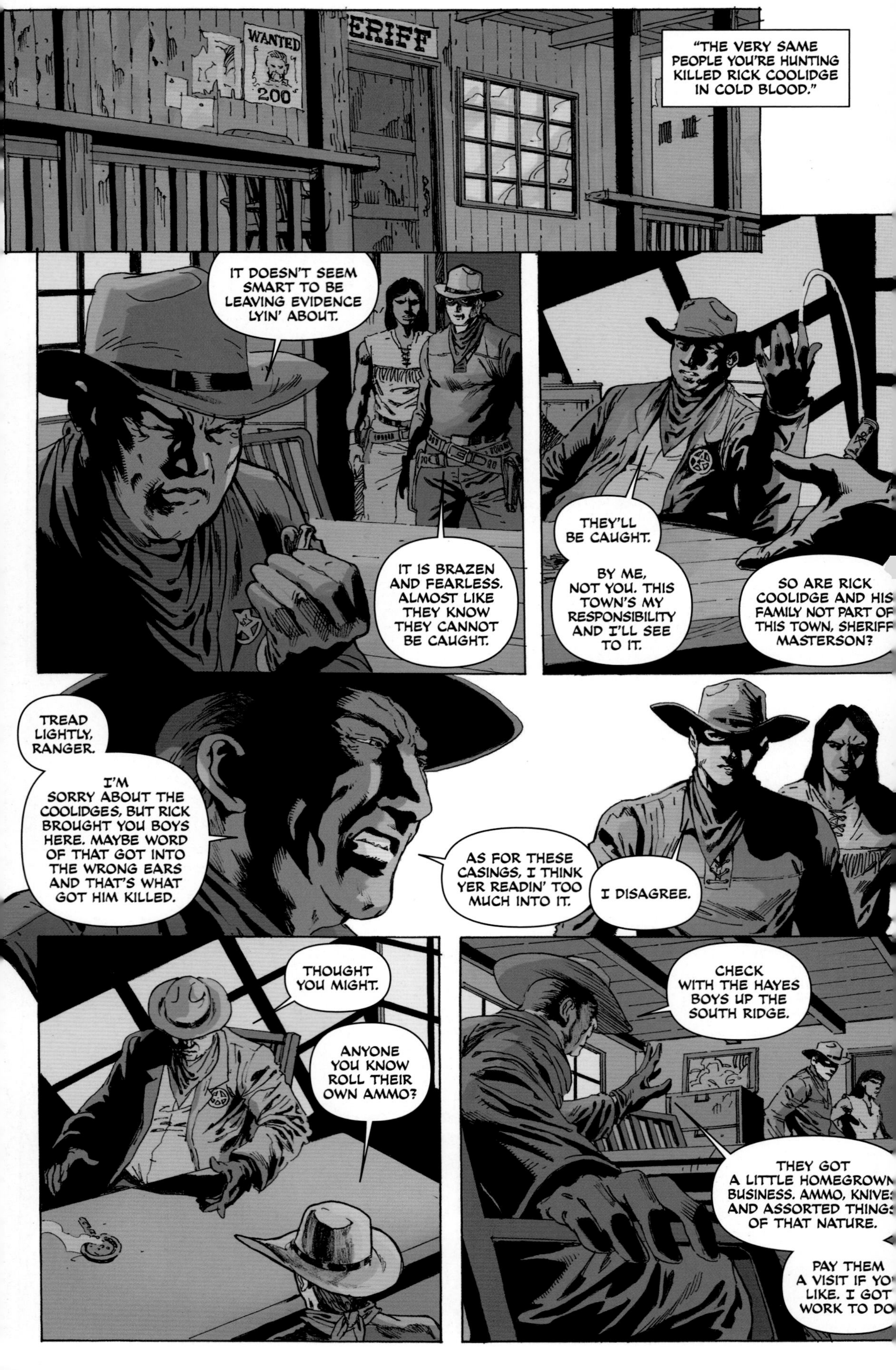
WANTED
200
ERIFF
"THE VERY SAME PEOPLE YOU'RE HUNTING KILLED RICK COOLIDGE IN COLD BLOOD."
IT DOESN'T SEEM SMART TO BE LEAVING EVIDENCE LYIN' ABOUT.
IT IS BRAZEN AND FEARLESS. ALMOST LIKE THEY KNOW THEY CANNOT BE CAUGHT.
THEY'LL BE CAUGHT.
BY ME, NOT YOU. THIS TOWN'S MY RESPONSIBILITY AND I'LL SEE TO IT.
SO ARE RICK COOLIDGE AND HIS FAMILY NOT PART OF THIS TOWN, SHERIFF MASTERSON?
TREAD LIGHTLY, RANGER.
I'M SORRY ABOUT THE COOLIDGES, BUT RICK BROUGHT YOU BOYS HERE. MAYBE WORD OF THAT GOT INTO THE WRONG EARS AND THAT'S WHAT GOT HIM KILLED.
AS FOR THESE CASINGS, I THINK YER READIN' TOO MUCH INTO IT.
I DISAGREE.
THOUGHT YOU MIGHT.
ANYONE YOU KNOW ROLL THEIR OWN AMMO?
CHECK WITH THE HAYES BOYS UP THE SOUTH RIDGE.
THEY GOT A LITTLE HOMEGROWN BUSINESS. AMMO, KNIVES AND ASSORTED THINGS OF THAT NATURE.
PAY THEM A VISIT IF YOU LIKE. I GOT WORK TO DO

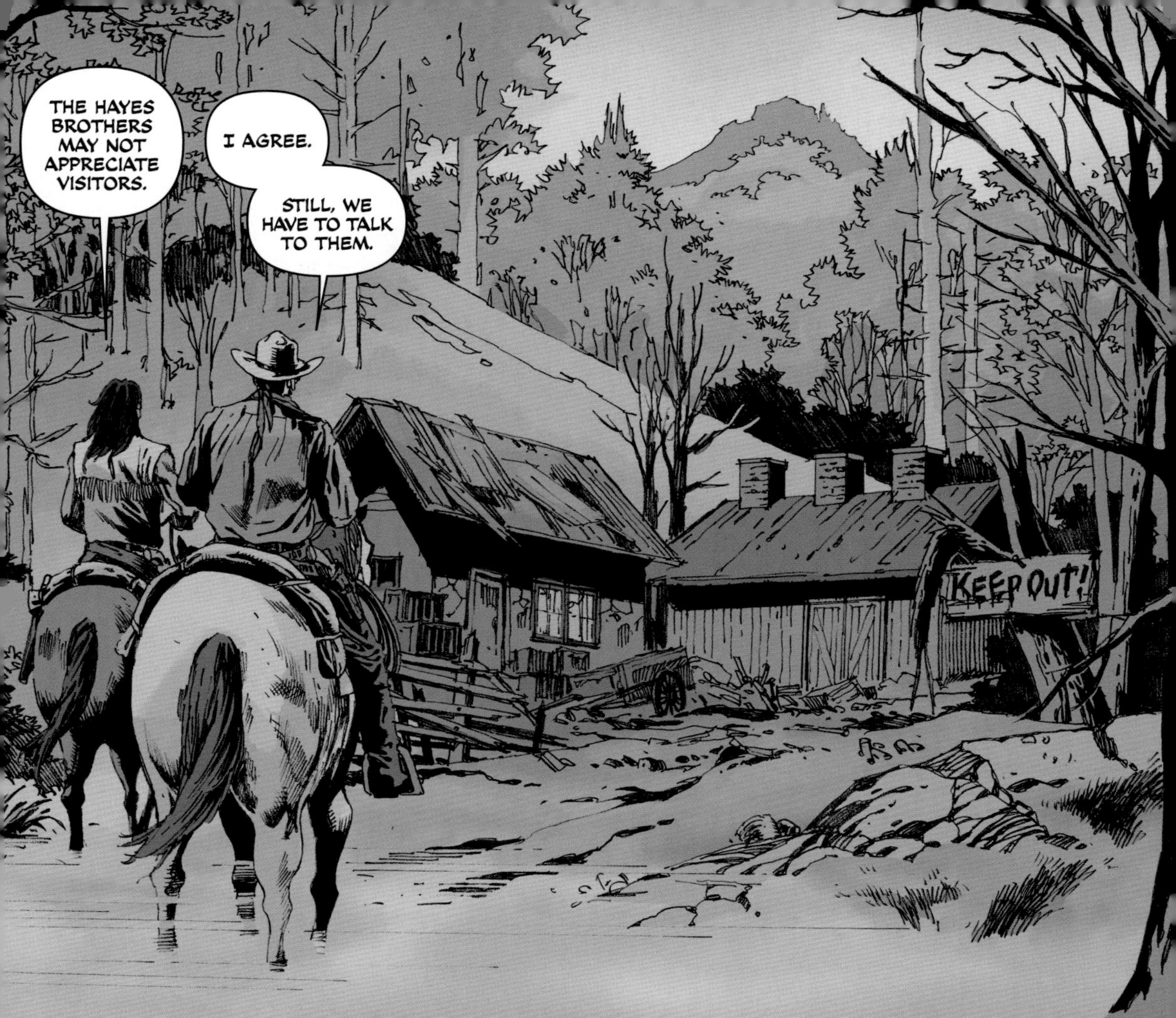
THE HAYES BROTHERS MAY NOT APPRECIATE VISITORS.
I AGREE.
STILL, WE HAVE TO TALK TO THEM.
KEEP OUT!

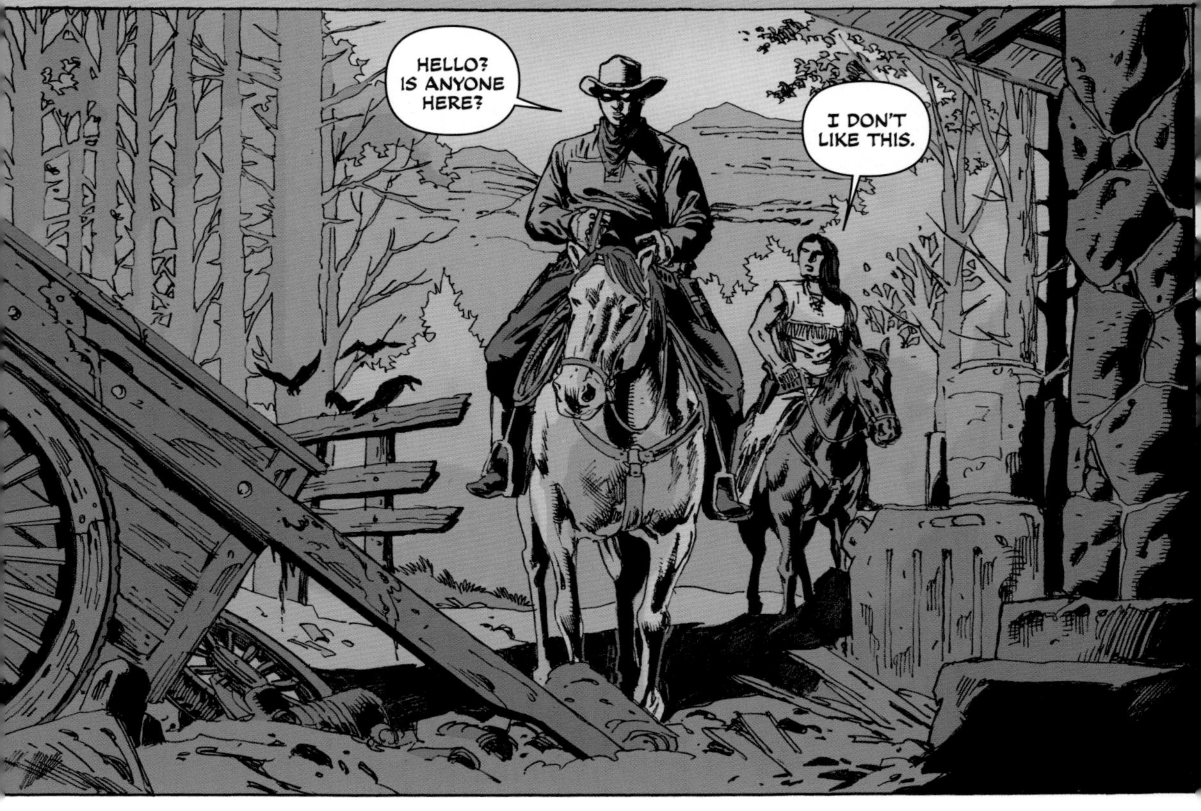
HELLO? IS ANYONE HERE?
I DON'T LIKE THIS.

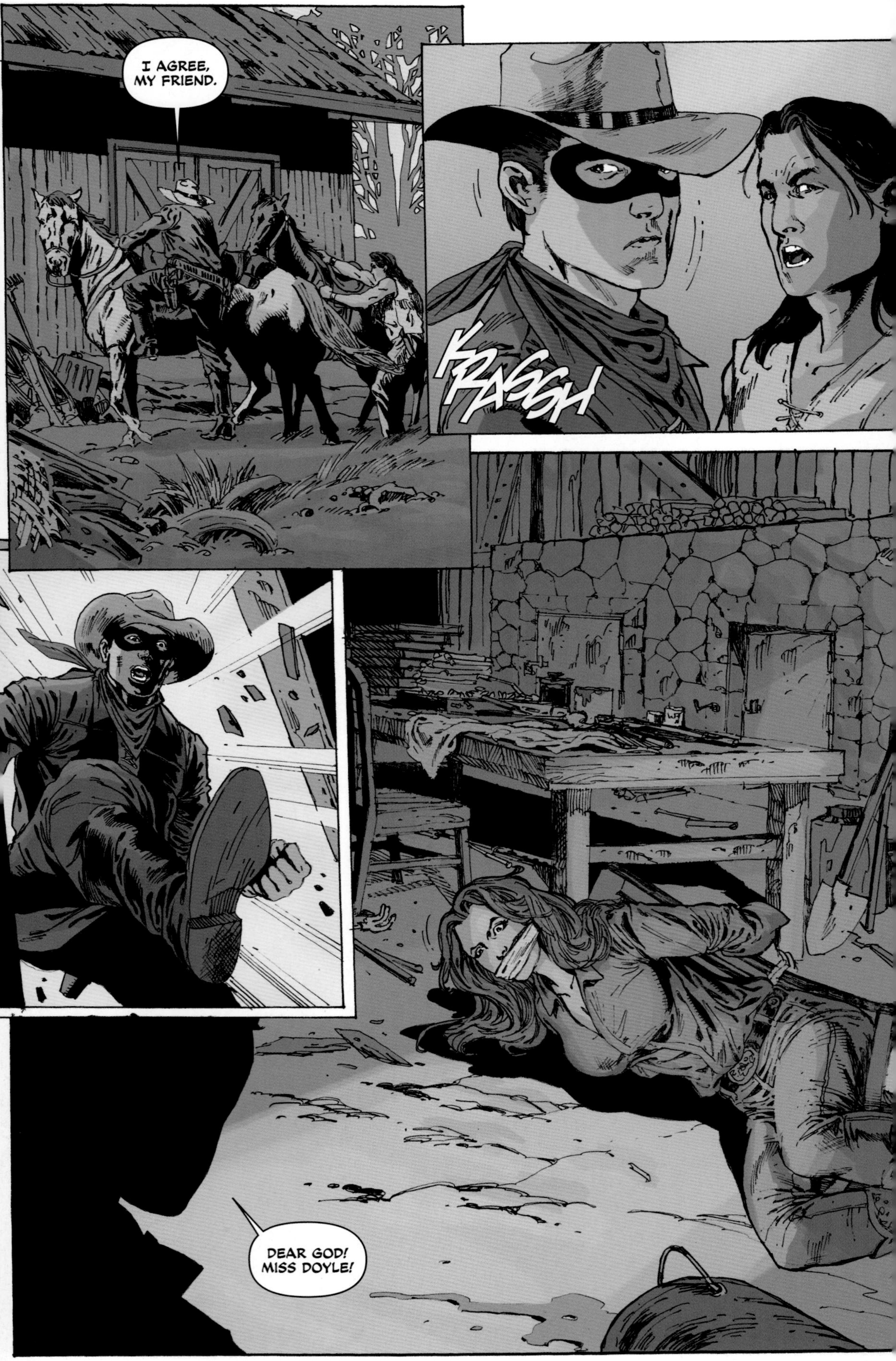
I AGREE, MY FRIEND.
KRASSH
DEAR GOD! MISS DOYLE!

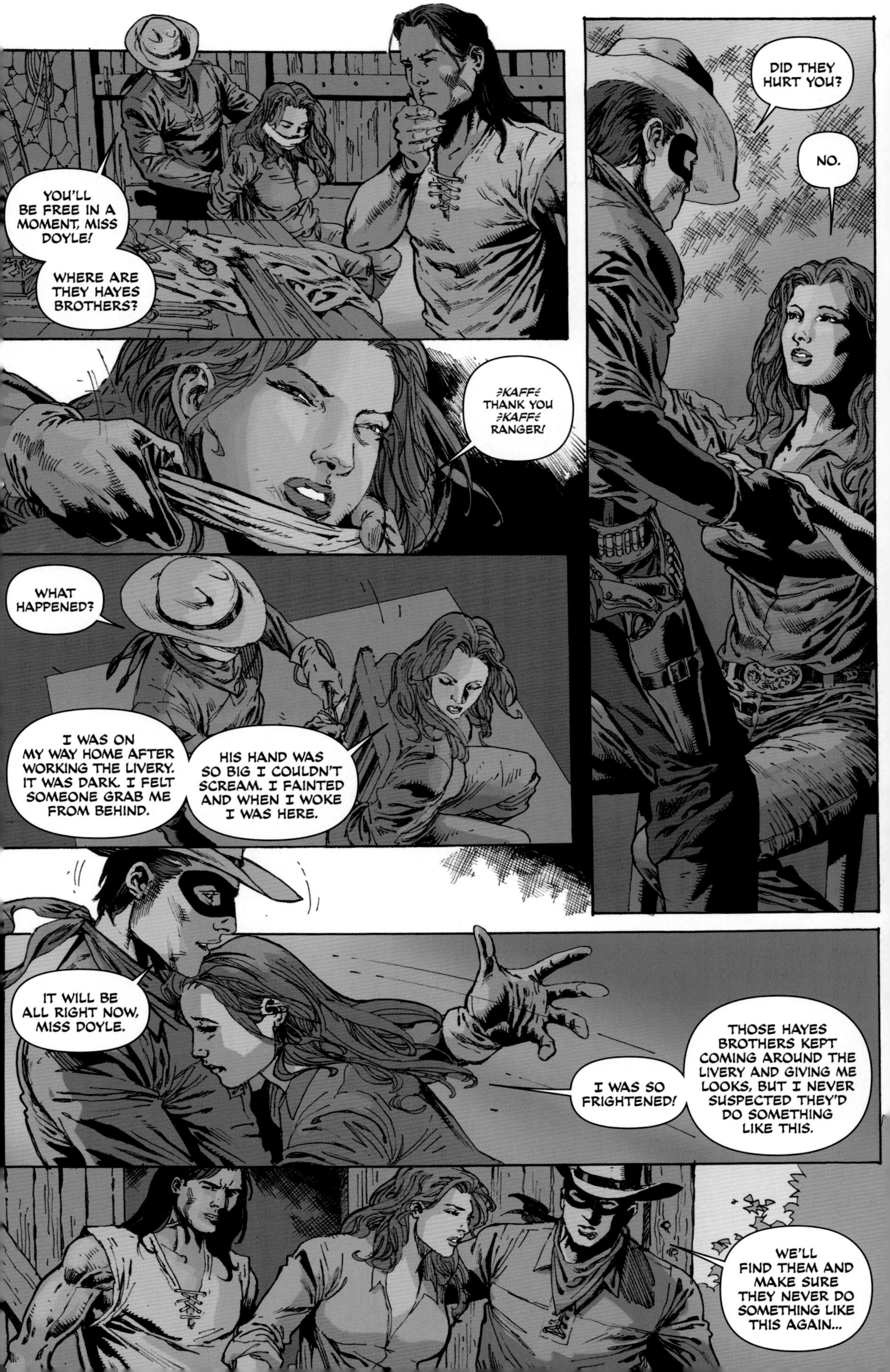
YOU'LL BE FREE IN A MOMENT, MISS DOYLE!
WHERE ARE THEY HAYES BROTHERS?
DID THEY HURT YOU?
NO.
≠KAFF≠ THANK YOU ≠KAFF≠ RANGER!
WHAT HAPPENED?
I WAS ON MY WAY HOME AFTER WORKING THE LIVERY. IT WAS DARK. I FELT SOMEONE GRAB ME FROM BEHIND.
HIS HAND WAS SO BIG I COULDN'T SCREAM. I FAINTED AND WHEN I WOKE I WAS HERE.
IT WILL BE ALL RIGHT NOW, MISS DOYLE.
I WAS SO FRIGHTENED!
THOSE HAYES BROTHERS KEPT COMING AROUND THE LIVERY AND GIVING ME LOOKS, BUT I NEVER SUSPECTED THEY'D DO SOMETHING LIKE THIS.
WE'LL FIND THEM AND MAKE SURE THEY NEVER DO SOMETHING LIKE THIS AGAIN...

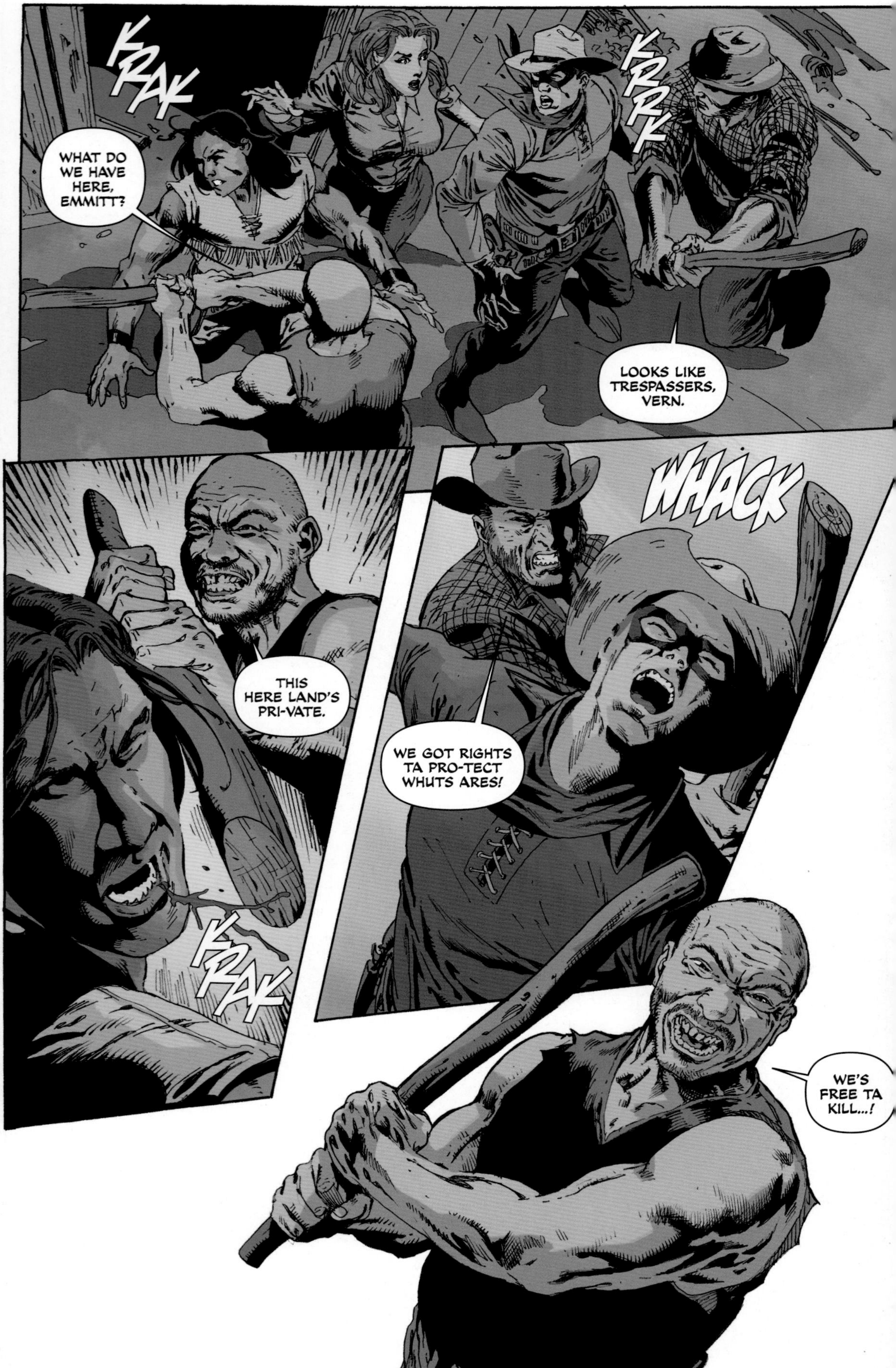
KRAK
KRRK
WHAT DO WE HAVE HERE, EMMITT?
LOOKS LIKE TRESPASSERS, VERN.
THIS HERE LAND'S PRI-VATE.
KRAK
WHACK
WE GOT RIGHTS TA PRO-TECT WHUTS ARES!
WE'S FREE TA KILL...!

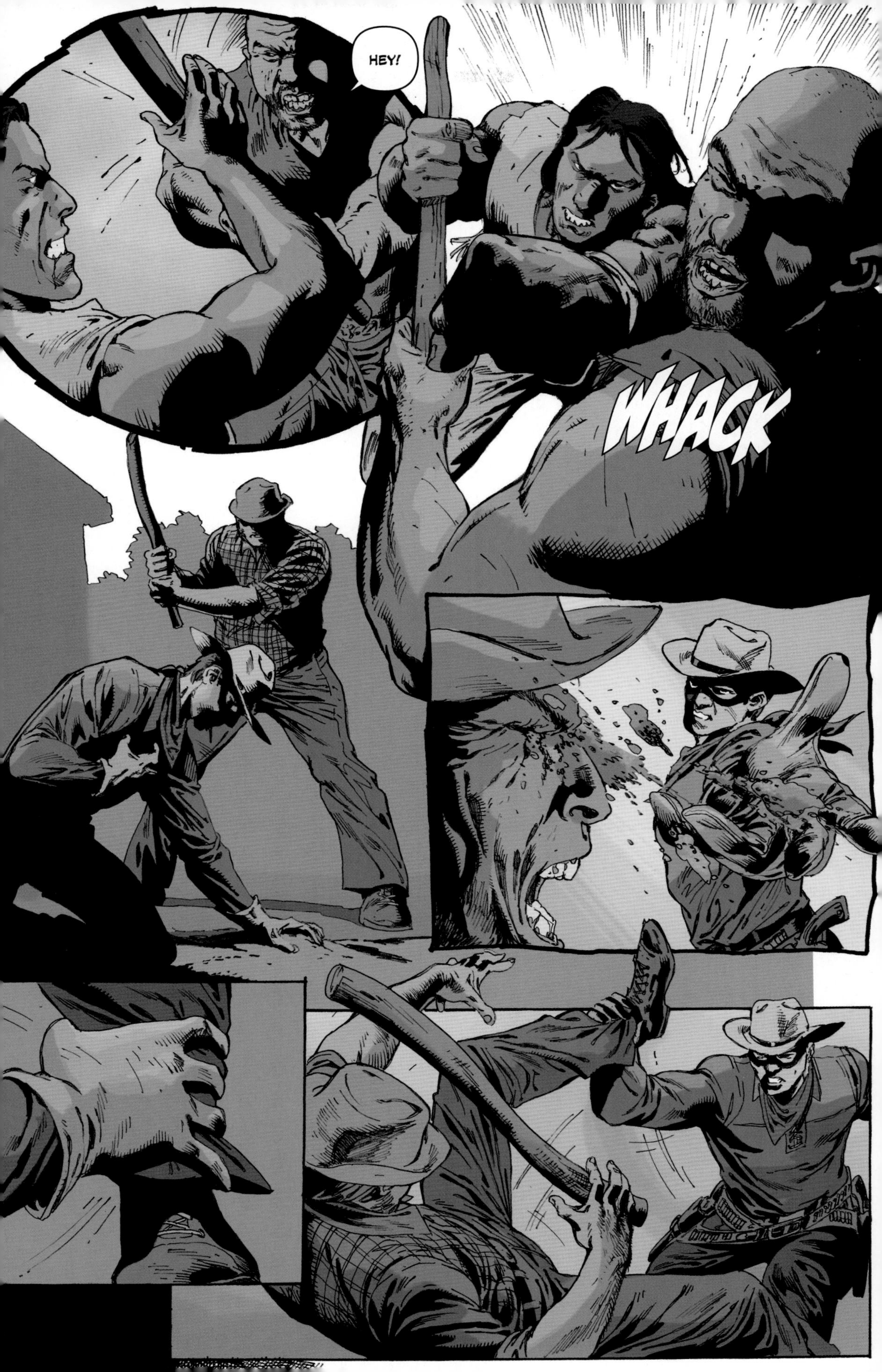
HEY!
WHACK

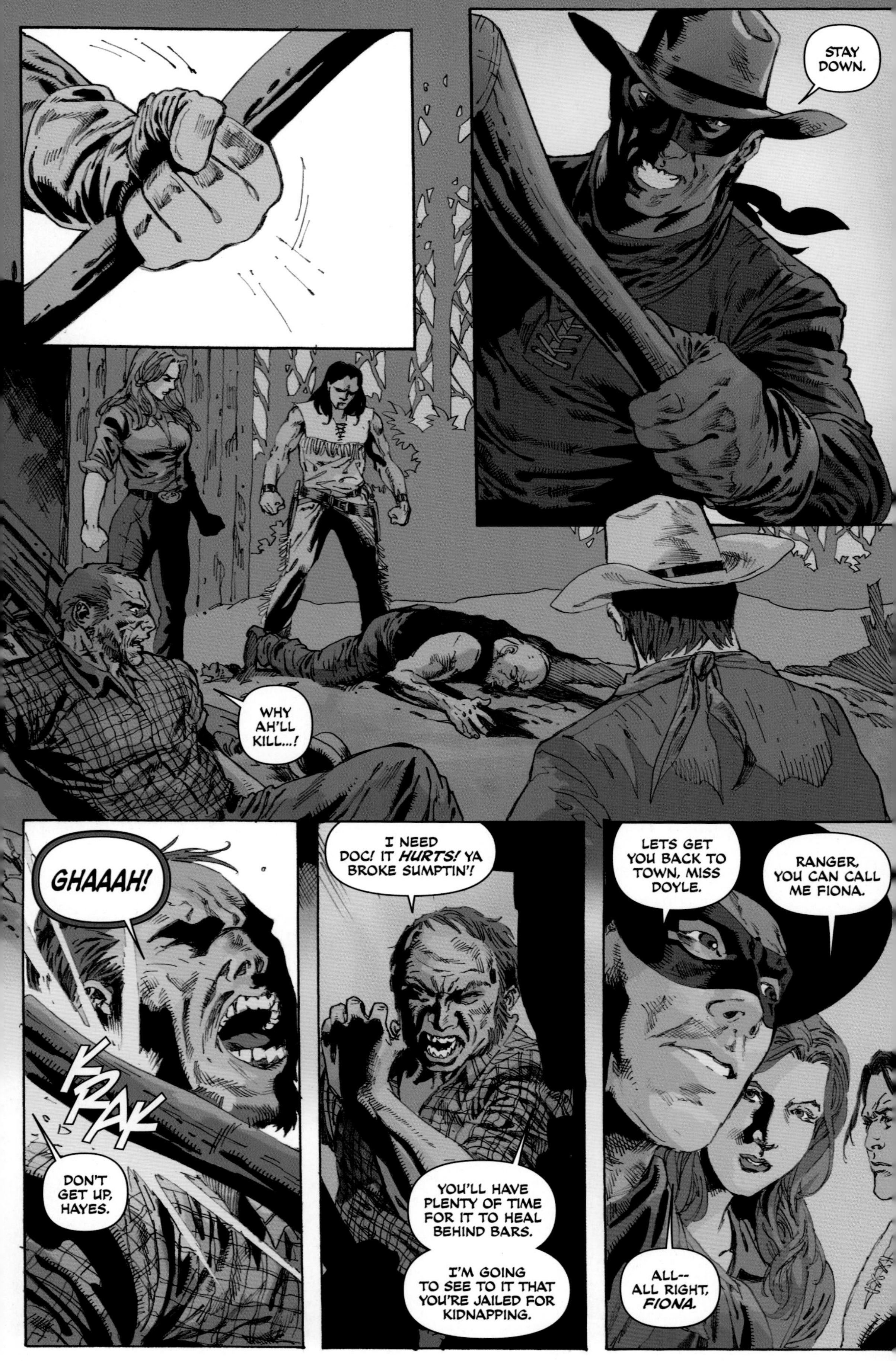
STAY DOWN.
WHY AH'LL KILL...!
GHAAAH!
KRAK
DON'T GET UP, HAYES.
I NEED DOC! IT *HURTS!* YA BROKE SUMPTIN'!
YOU'LL HAVE PLENTY OF TIME FOR IT TO HEAL BEHIND BARS.
I'M GOING TO SEE TO IT THAT YOU'RE JAILED FOR KIDNAPPING.
LETS GET YOU BACK TO TOWN, MISS DOYLE.
RANGER, YOU CAN CALL ME FIONA.
ALL-- ALL RIGHT, *FIONA.*

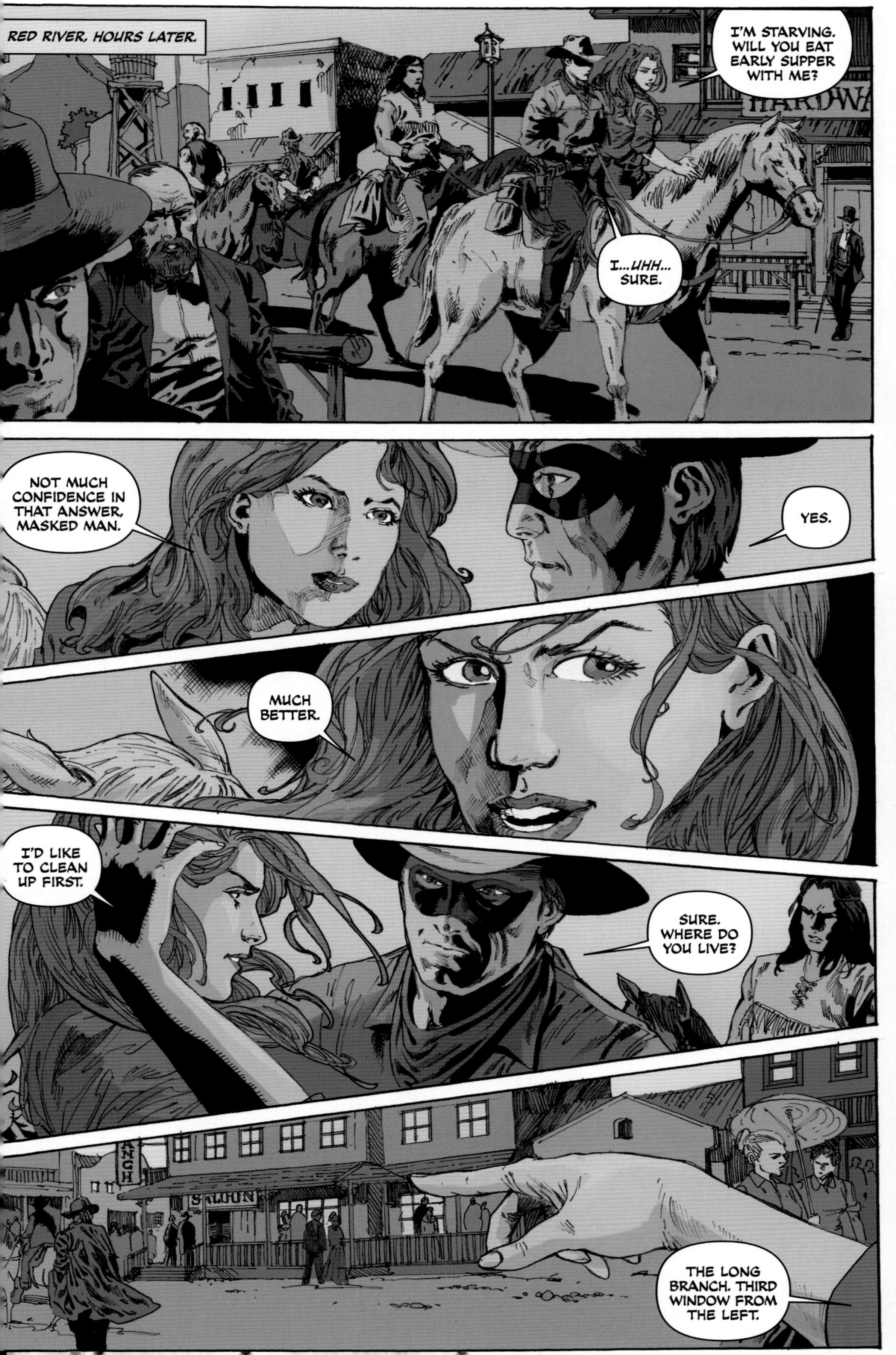
RED RIVER, HOURS LATER.
I'M STARVING. WILL YOU EAT EARLY SUPPER WITH ME?
I...UHH... SURE.
HARDWA
NOT MUCH CONFIDENCE IN THAT ANSWER, MASKED MAN.
YES.
MUCH BETTER.
I'D LIKE TO CLEAN UP FIRST.
SURE. WHERE DO YOU LIVE?
THE LONG BRANCH. THIRD WINDOW FROM THE LEFT.

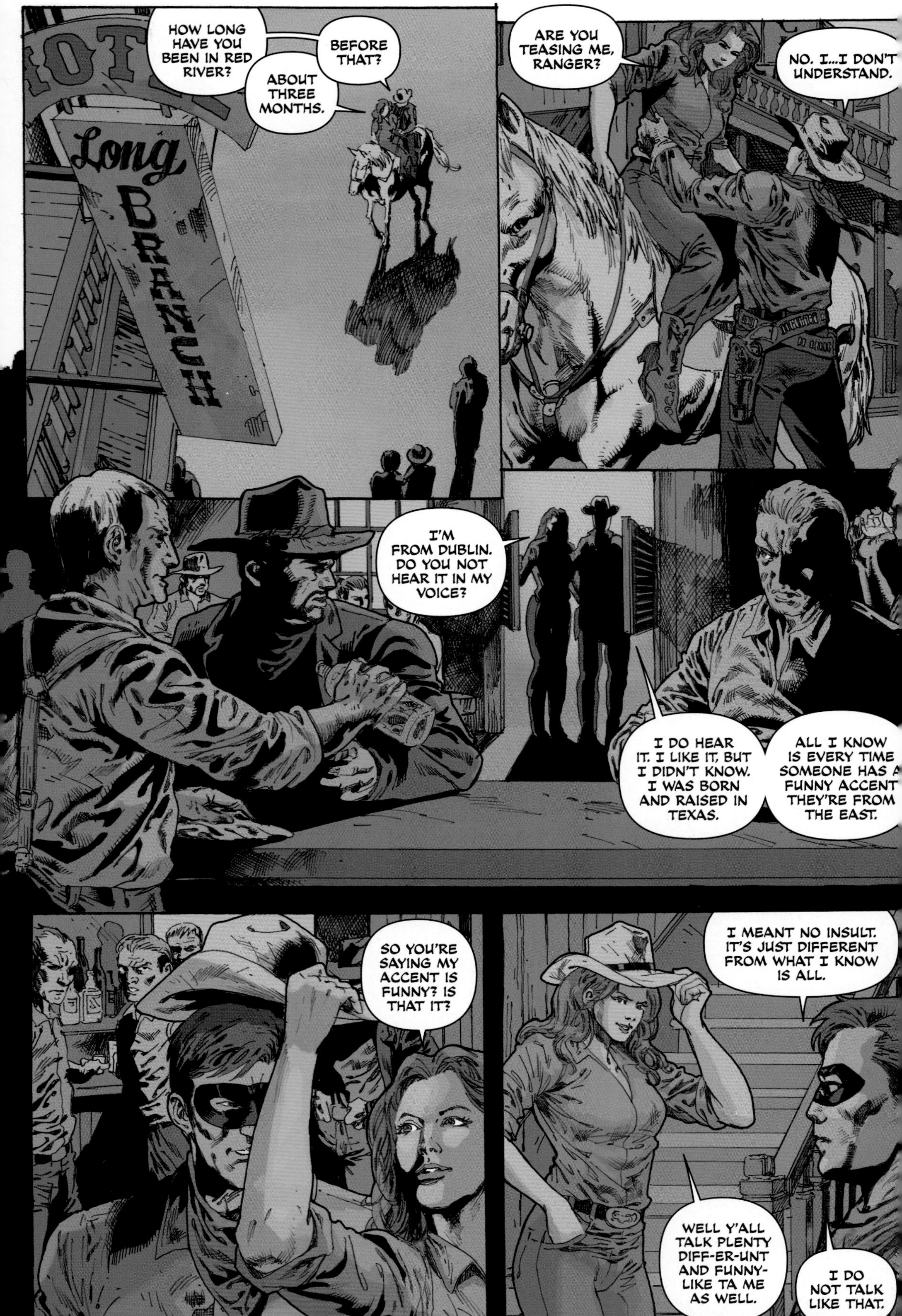
HOTEL
Long BRANCH
HOW LONG HAVE YOU BEEN IN RED RIVER?
ABOUT THREE MONTHS.
BEFORE THAT?
ARE YOU TEASING ME, RANGER?
NO. I...I DON'T UNDERSTAND.
I'M FROM DUBLIN. DO YOU NOT HEAR IT IN MY VOICE?
I DO HEAR IT. I LIKE IT, BUT I DIDN'T KNOW. I WAS BORN AND RAISED IN TEXAS.
ALL I KNOW IS EVERY TIME SOMEONE HAS A FUNNY ACCENT THEY'RE FROM THE EAST.
SO YOU'RE SAYING MY ACCENT IS FUNNY? IS THAT IT?
I MEANT NO INSULT. IT'S JUST DIFFERENT FROM WHAT I KNOW IS ALL.
WELL Y'ALL TALK PLENTY DIFF-ER-UNT AND FUNNY-LIKE TA ME AS WELL.
I DO NOT TALK LIKE THAT.

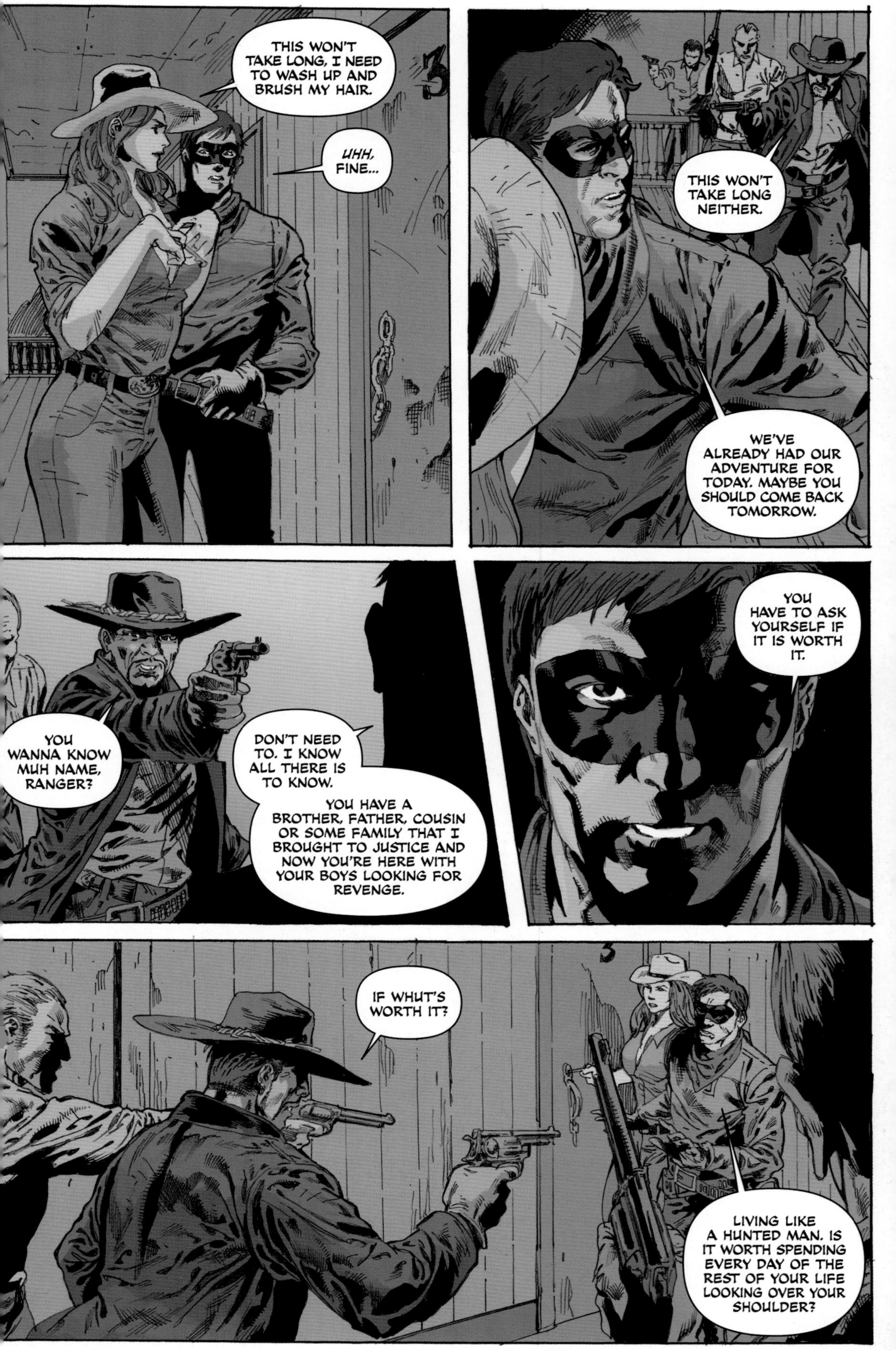
THIS WON'T TAKE LONG, I NEED TO WASH UP AND BRUSH MY HAIR.
UHH, FINE...
THIS WON'T TAKE LONG NEITHER.
WE'VE ALREADY HAD OUR ADVENTURE FOR TODAY. MAYBE YOU SHOULD COME BACK TOMORROW.
YOU WANNA KNOW MUH NAME, RANGER?
DON'T NEED TO. I KNOW ALL THERE IS TO KNOW.
YOU HAVE A BROTHER, FATHER, COUSIN OR SOME FAMILY THAT I BROUGHT TO JUSTICE AND NOW YOU'RE HERE WITH YOUR BOYS LOOKING FOR REVENGE.
YOU HAVE TO ASK YOURSELF IF IT IS WORTH IT.
IF WHUT'S WORTH IT?
LIVING LIKE A HUNTED MAN. IS IT WORTH SPENDING EVERY DAY OF THE REST OF YOUR LIFE LOOKING OVER YOUR SHOULDER?

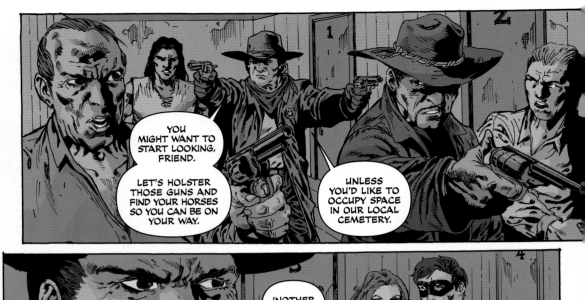

YOU MIGHT WANT TO START LOOKING, FRIEND.

LET'S HOLSTER THOSE GUNS AND FIND YOUR HORSES SO YOU CAN BE ON YOUR WAY.

UNLESS YOU'D LIKE TO OCCUPY SPACE IN OUR LOCAL CEMETERY.

'NOTHER TIME, RANGER.

DEAR ME, WHAT WILL THE NEIGHBORS SAY WHEN THEY SEE THREE STRAPPING YOUNG MEN ENTERING MY ROOM?

I JUST CAME BY TO SEE HOW YOU WERE, MISS DOYLE.

I WAS SHAKEN AND QUITE FRIGHTENED AT THE TIME, BUT THESE HEROIC MEN SAVED ME FROM UNIMAGINABLE HORRORS.

I ASSURE YOU THOSE DIMWITTED HAYES BOYS WILL STEER CLEAR OF YOU AND RED RIVER ENTIRELY.

GOOD TO KNOW YOU'RE RUNNING THEM OUT OF TOWN.

I SENT MY DEPUTY FOR JUDGE CARSON OVER IN ABELINE. I AIM TO STRETCH THEIR NECKS.

WAIT, YOU'RE GOING TO HANG THEM?

THAT'S RIGHT.

YOU SAID IT YOURSELF. THEY'RE DIMWITTED, MAYBE EVEN TOO STUPID TO KNOW BETTER WHICH MAKES KILLING THEM SOMEWHAT UNFAIR. WOULDN'T YOU AGREE?

I DON'T GET YOU, RANGER.

THESE MEN KIDNAP MISS DOYLE AND HOLD HER HOSTAGE WITH BAD INTENTIONS. ARE YOU SUGGESTING I SHOULD MAKE THEM SOMEONE ELSE'S PROBLEM?

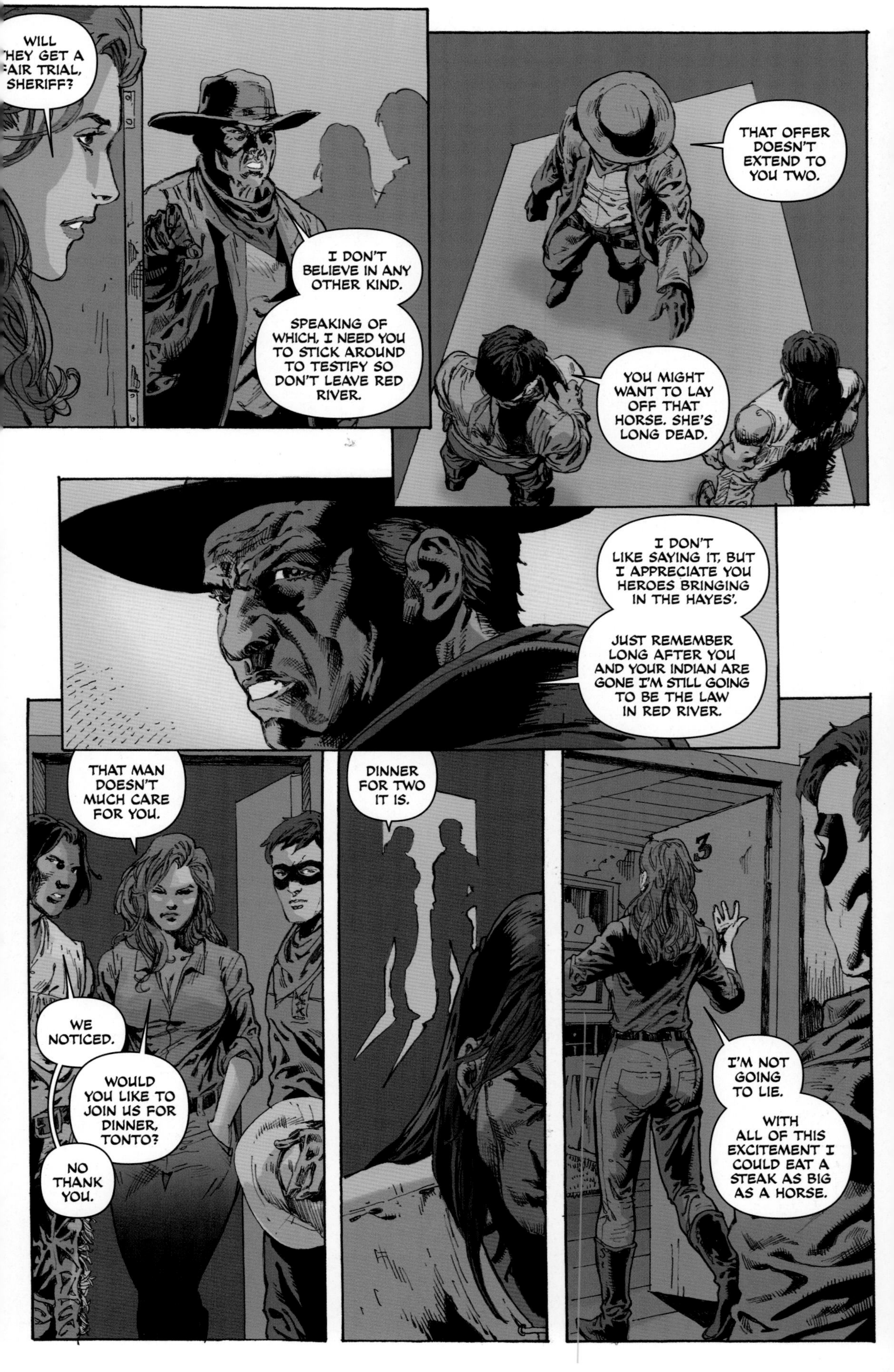

WILL THEY GET A FAIR TRIAL, SHERIFF?
I DON'T BELIEVE IN ANY OTHER KIND.
SPEAKING OF WHICH, I NEED YOU TO STICK AROUND TO TESTIFY SO DON'T LEAVE RED RIVER.
THAT OFFER DOESN'T EXTEND TO YOU TWO.
YOU MIGHT WANT TO LAY OFF THAT HORSE. SHE'S LONG DEAD.
I DON'T LIKE SAYING IT, BUT I APPRECIATE YOU HEROES BRINGING IN THE HAYES'.
JUST REMEMBER LONG AFTER YOU AND YOUR INDIAN ARE GONE I'M STILL GOING TO BE THE LAW IN RED RIVER.
THAT MAN DOESN'T MUCH CARE FOR YOU.
WE NOTICED.
WOULD YOU LIKE TO JOIN US FOR DINNER, TONTO?
NO THANK YOU.
DINNER FOR TWO IT IS.
I'M NOT GOING TO LIE.
WITH ALL OF THIS EXCITEMENT I COULD EAT A STEAK AS BIG AS A HORSE.

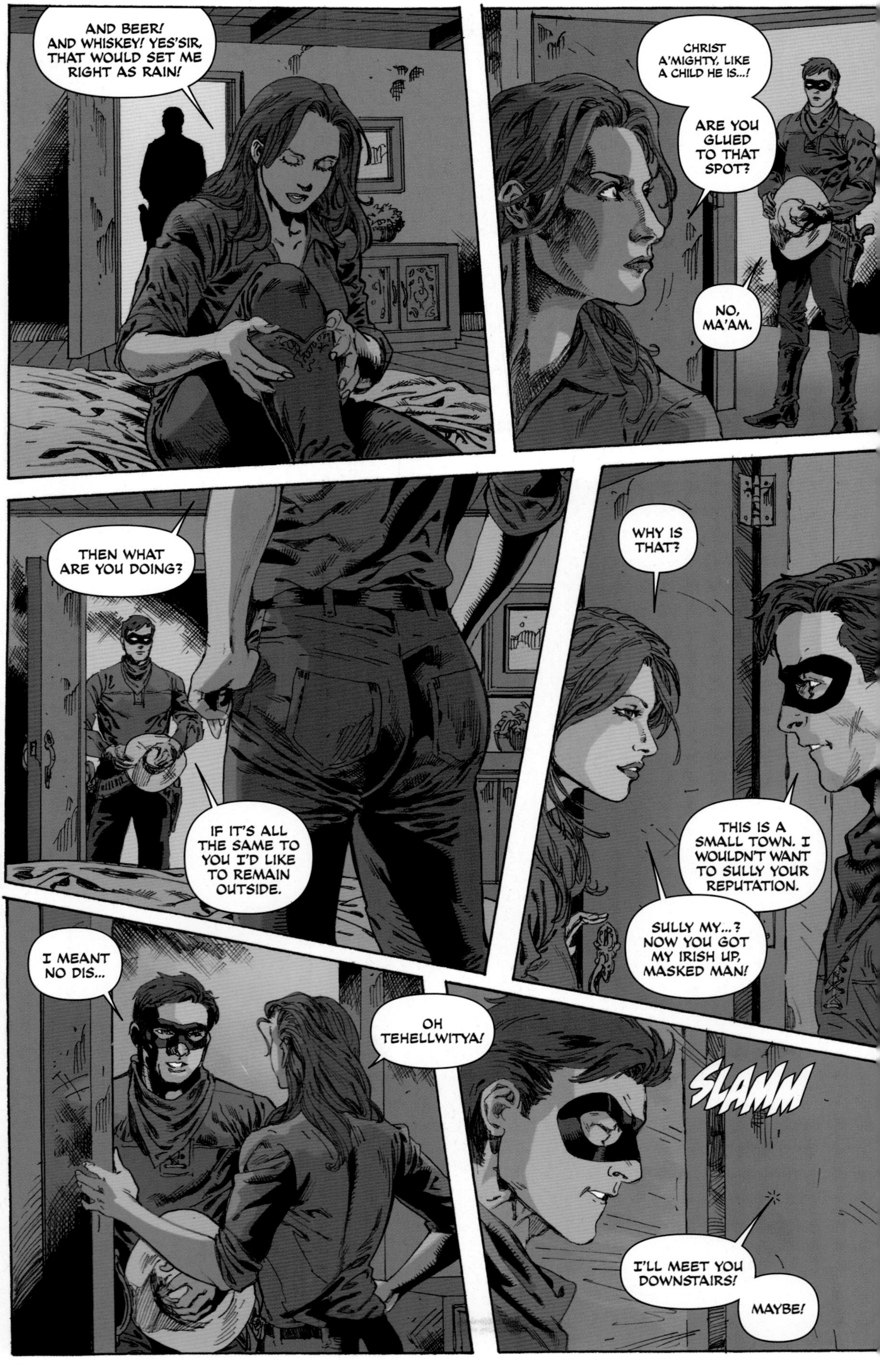
AND BEER! AND WHISKEY! YES'SIR, THAT WOULD SET ME RIGHT AS RAIN!
CHRIST A'MIGHTY, LIKE A CHILD HE IS...!
ARE YOU GLUED TO THAT SPOT?
NO, MA'AM.
THEN WHAT ARE YOU DOING?
IF IT'S ALL THE SAME TO YOU I'D LIKE TO REMAIN OUTSIDE.
WHY IS THAT?
THIS IS A SMALL TOWN. I WOULDN'T WANT TO SULLY YOUR REPUTATION.
SULLY MY...? NOW YOU GOT MY IRISH UP, MASKED MAN!
I MEANT NO DIS...
OH TEHELLWITYA!
SLAMM
I'LL MEET YOU DOWNSTAIRS!
MAYBE!

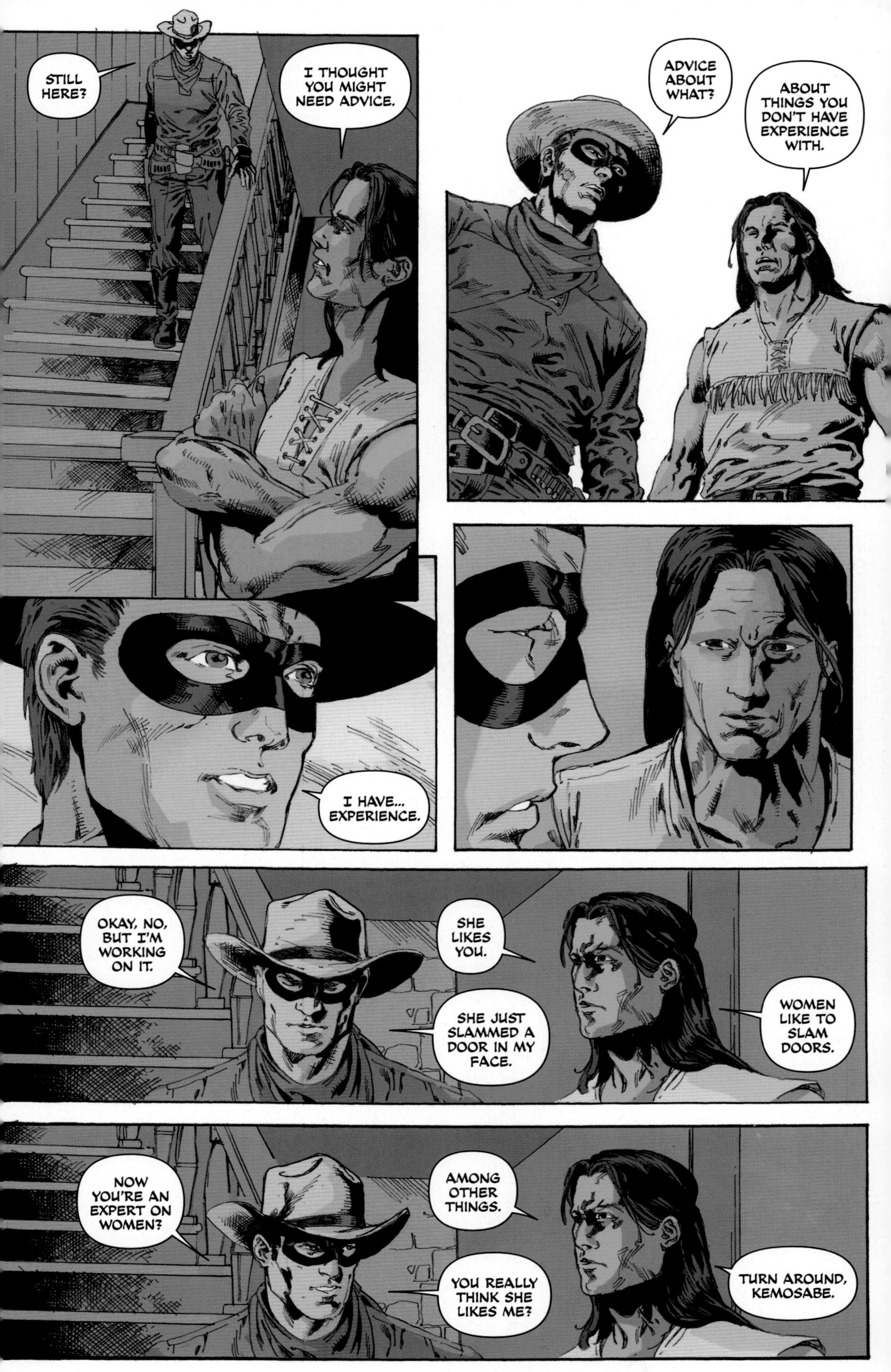
STILL HERE?
I THOUGHT YOU MIGHT NEED ADVICE.
ADVICE ABOUT WHAT?
ABOUT THINGS YOU DON'T HAVE EXPERIENCE WITH.
I HAVE... EXPERIENCE.
OKAY, NO, BUT I'M WORKING ON IT.
SHE LIKES YOU.
SHE JUST SLAMMED A DOOR IN MY FACE.
WOMEN LIKE TO SLAM DOORS.
NOW YOU'RE AN EXPERT ON WOMEN?
AMONG OTHER THINGS.
YOU REALLY THINK SHE LIKES ME?
TURN AROUND, KEMOSABE.

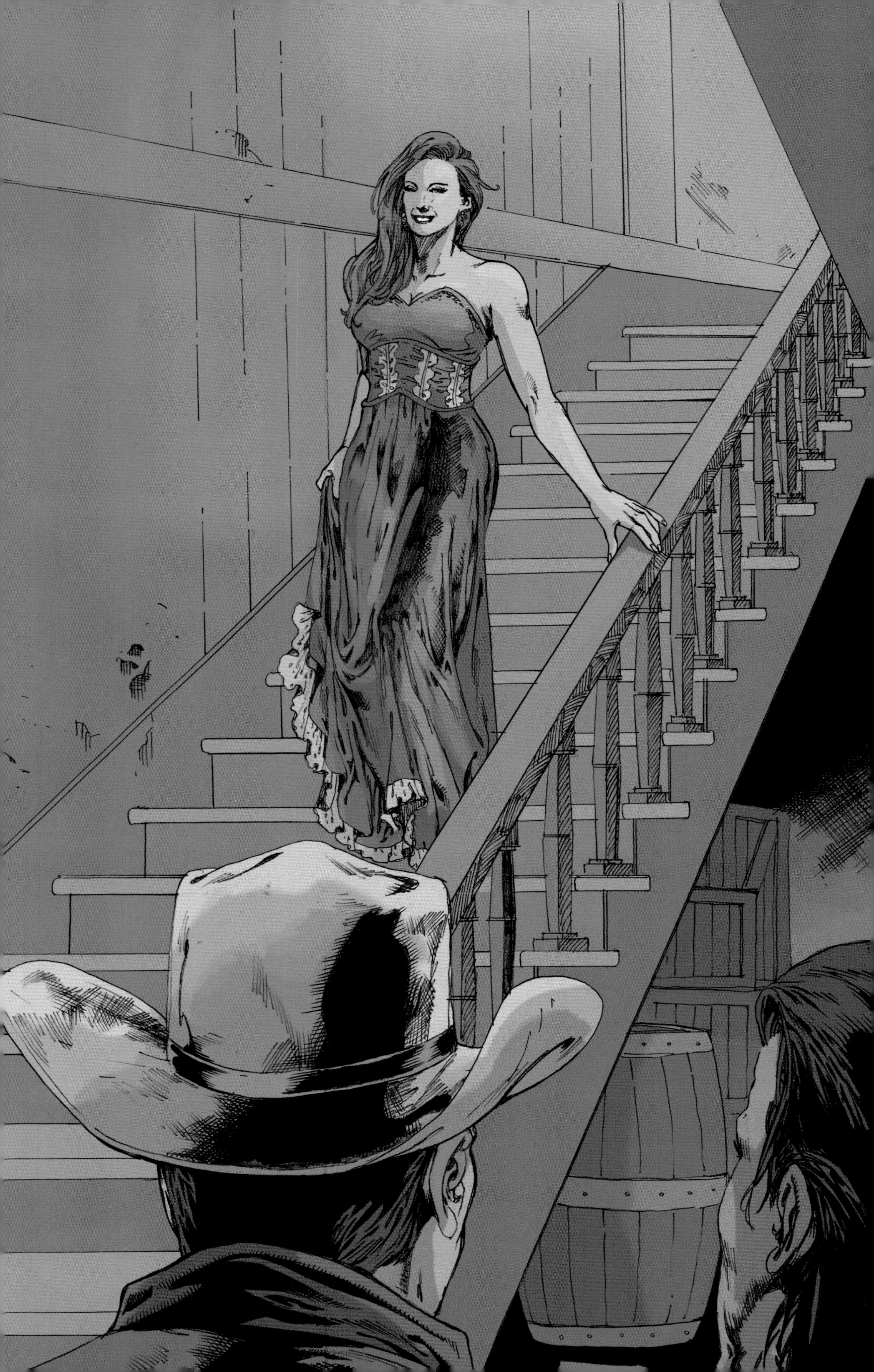

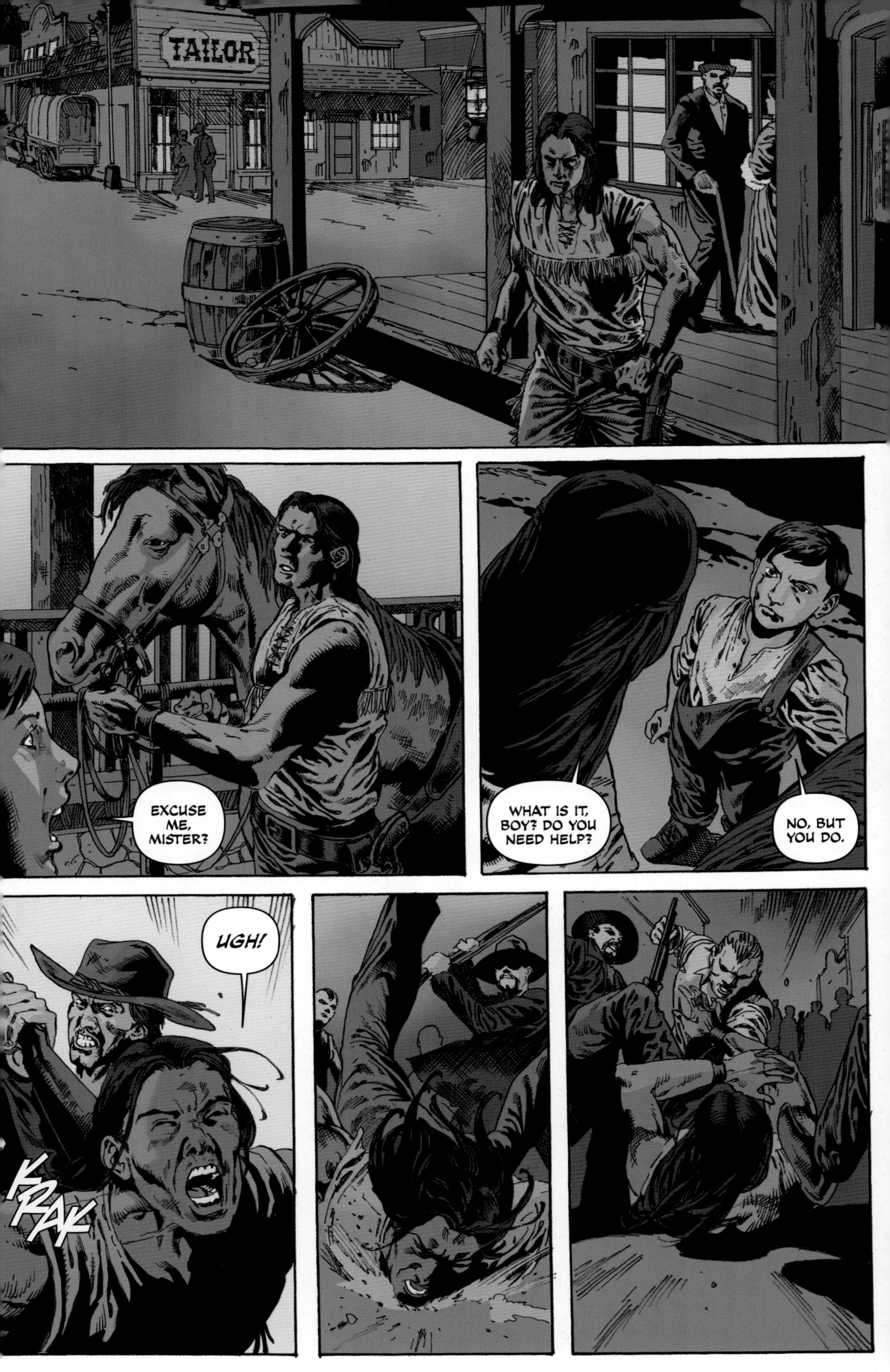
TAILOR
EXCUSE ME, MISTER?
WHAT IS IT, BOY? DO YOU NEED HELP?
NO, BUT YOU DO.
UGH!
KRAK

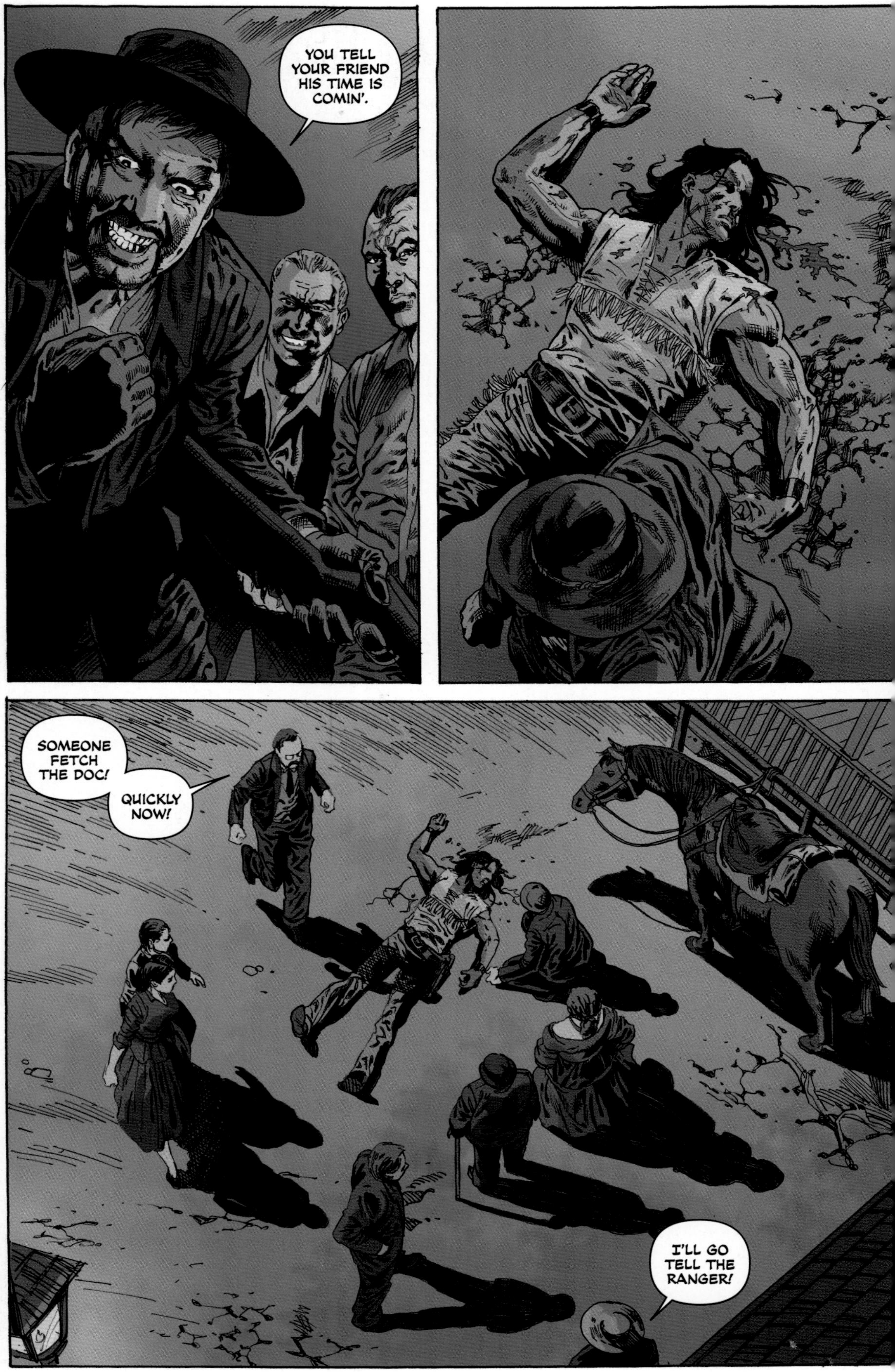
YOU TELL YOUR FRIEND HIS TIME IS COMIN'.
SOMEONE FETCH THE DOC!
QUICKLY NOW!
I'LL GO TELL THE RANGER!

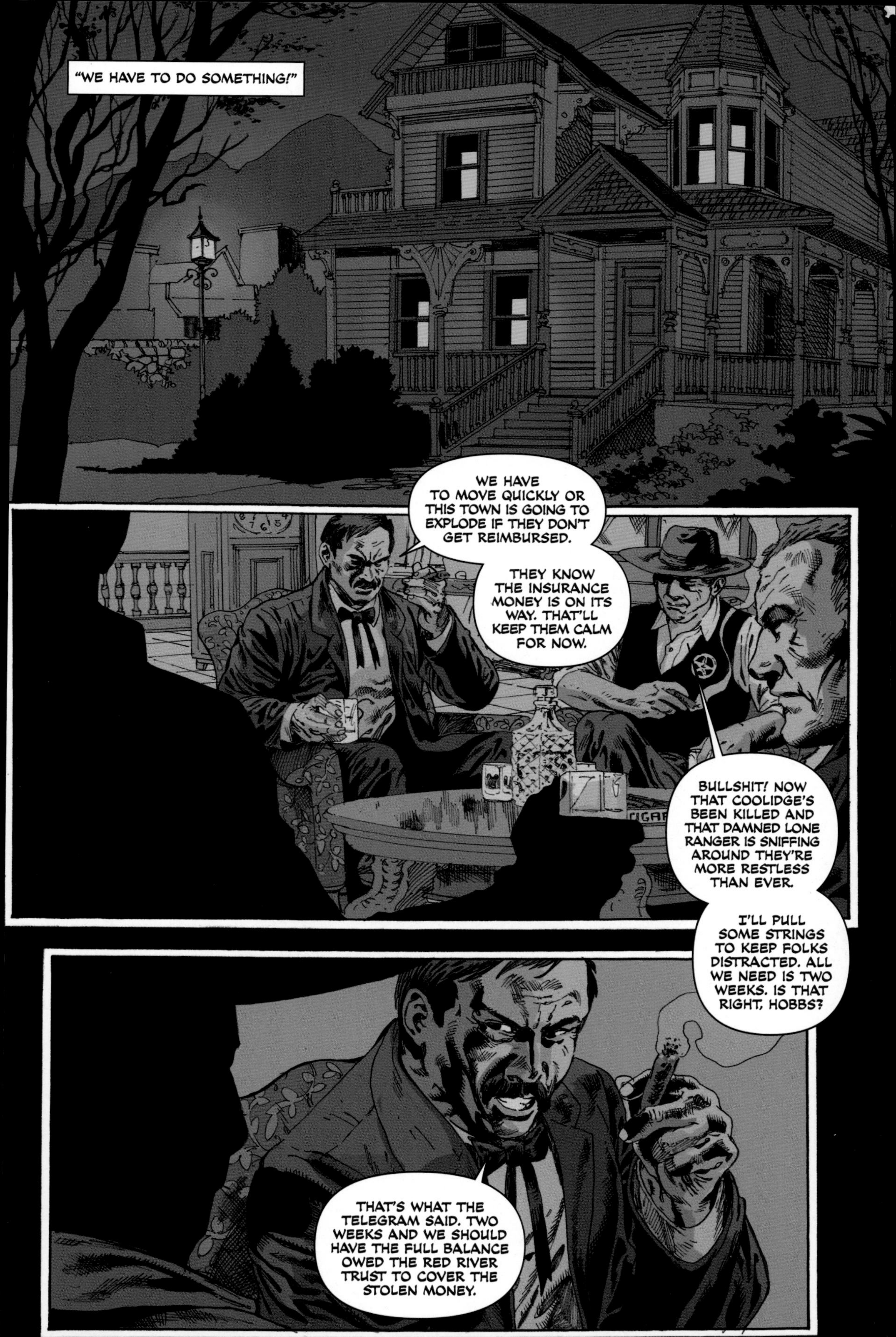
"WE HAVE TO DO SOMETHING!"
WE HAVE TO MOVE QUICKLY OR THIS TOWN IS GOING TO EXPLODE IF THEY DON'T GET REIMBURSED.
THEY KNOW THE INSURANCE MONEY IS ON ITS WAY. THAT'LL KEEP THEM CALM FOR NOW.
BULLSHIT! NOW THAT COOLIDGE'S BEEN KILLED AND THAT DAMNED LONE RANGER IS SNIFFING AROUND THEY'RE MORE RESTLESS THAN EVER.
I'LL PULL SOME STRINGS TO KEEP FOLKS DISTRACTED. ALL WE NEED IS TWO WEEKS. IS THAT RIGHT, HOBBS?
THAT'S WHAT THE TELEGRAM SAID. TWO WEEKS AND WE SHOULD HAVE THE FULL BALANCE OWED THE RED RIVER TRUST TO COVER THE STOLEN MONEY.

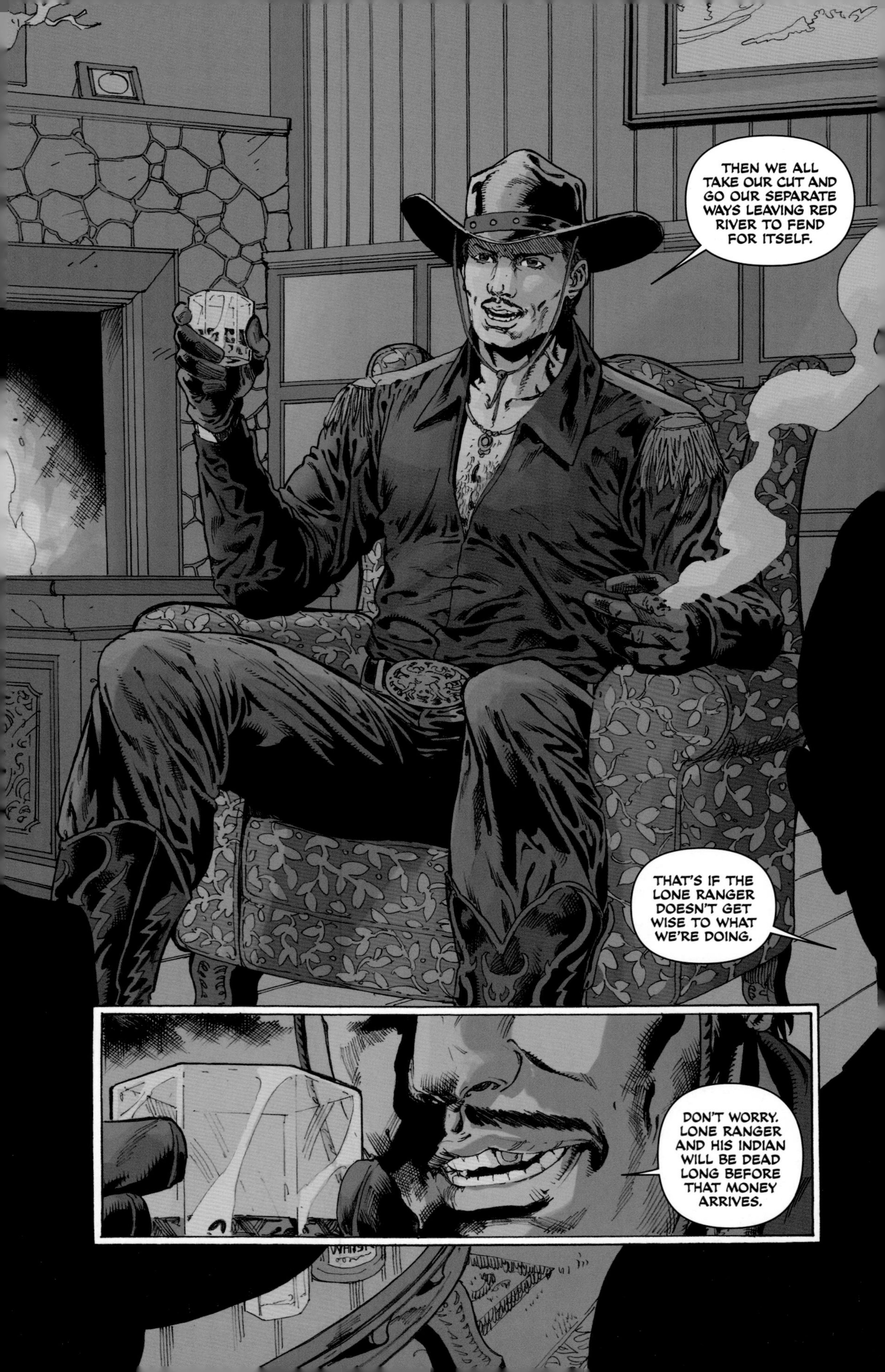
THEN WE ALL TAKE OUR CUT AND GO OUR SEPARATE WAYS LEAVING RED RIVER TO FEND FOR ITSELF.
THAT'S IF THE LONE RANGER DOESN'T GET WISE TO WHAT WE'RE DOING.
DON'T WORRY. LONE RANGER AND HIS INDIAN WILL BE DEAD LONG BEFORE THAT MONEY ARRIVES.

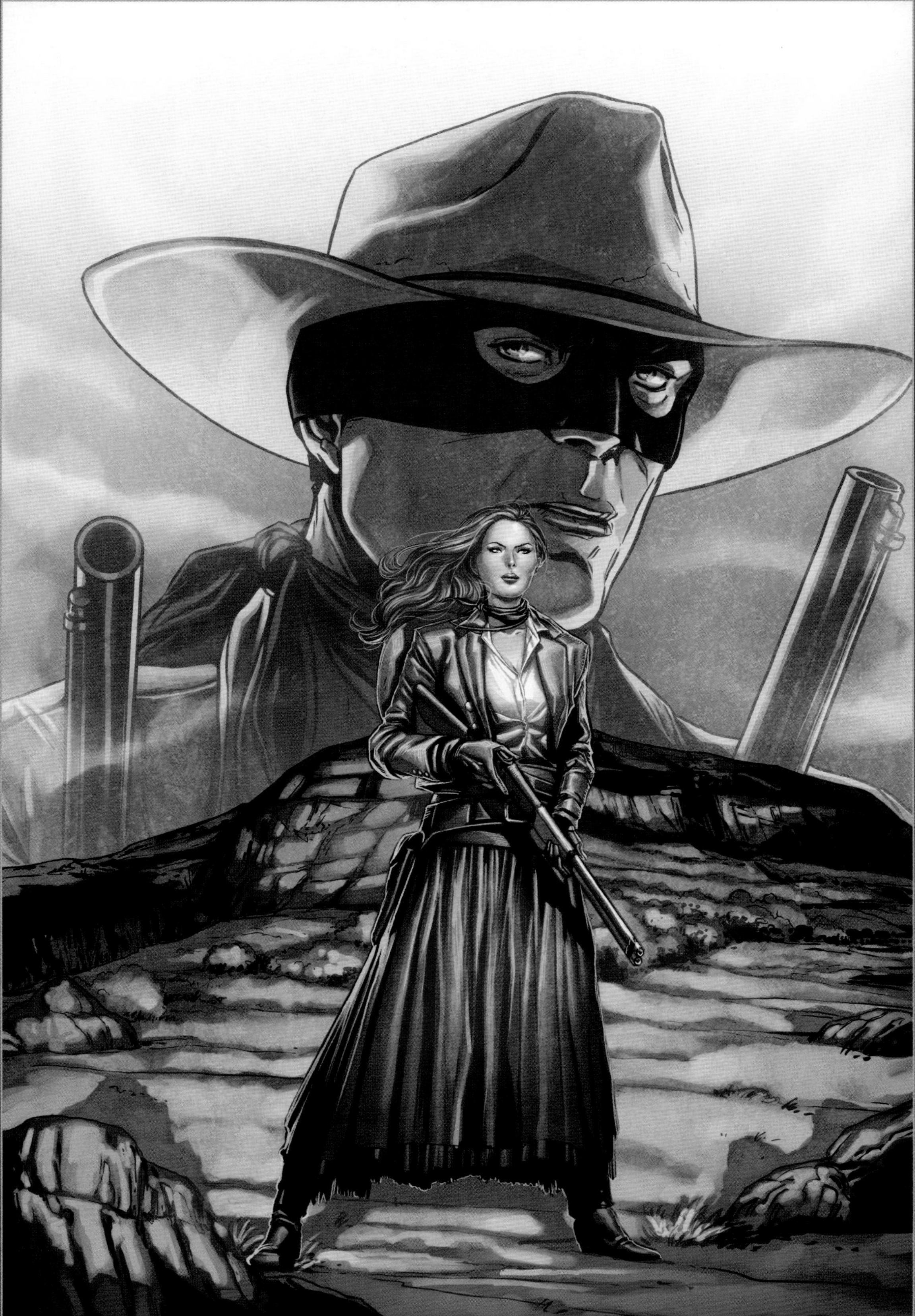

issue #3 cover by **MARC LAMING**
colors by **ELMER SANTOS**

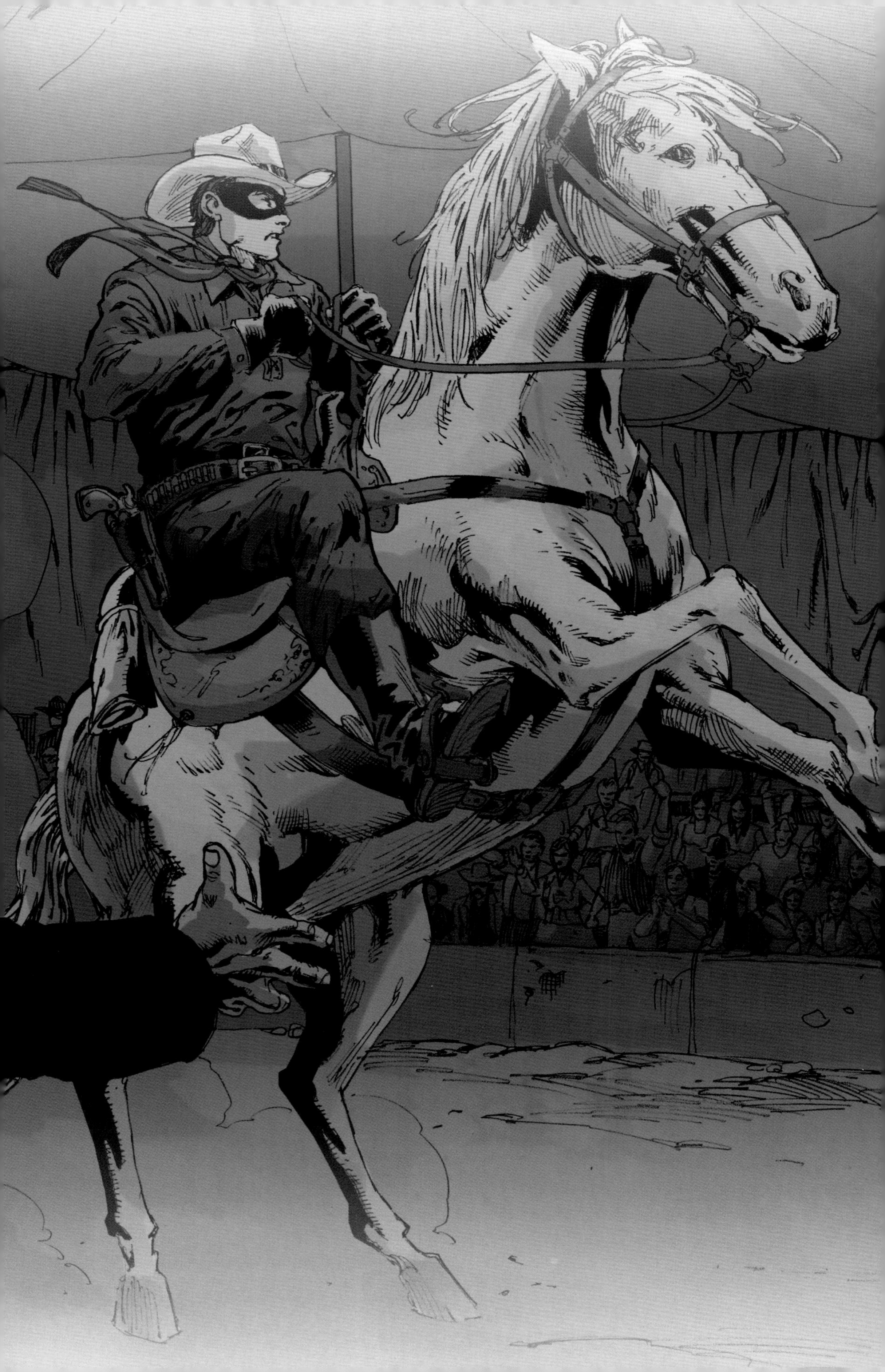

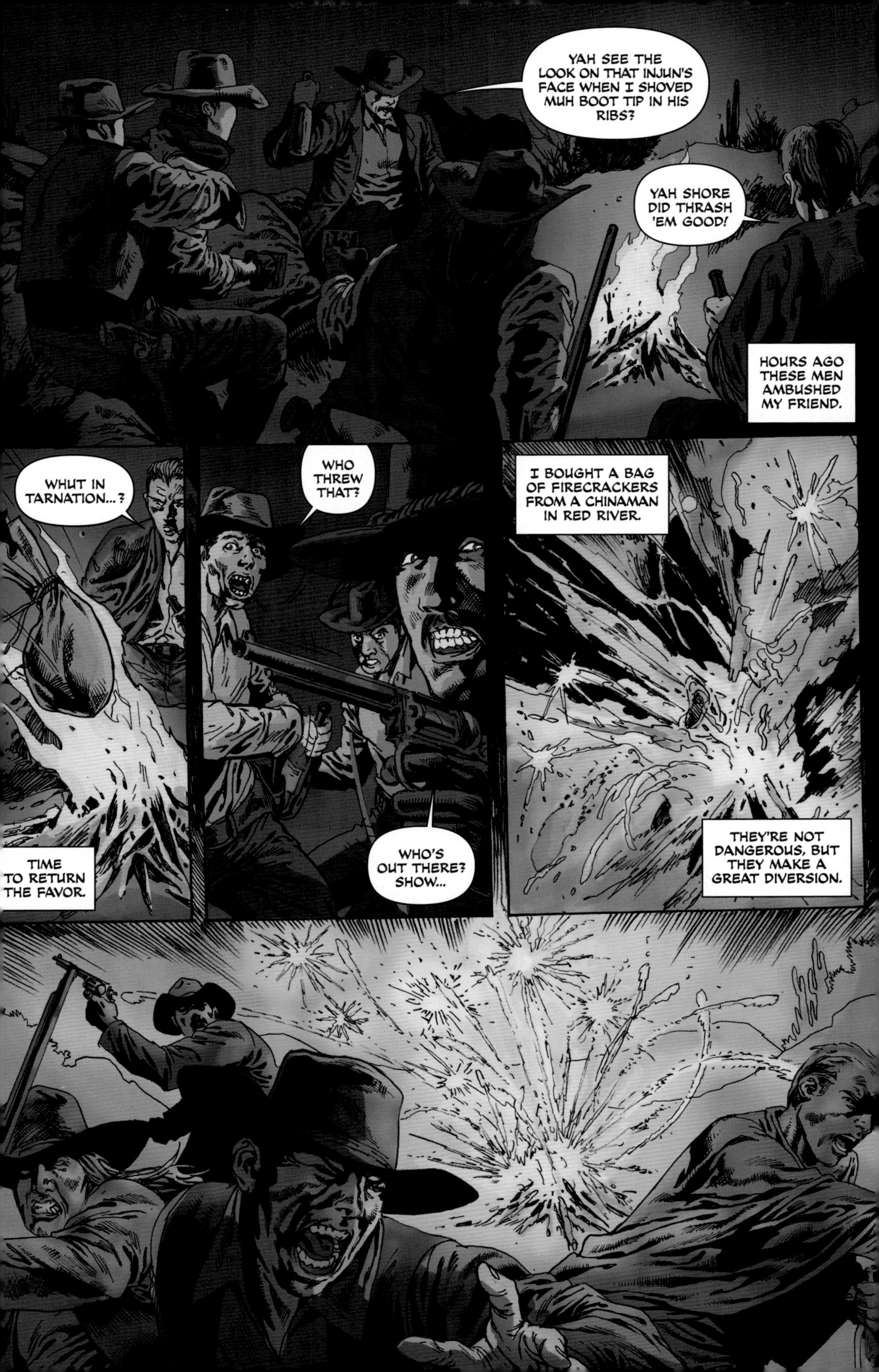
YAH SEE THE LOOK ON THAT INJUN'S FACE WHEN I SHOVED MUH BOOT TIP IN HIS RIBS?
YAH SHORE DID THRASH 'EM GOOD!
HOURS AGO THESE MEN AMBUSHED MY FRIEND.
WHUT IN TARNATION...?
TIME TO RETURN THE FAVOR.
WHO THREW THAT?
WHO'S OUT THERE? SHOW...
I BOUGHT A BAG OF FIRECRACKERS FROM A CHINAMAN IN RED RIVER.
THEY'RE NOT DANGEROUS, BUT THEY MAKE A GREAT DIVERSION.

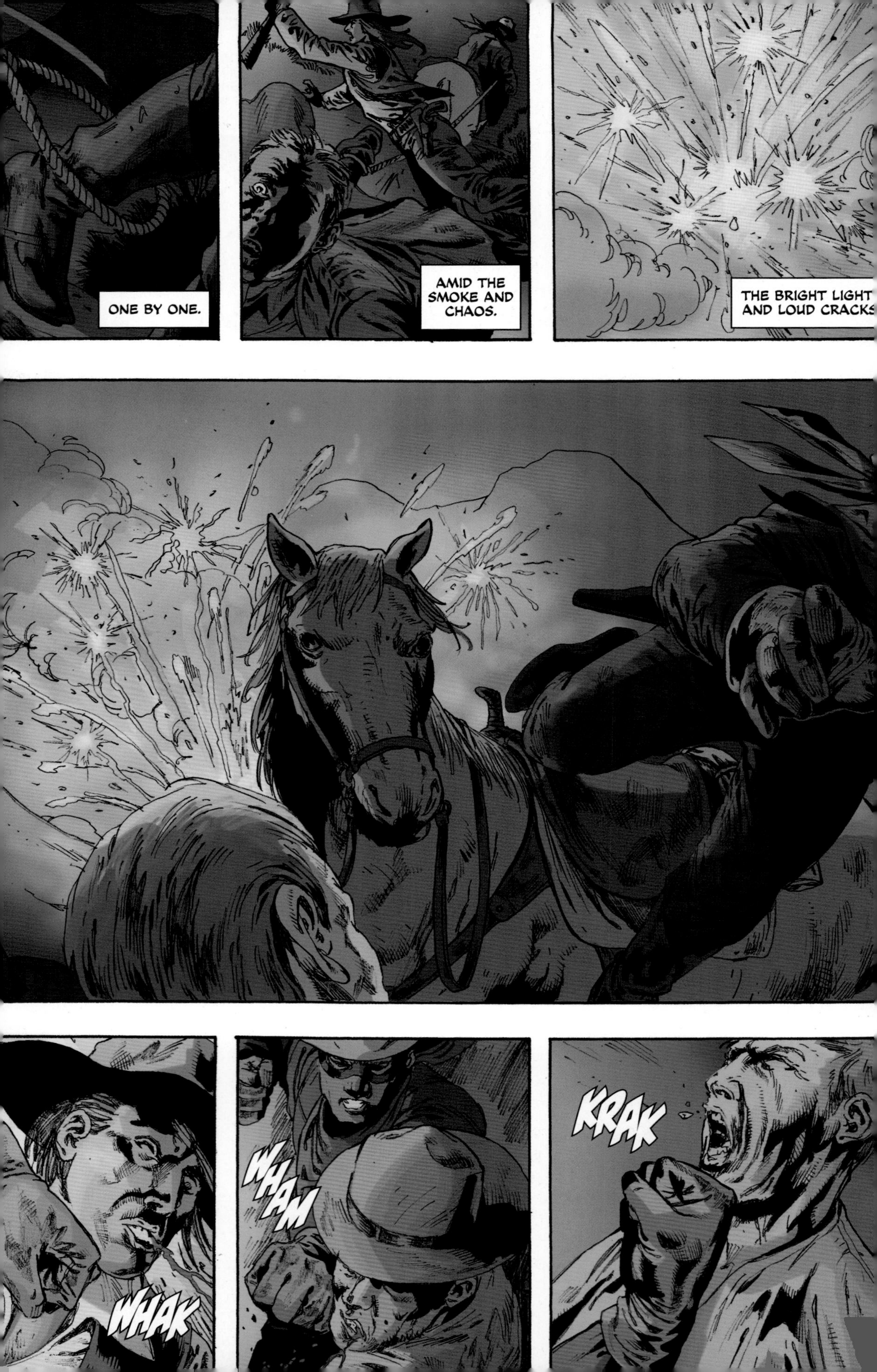
ONE BY ONE.
AMID THE SMOKE AND CHAOS.
THE BRIGHT LIGHT AND LOUD CRACKS
WHAK
WHAM
KRAK

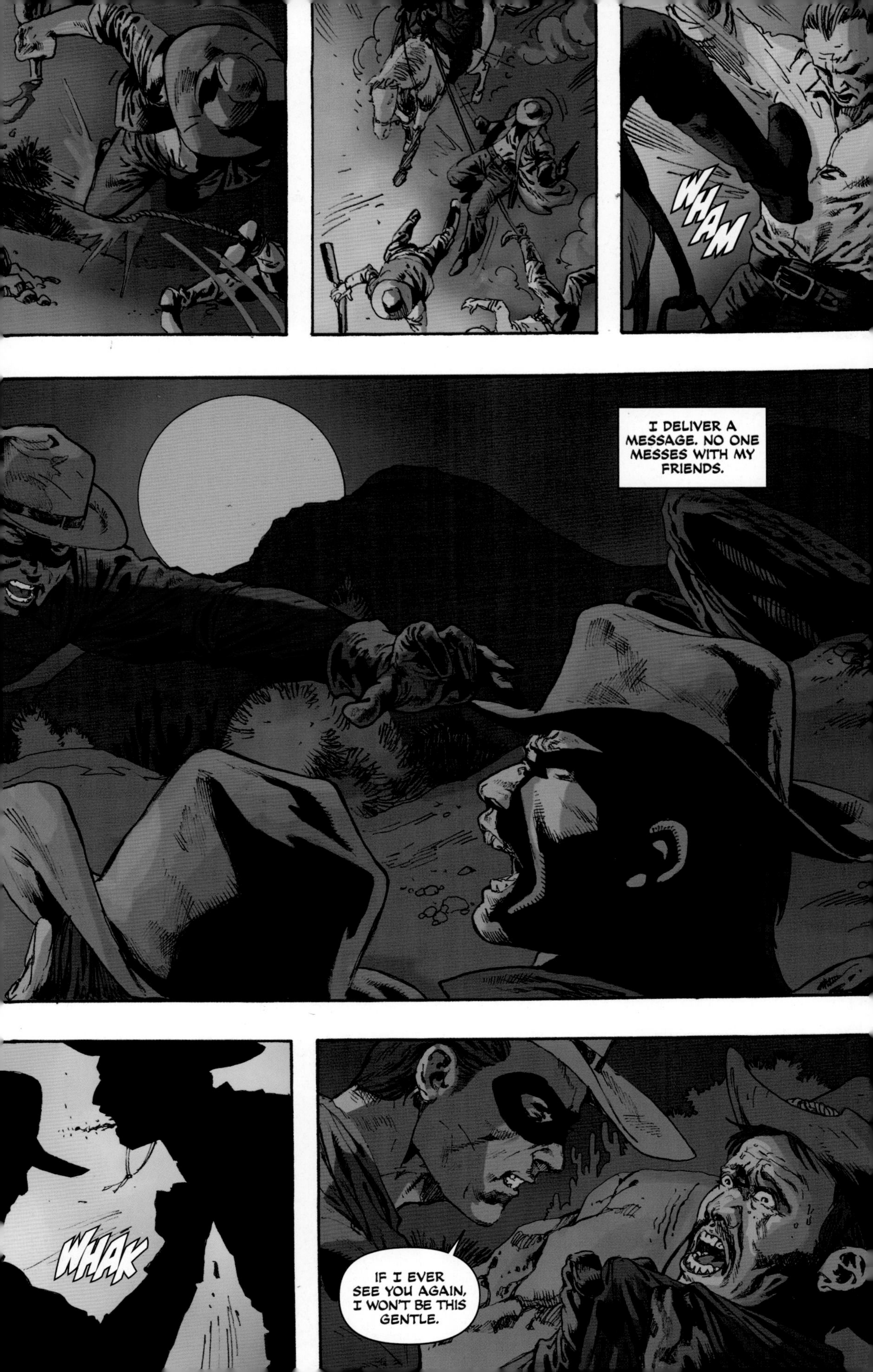
WHAM
I DELIVER A MESSAGE. NO ONE MESSES WITH MY FRIENDS.
WHAK
IF I EVER SEE YOU AGAIN, I WON'T BE THIS GENTLE.

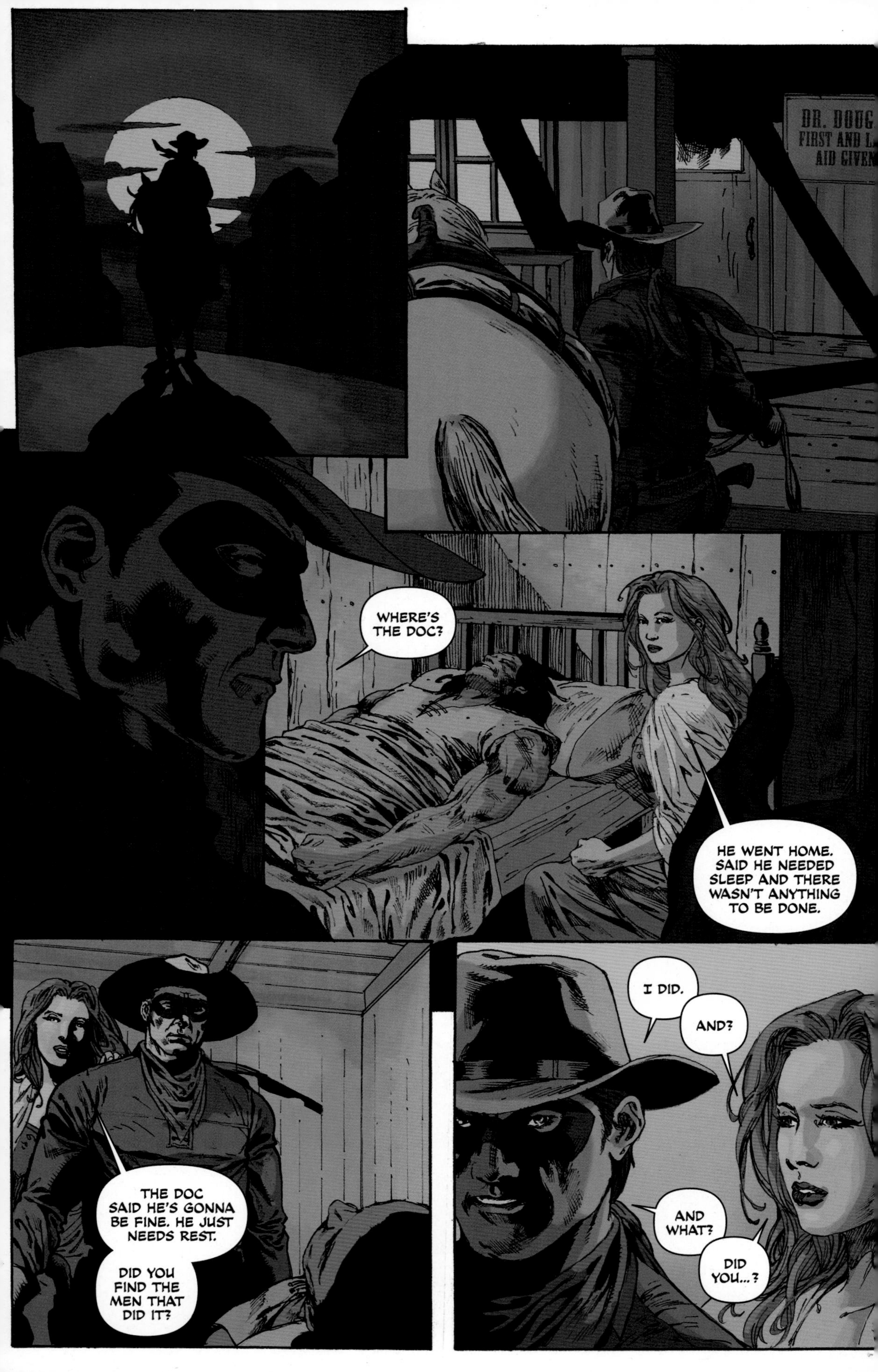

DR. DOUG
FIRST AND L
AID GIVEN
WHERE'S THE DOC?
HE WENT HOME. SAID HE NEEDED SLEEP AND THERE WASN'T ANYTHING TO BE DONE.
THE DOC SAID HE'S GONNA BE FINE. HE JUST NEEDS REST.
DID YOU FIND THE MEN THAT DID IT?
I DID.
AND?
AND WHAT?
DID YOU...?

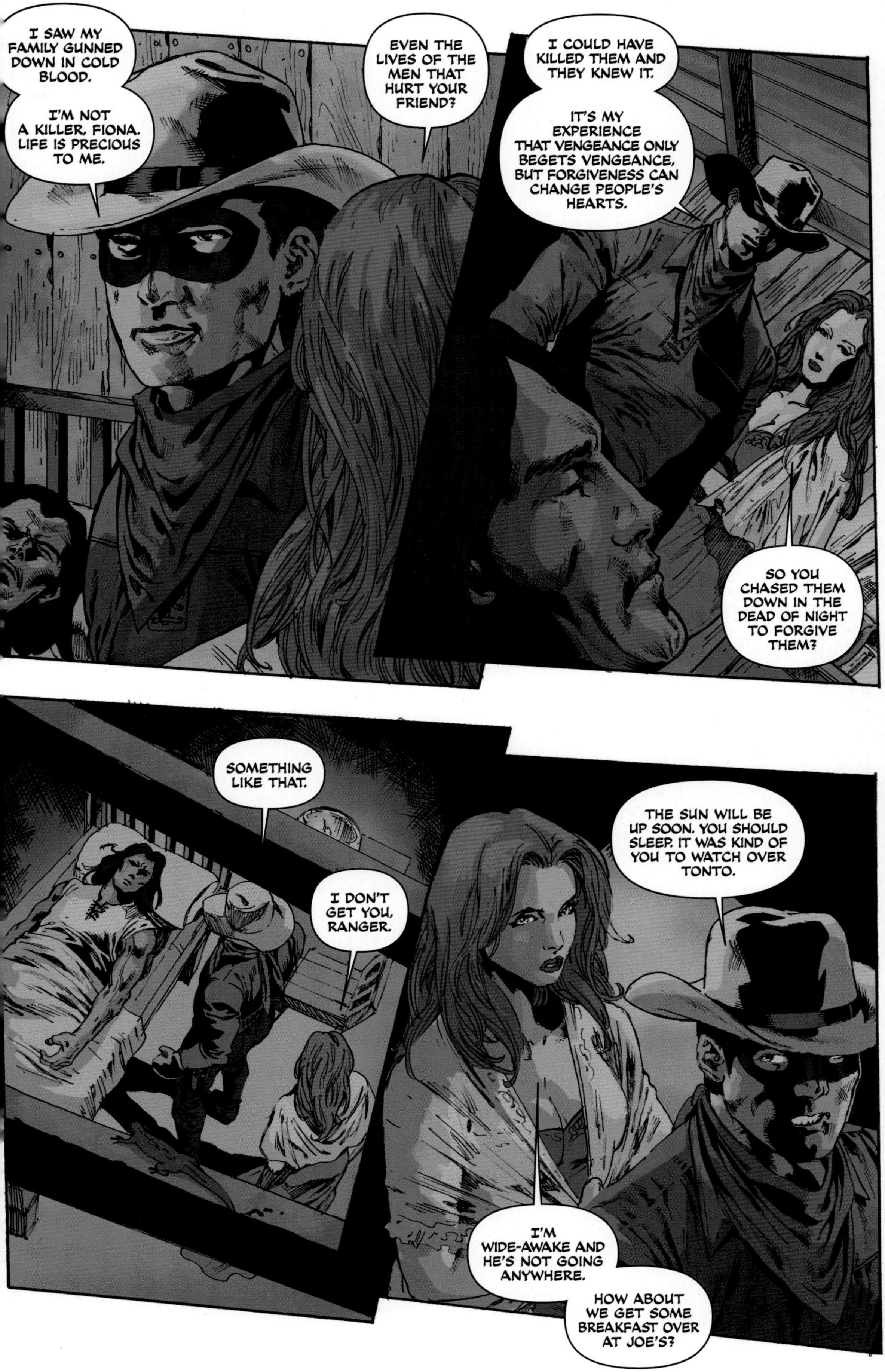

I SAW MY FAMILY GUNNED DOWN IN COLD BLOOD.
I'M NOT A KILLER, FIONA. LIFE IS PRECIOUS TO ME.
EVEN THE LIVES OF THE MEN THAT HURT YOUR FRIEND?
I COULD HAVE KILLED THEM AND THEY KNEW IT.
IT'S MY EXPERIENCE THAT VENGEANCE ONLY BEGETS VENGEANCE, BUT FORGIVENESS CAN CHANGE PEOPLE'S HEARTS.
SO YOU CHASED THEM DOWN IN THE DEAD OF NIGHT TO FORGIVE THEM?
SOMETHING LIKE THAT.
I DON'T GET YOU, RANGER.
THE SUN WILL BE UP SOON. YOU SHOULD SLEEP. IT WAS KIND OF YOU TO WATCH OVER TONTO.
I'M WIDE-AWAKE AND HE'S NOT GOING ANYWHERE.
HOW ABOUT WE GET SOME BREAKFAST OVER AT JOE'S?

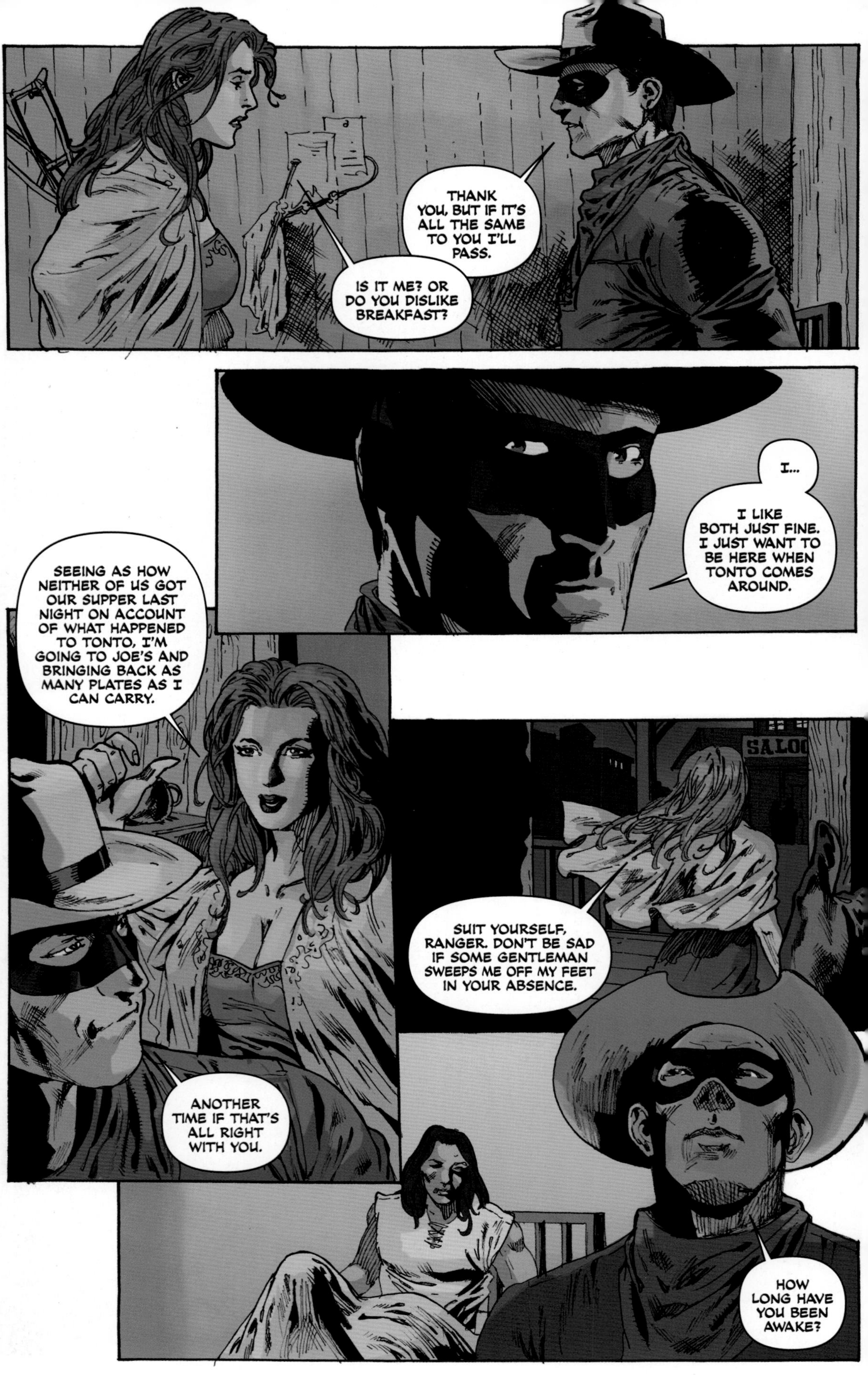
IS IT ME? OR DO YOU DISLIKE BREAKFAST?
THANK YOU, BUT IF IT'S ALL THE SAME TO YOU I'LL PASS.
I...
I LIKE BOTH JUST FINE. I JUST WANT TO BE HERE WHEN TONTO COMES AROUND.
SEEING AS HOW NEITHER OF US GOT OUR SUPPER LAST NIGHT ON ACCOUNT OF WHAT HAPPENED TO TONTO, I'M GOING TO JOE'S AND BRINGING BACK AS MANY PLATES AS I CAN CARRY.
ANOTHER TIME IF THAT'S ALL RIGHT WITH YOU.
SALOO
SUIT YOURSELF, RANGER. DON'T BE SAD IF SOME GENTLEMAN SWEEPS ME OFF MY FEET IN YOUR ABSENCE.
HOW LONG HAVE YOU BEEN AWAKE?

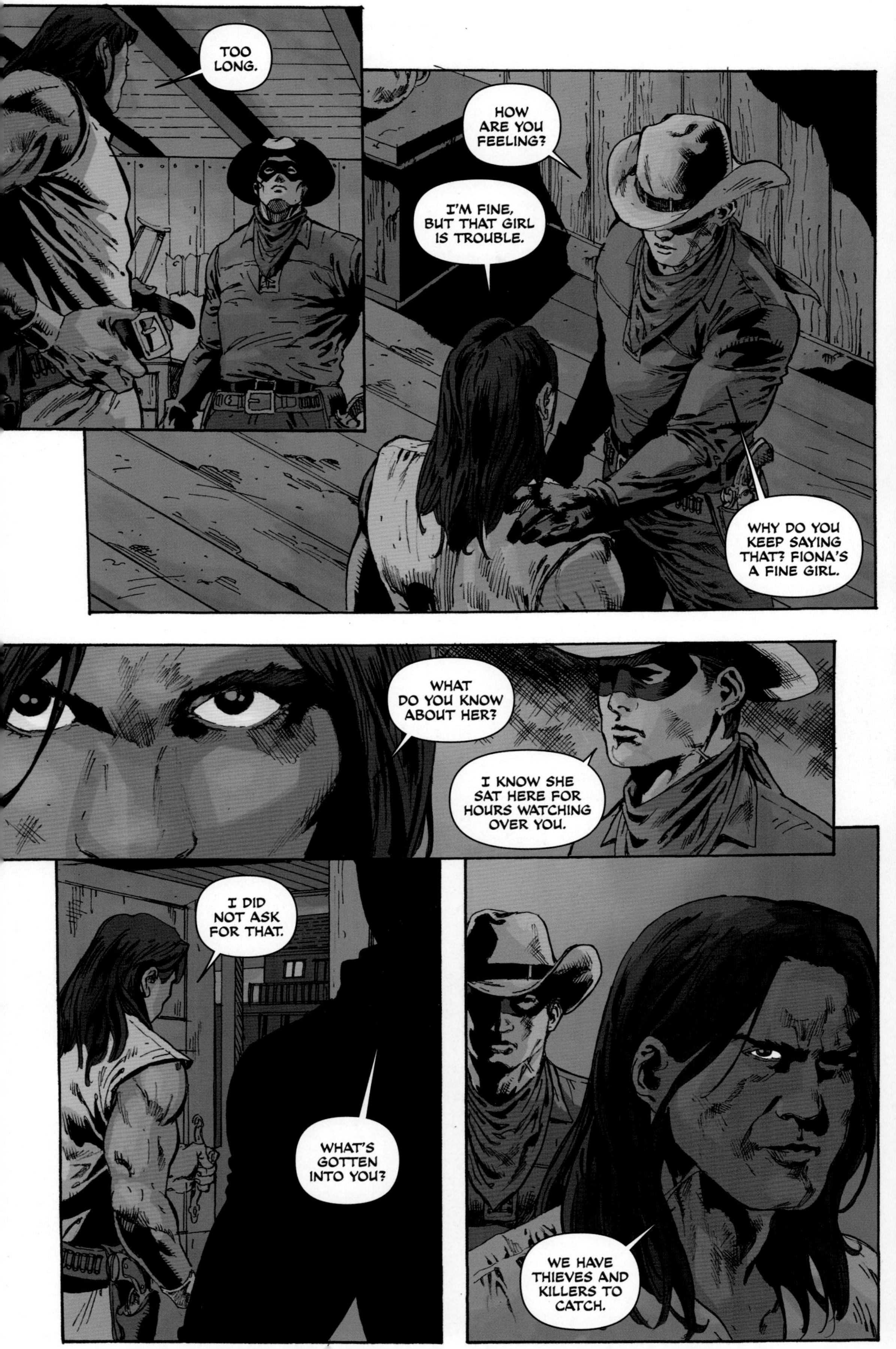
TOO LONG.
HOW ARE YOU FEELING?
I'M FINE, BUT THAT GIRL IS TROUBLE.
WHY DO YOU KEEP SAYING THAT? FIONA'S A FINE GIRL.
WHAT DO YOU KNOW ABOUT HER?
I KNOW SHE SAT HERE FOR HOURS WATCHING OVER YOU.
I DID NOT ASK FOR THAT.
WHAT'S GOTTEN INTO YOU?
WE HAVE THIEVES AND KILLERS TO CATCH.

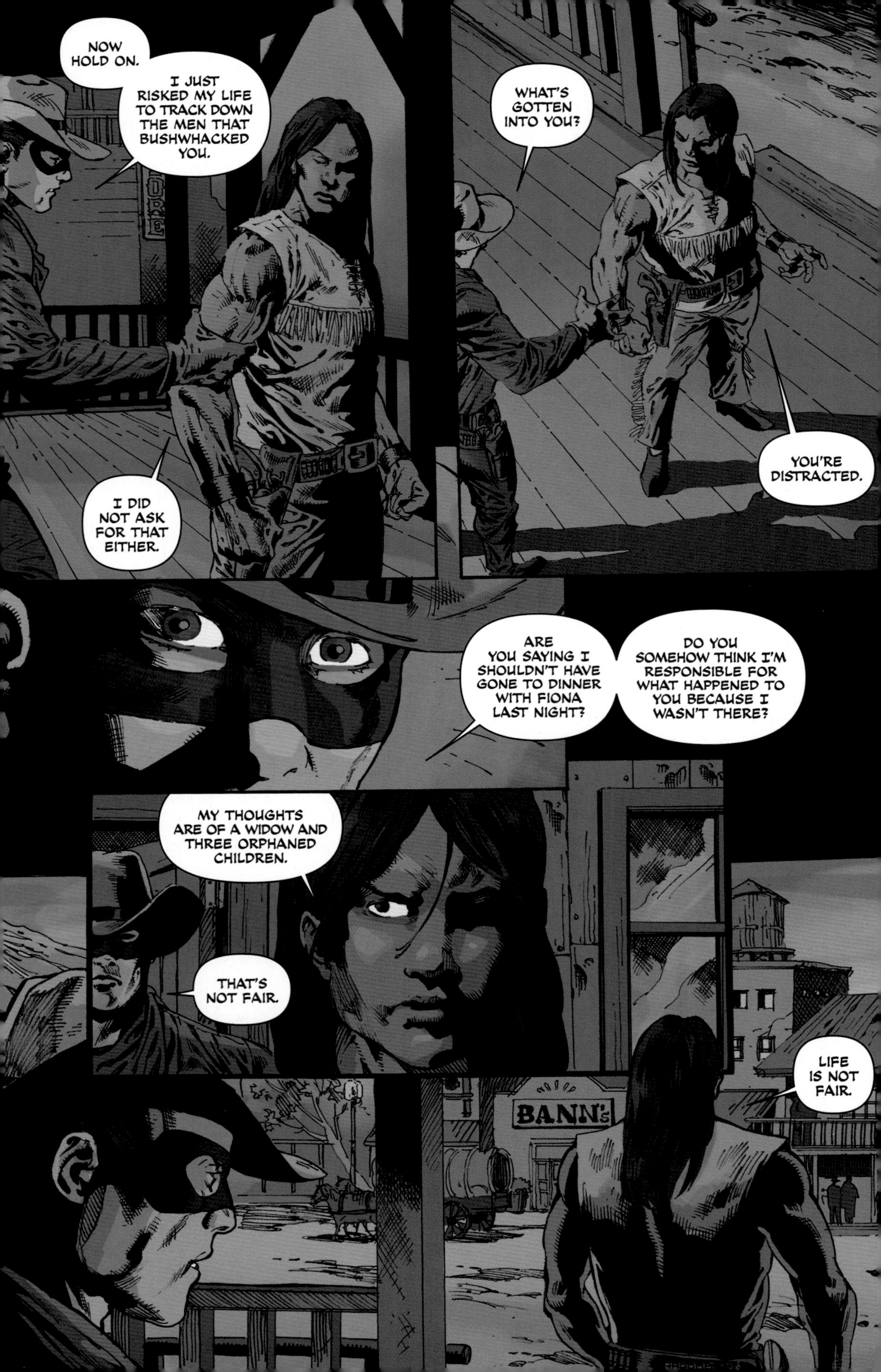
NOW HOLD ON.
I JUST RISKED MY LIFE TO TRACK DOWN THE MEN THAT BUSHWHACKED YOU.
I DID NOT ASK FOR THAT EITHER.
WHAT'S GOTTEN INTO YOU?
YOU'RE DISTRACTED.
ARE YOU SAYING I SHOULDN'T HAVE GONE TO DINNER WITH FIONA LAST NIGHT?
DO YOU SOMEHOW THINK I'M RESPONSIBLE FOR WHAT HAPPENED TO YOU BECAUSE I WASN'T THERE?
MY THOUGHTS ARE OF A WIDOW AND THREE ORPHANED CHILDREN.
THAT'S NOT FAIR.
BANN'S
LIFE IS NOT FAIR.

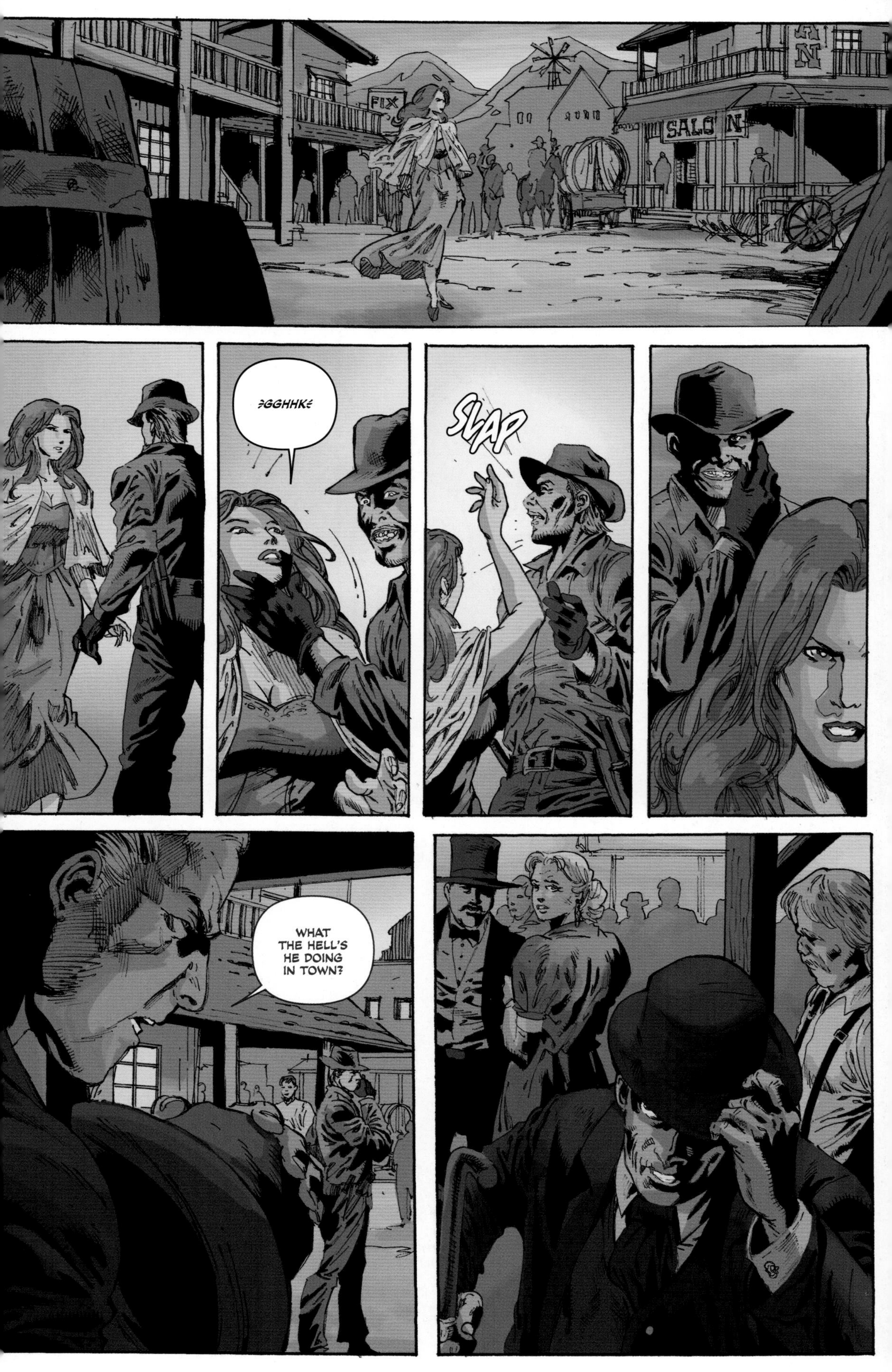
FIX
SALO N
≥GGHHK≤
SLAP
WHAT THE HELL'S HE DOING IN TOWN?

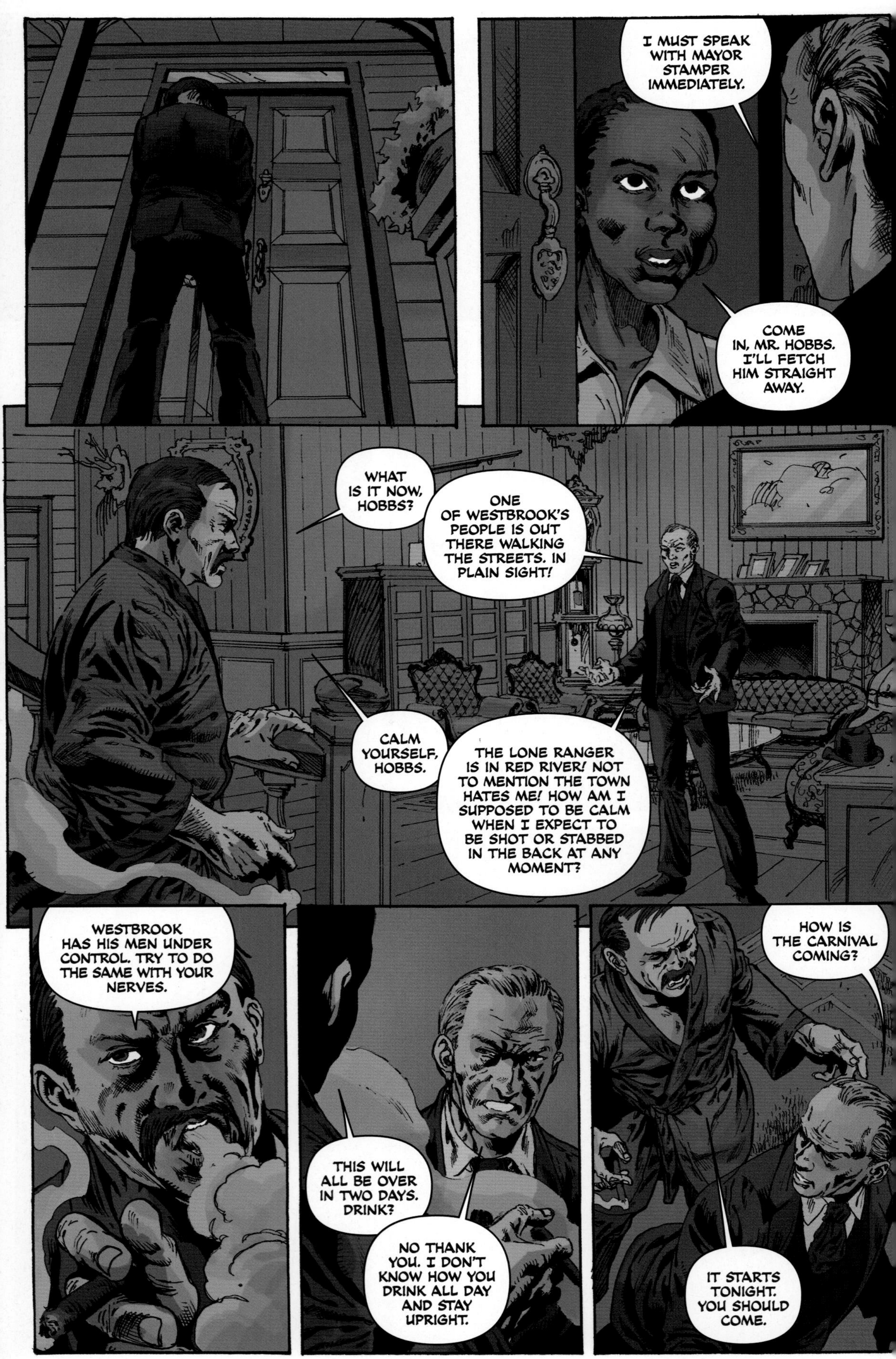
I MUST SPEAK WITH MAYOR STAMPER IMMEDIATELY.
COME IN, MR. HOBBS. I'LL FETCH HIM STRAIGHT AWAY.
WHAT IS IT NOW, HOBBS?
ONE OF WESTBROOK'S PEOPLE IS OUT THERE WALKING THE STREETS. IN PLAIN SIGHT!
CALM YOURSELF, HOBBS.
THE LONE RANGER IS IN RED RIVER! NOT TO MENTION THE TOWN HATES ME! HOW AM I SUPPOSED TO BE CALM WHEN I EXPECT TO BE SHOT OR STABBED IN THE BACK AT ANY MOMENT?
WESTBROOK HAS HIS MEN UNDER CONTROL. TRY TO DO THE SAME WITH YOUR NERVES.
THIS WILL ALL BE OVER IN TWO DAYS. DRINK?
NO THANK YOU. I DON'T KNOW HOW YOU DRINK ALL DAY AND STAY UPRIGHT.
HOW IS THE CARNIVAL COMING?
IT STARTS TONIGHT. YOU SHOULD COME.

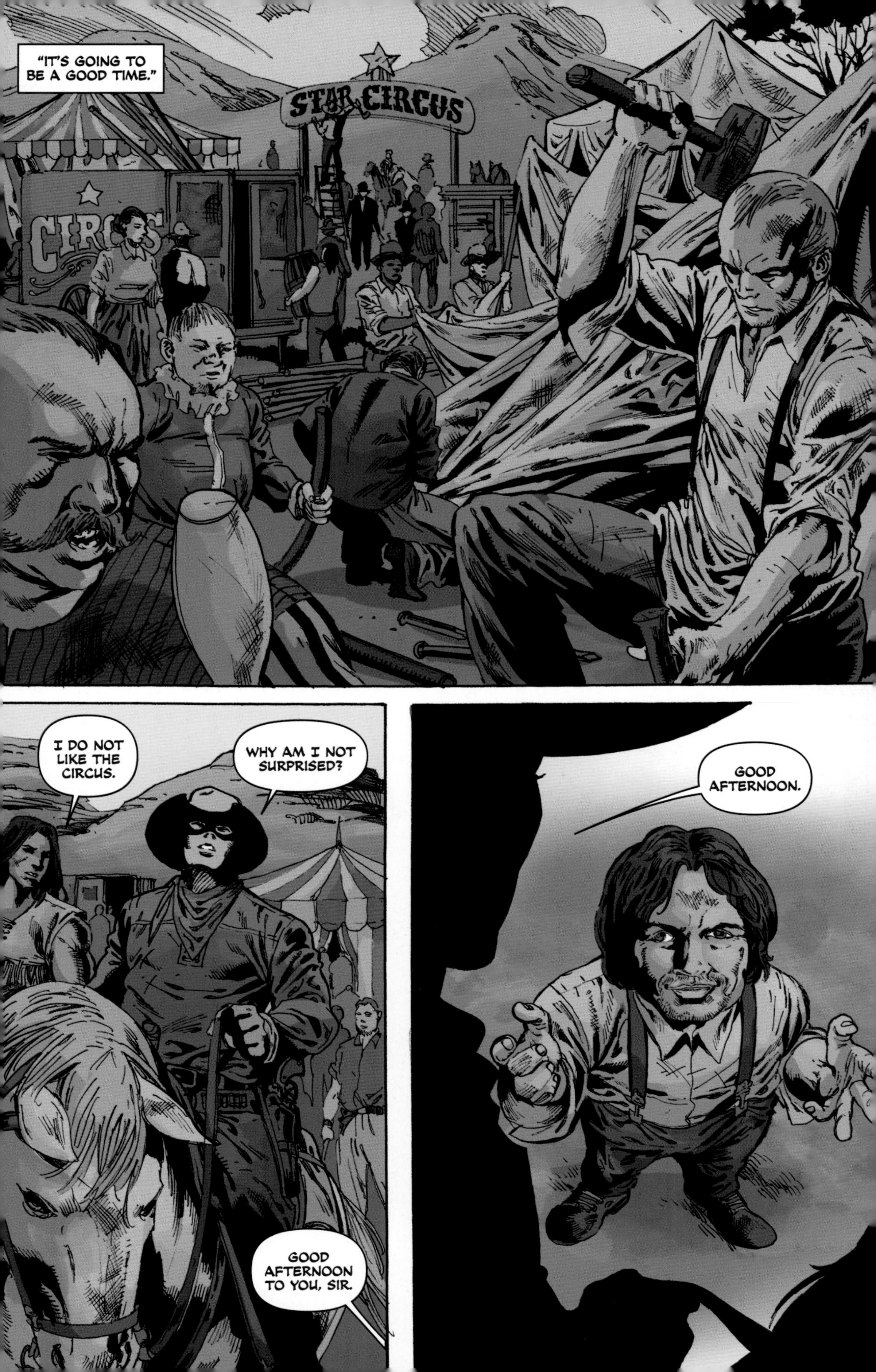
"IT'S GOING TO BE A GOOD TIME."
STAR CIRCUS
CIRCUS
I DO NOT LIKE THE CIRCUS.
WHY AM I NOT SURPRISED?
GOOD AFTERNOON TO YOU, SIR.
GOOD AFTERNOON.

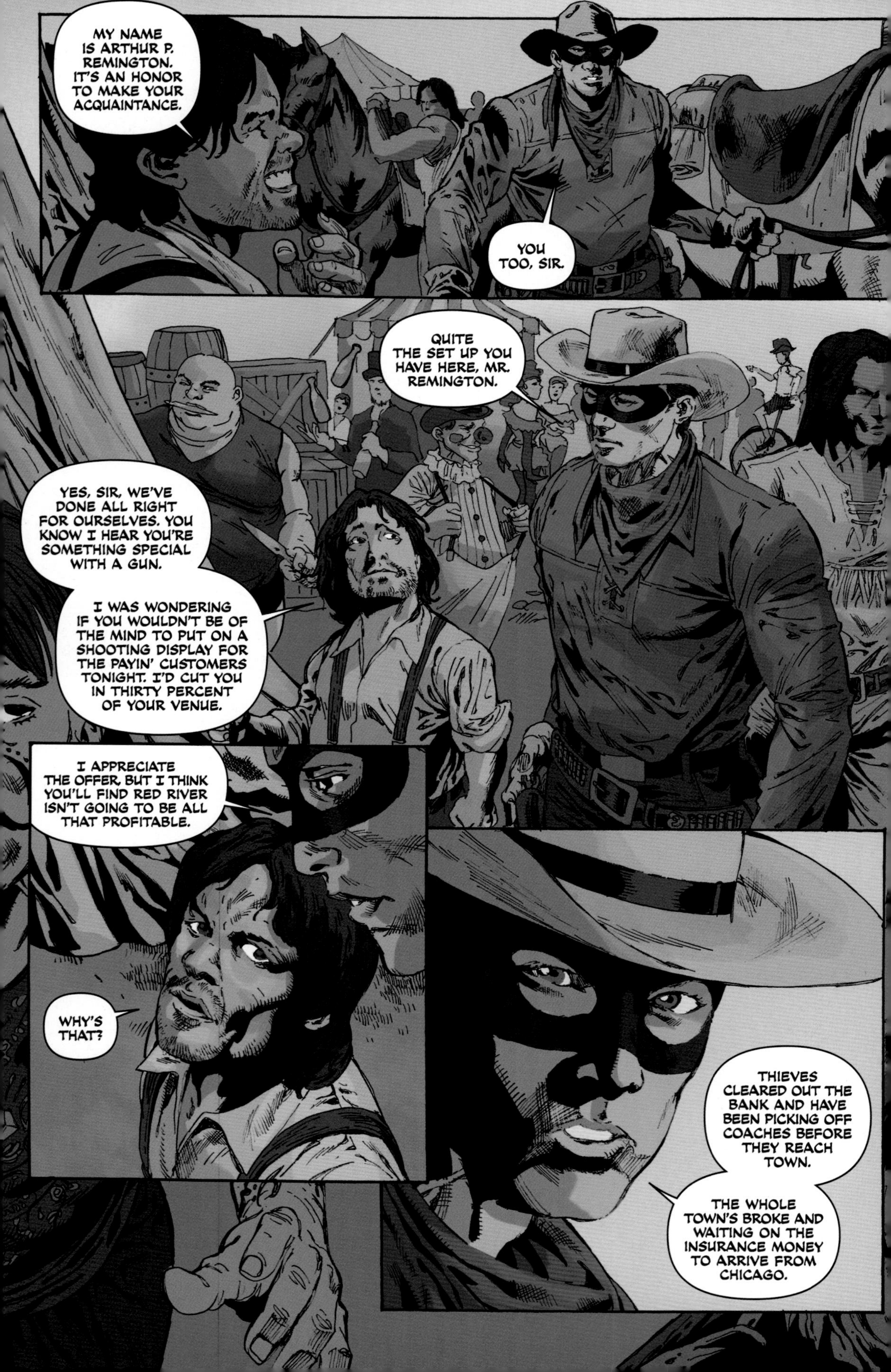
MY NAME IS ARTHUR P. REMINGTON. IT'S AN HONOR TO MAKE YOUR ACQUAINTANCE.
YOU TOO, SIR.
QUITE THE SET UP YOU HAVE HERE, MR. REMINGTON.
YES, SIR, WE'VE DONE ALL RIGHT FOR OURSELVES. YOU KNOW I HEAR YOU'RE SOMETHING SPECIAL WITH A GUN.
I WAS WONDERING IF YOU WOULDN'T BE OF THE MIND TO PUT ON A SHOOTING DISPLAY FOR THE PAYIN' CUSTOMERS TONIGHT. I'D CUT YOU IN THIRTY PERCENT OF YOUR VENUE.
I APPRECIATE THE OFFER, BUT I THINK YOU'LL FIND RED RIVER ISN'T GOING TO BE ALL THAT PROFITABLE.
WHY'S THAT?
THIEVES CLEARED OUT THE BANK AND HAVE BEEN PICKING OFF COACHES BEFORE THEY REACH TOWN.
THE WHOLE TOWN'S BROKE AND WAITING ON THE INSURANCE MONEY TO ARRIVE FROM CHICAGO.

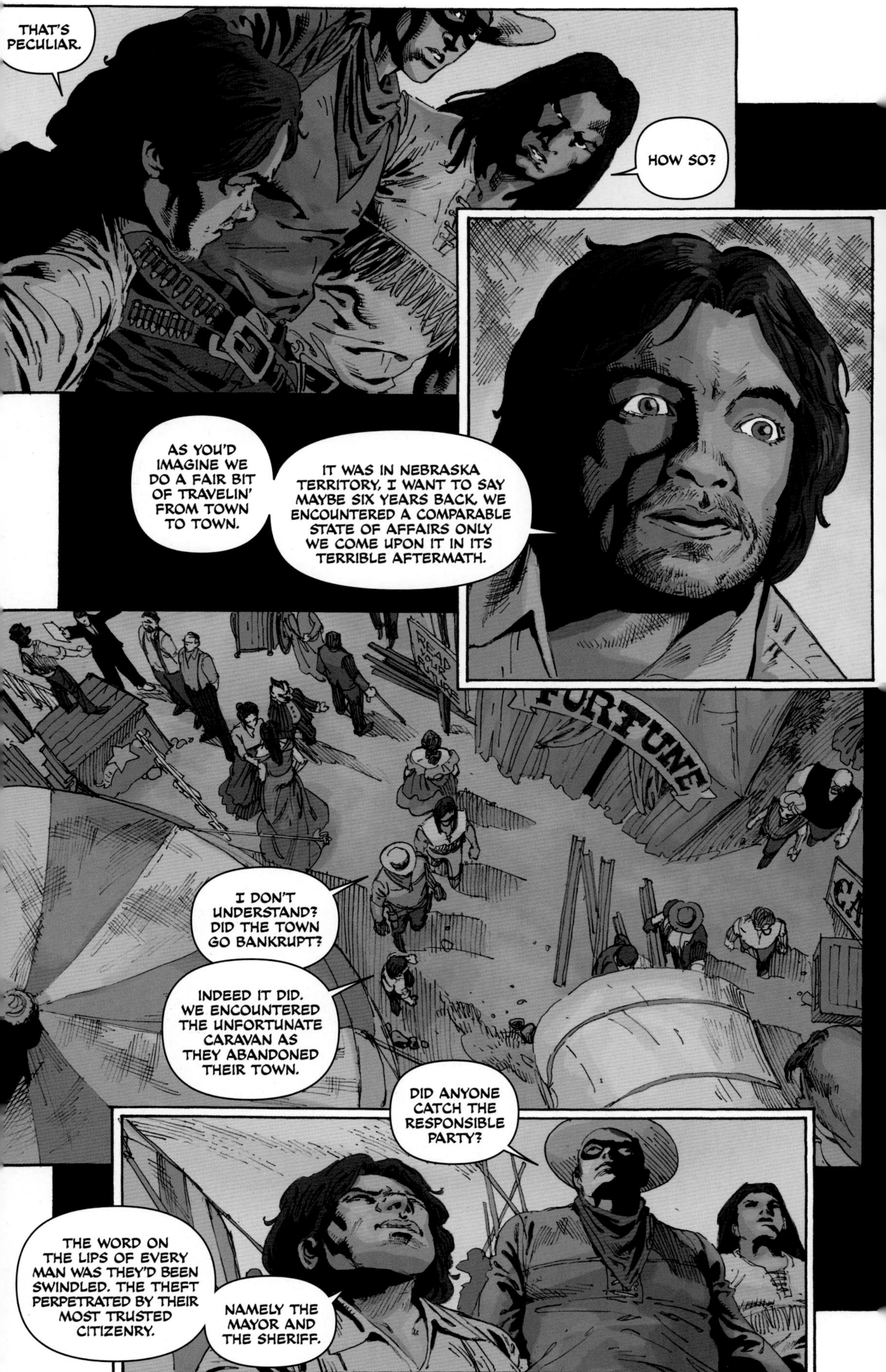

THAT'S PECULIAR.
HOW SO?
AS YOU'D IMAGINE WE DO A FAIR BIT OF TRAVELIN' FROM TOWN TO TOWN.
IT WAS IN NEBRASKA TERRITORY, I WANT TO SAY MAYBE SIX YEARS BACK, WE ENCOUNTERED A COMPARABLE STATE OF AFFAIRS ONLY WE COME UPON IT IN ITS TERRIBLE AFTERMATH.
READ YOUR FUTURE
FORTUNE
I DON'T UNDERSTAND? DID THE TOWN GO BANKRUPT?
INDEED IT DID. WE ENCOUNTERED THE UNFORTUNATE CARAVAN AS THEY ABANDONED THEIR TOWN.
DID ANYONE CATCH THE RESPONSIBLE PARTY?
THE WORD ON THE LIPS OF EVERY MAN WAS THEY'D BEEN SWINDLED. THE THEFT PERPETRATED BY THEIR MOST TRUSTED CITIZENRY.
NAMELY THE MAYOR AND THE SHERIFF.

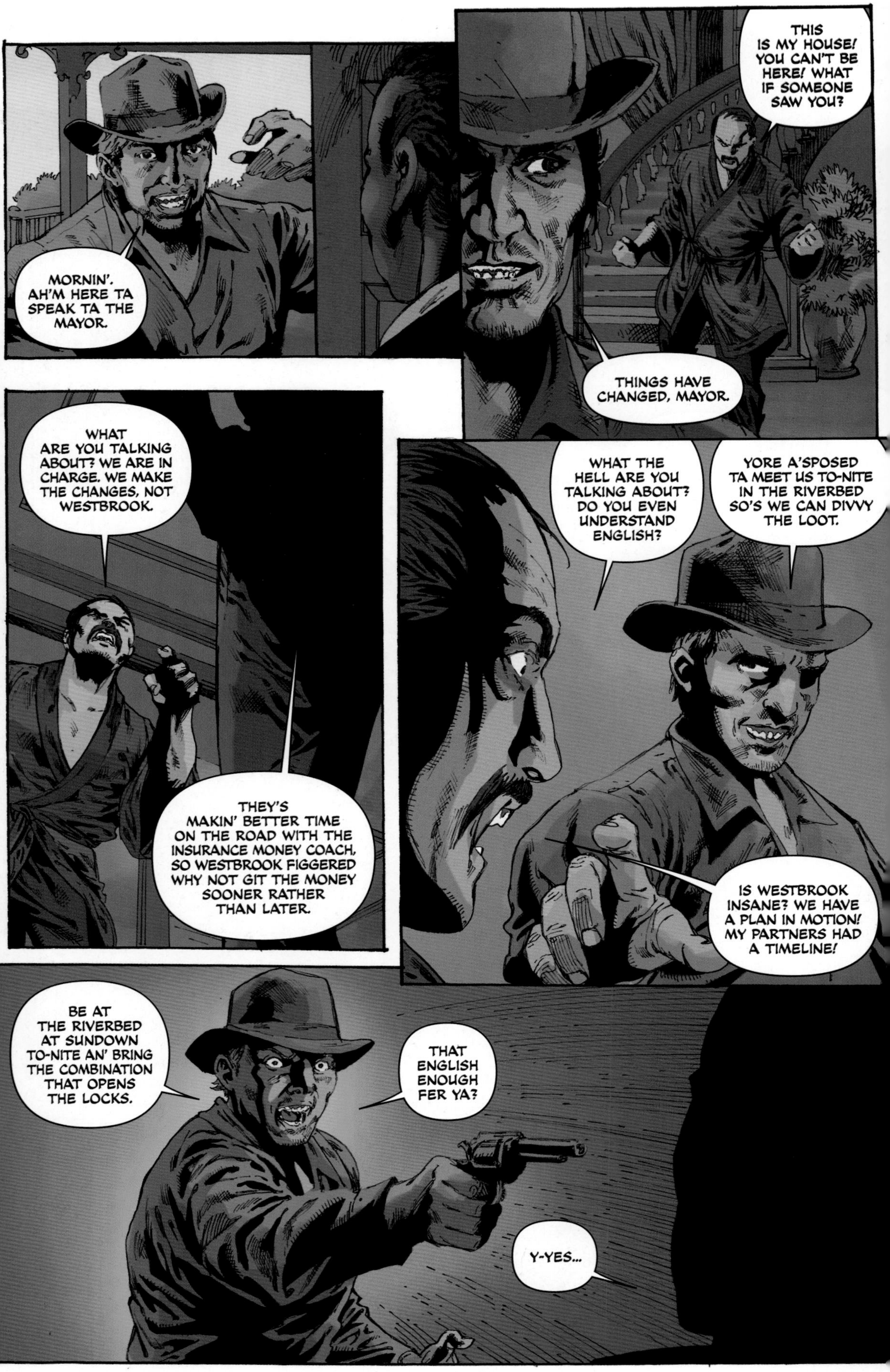
MORNIN'. AH'M HERE TA SPEAK TA THE MAYOR.
THIS IS MY HOUSE! YOU CAN'T BE HERE! WHAT IF SOMEONE SAW YOU?
THINGS HAVE CHANGED, MAYOR.
WHAT ARE YOU TALKING ABOUT? WE ARE IN CHARGE. WE MAKE THE CHANGES, NOT WESTBROOK.
THEY'S MAKIN' BETTER TIME ON THE ROAD WITH THE INSURANCE MONEY COACH, SO WESTBROOK FIGGERED WHY NOT GIT THE MONEY SOONER RATHER THAN LATER.
IS WESTBROOK INSANE? WE HAVE A PLAN IN MOTION! MY PARTNERS HAD A TIMELINE!
YORE A'SPOSED TA MEET US TO-NITE IN THE RIVERBED SO'S WE CAN DIVVY THE LOOT.
WHAT THE HELL ARE YOU TALKING ABOUT? DO YOU EVEN UNDERSTAND ENGLISH?
BE AT THE RIVERBED AT SUNDOWN TO-NITE AN' BRING THE COMBINATION THAT OPENS THE LOCKS.
THAT ENGLISH ENOUGH FER YA?
Y-YES...

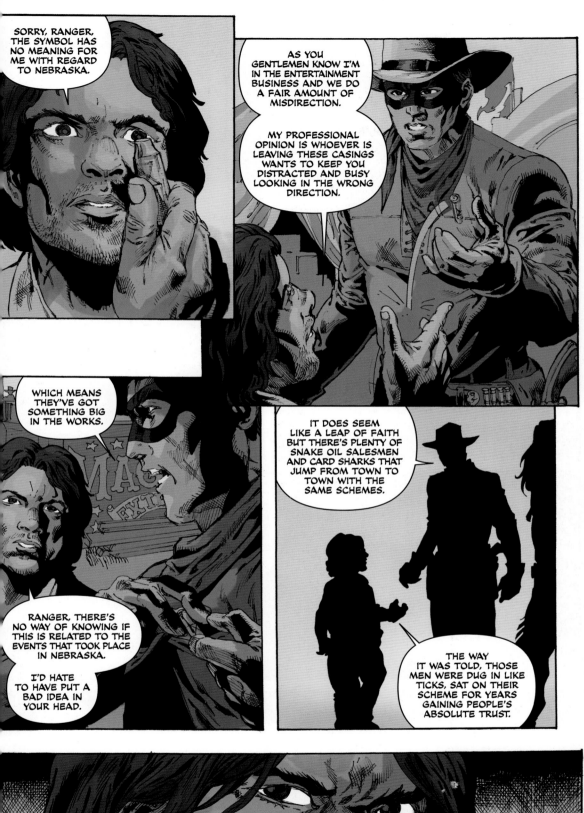

SORRY, RANGER, THE SYMBOL HAS NO MEANING FOR ME WITH REGARD TO NEBRASKA.

AS YOU GENTLEMEN KNOW I'M IN THE ENTERTAINMENT BUSINESS AND WE DO A FAIR AMOUNT OF MISDIRECTION.

MY PROFESSIONAL OPINION IS WHOEVER IS LEAVING THESE CASINGS WANTS TO KEEP YOU DISTRACTED AND BUSY LOOKING IN THE WRONG DIRECTION.

WHICH MEANS THEY'VE GOT SOMETHING BIG IN THE WORKS.

RANGER, THERE'S NO WAY OF KNOWING IF THIS IS RELATED TO THE EVENTS THAT TOOK PLACE IN NEBRASKA.

I'D HATE TO HAVE PUT A BAD IDEA IN YOUR HEAD.

IT DOES SEEM LIKE A LEAP OF FAITH BUT THERE'S PLENTY OF SNAKE OIL SALESMEN AND CARD SHARKS THAT JUMP FROM TOWN TO TOWN WITH THE SAME SCHEMES.

THE WAY IT WAS TOLD, THOSE MEN WERE DUG IN LIKE TICKS, SAT ON THEIR SCHEME FOR YEARS GAINING PEOPLE'S ABSOLUTE TRUST.

MAYBE WE SHOULD SEE HOW TRUSTWORTHY THIS MAYOR IS.

NO, SIR, MR. STAMPER ISN'T HERE.

BEEN A BUSY DAY THOUGH.

DO YOU KNOW WHERE WE COULD FIND HIM?

HE ONLY TELLS ME WHAT HE WANTS DOIN' AND NEVER WHERE HE'S GOIN'.

MIGHT BE HE'S AT HIS OFFICE, I RECKON THAT'S WHERE HE IS MOST DAYS.

THANK YOU KINDLY, MA'AM.

YOU FIGURE REMINGTON MIGHT BE RIGHT? COULD IT BE THE SAME MEN HAVE SET UP HERE IN RED RIVER?

THE BETTER QUESTION IS COULD TWO MEN KILL AND ROB AS THEY HAVE DONE WHILE HOLDING SUCH PROMINENT POSITIONS IN TOWN.

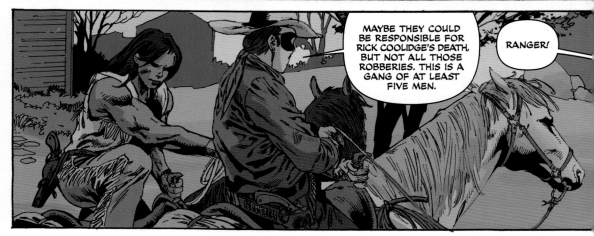

MAYBE THEY COULD BE RESPONSIBLE FOR RICK COOLIDGE'S DEATH, BUT NOT ALL THOSE ROBBERIES. THIS IS A GANG OF AT LEAST FIVE MEN.

RANGER!

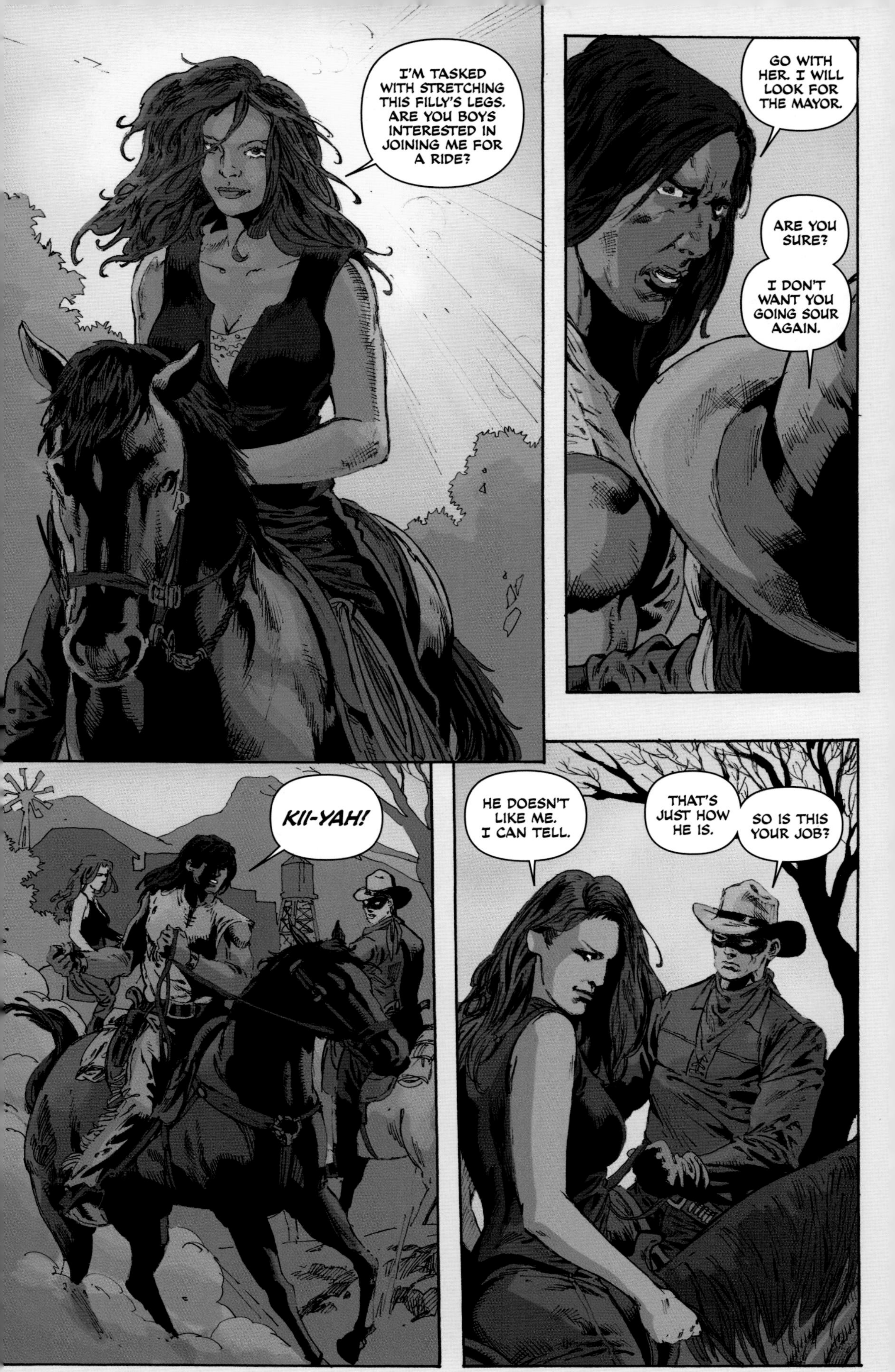
I'M TASKED WITH STRETCHING THIS FILLY'S LEGS. ARE YOU BOYS INTERESTED IN JOINING ME FOR A RIDE?
GO WITH HER. I WILL LOOK FOR THE MAYOR.
ARE YOU SURE?
I DON'T WANT YOU GOING SOUR AGAIN.
KII-YAH!
HE DOESN'T LIKE ME. I CAN TELL.
THAT'S JUST HOW HE IS.
SO IS THIS YOUR JOB?

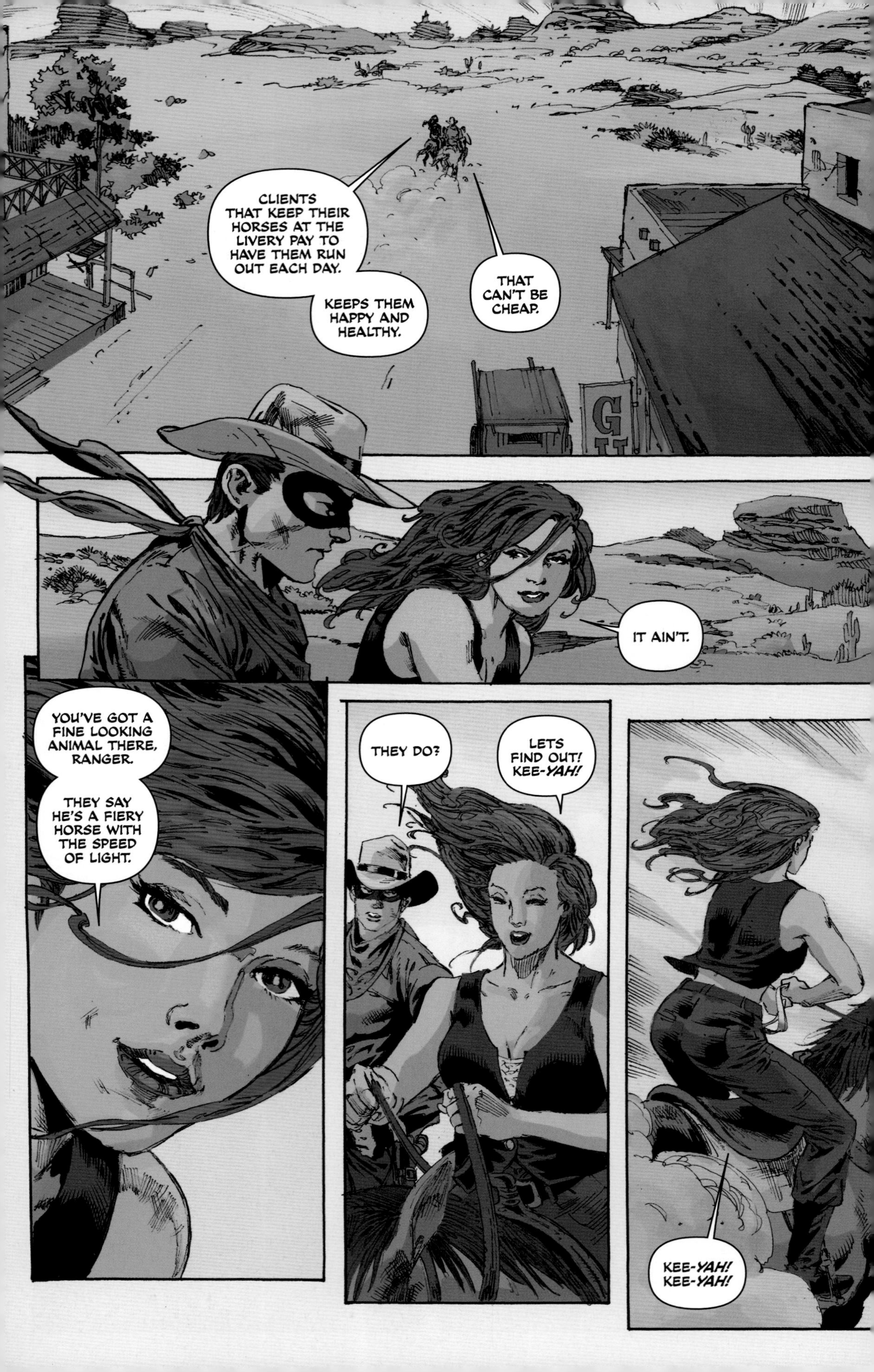
CLIENTS THAT KEEP THEIR HORSES AT THE LIVERY PAY TO HAVE THEM RUN OUT EACH DAY.
KEEPS THEM HAPPY AND HEALTHY.
THAT CAN'T BE CHEAP.
IT AIN'T.
YOU'VE GOT A FINE LOOKING ANIMAL THERE, RANGER.
THEY SAY HE'S A FIERY HORSE WITH THE SPEED OF LIGHT.
THEY DO?
LETS FIND OUT! KEE-*YAH!*
KEE-*YAH!* KEE-*YAH!*

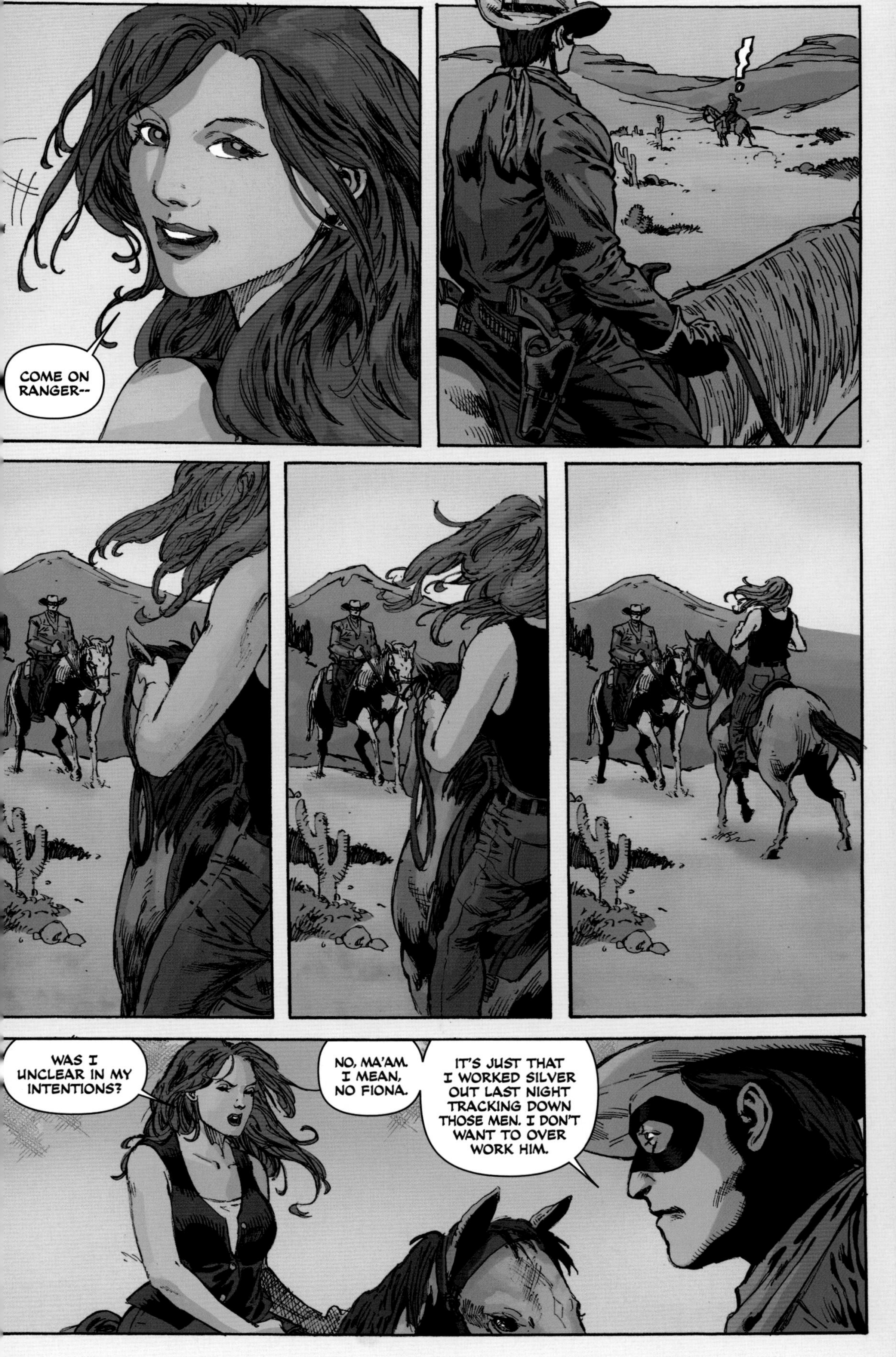
COME ON RANGER--
!
WAS I UNCLEAR IN MY INTENTIONS?
NO, MA'AM. I MEAN, NO FIONA.
IT'S JUST THAT I WORKED SILVER OUT LAST NIGHT TRACKING DOWN THOSE MEN. I DON'T WANT TO OVER WORK HIM.

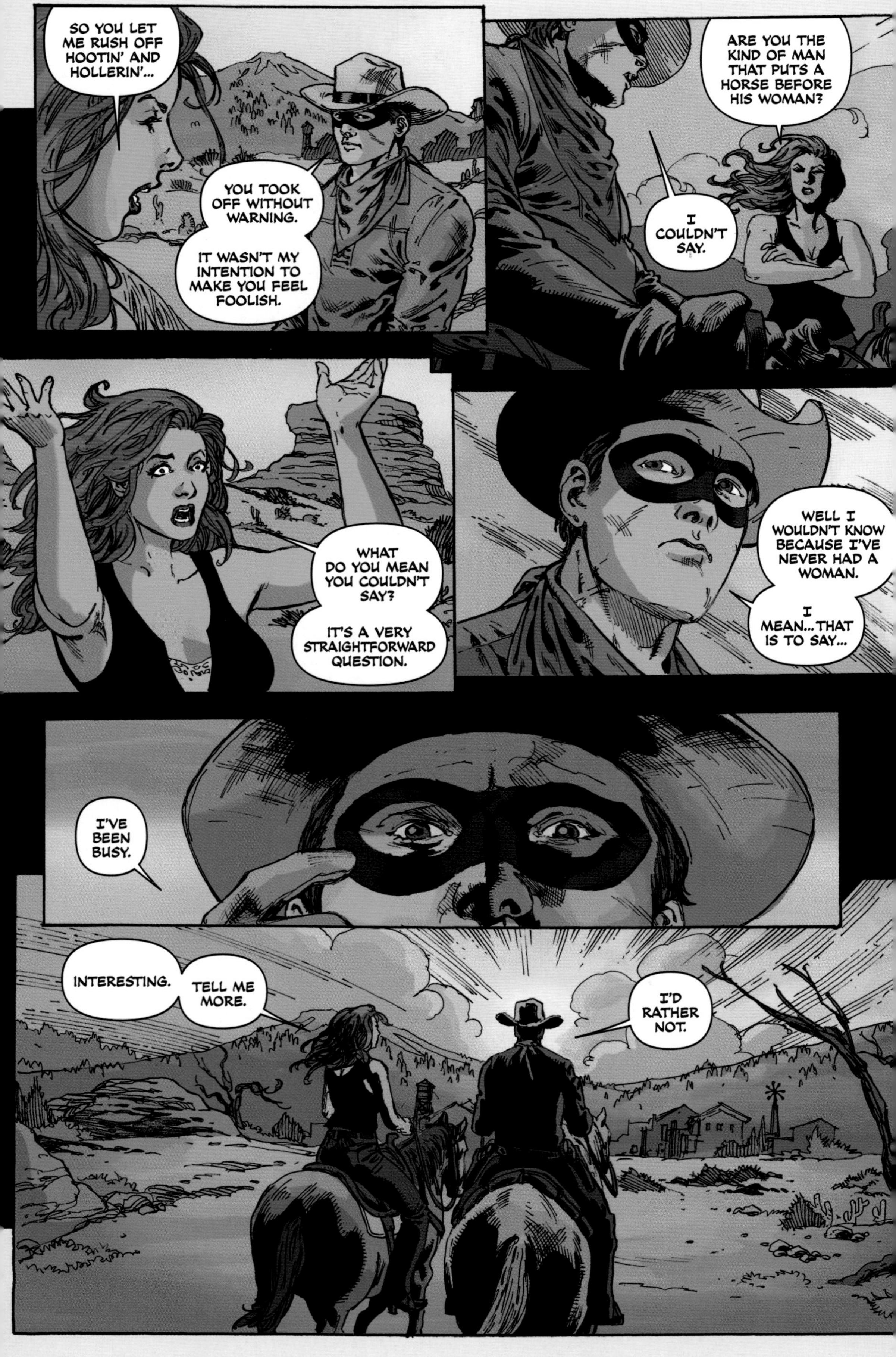
SO YOU LET ME RUSH OFF HOOTIN' AND HOLLERIN'...
YOU TOOK OFF WITHOUT WARNING.
IT WASN'T MY INTENTION TO MAKE YOU FEEL FOOLISH.
ARE YOU THE KIND OF MAN THAT PUTS A HORSE BEFORE HIS WOMAN?
I COULDN'T SAY.
WHAT DO YOU MEAN YOU COULDN'T SAY?
IT'S A VERY STRAIGHTFORWARD QUESTION.
WELL I WOULDN'T KNOW BECAUSE I'VE NEVER HAD A WOMAN.
I MEAN...THAT IS TO SAY...
I'VE BEEN BUSY.
INTERESTING.
TELL ME MORE.
I'D RATHER NOT.

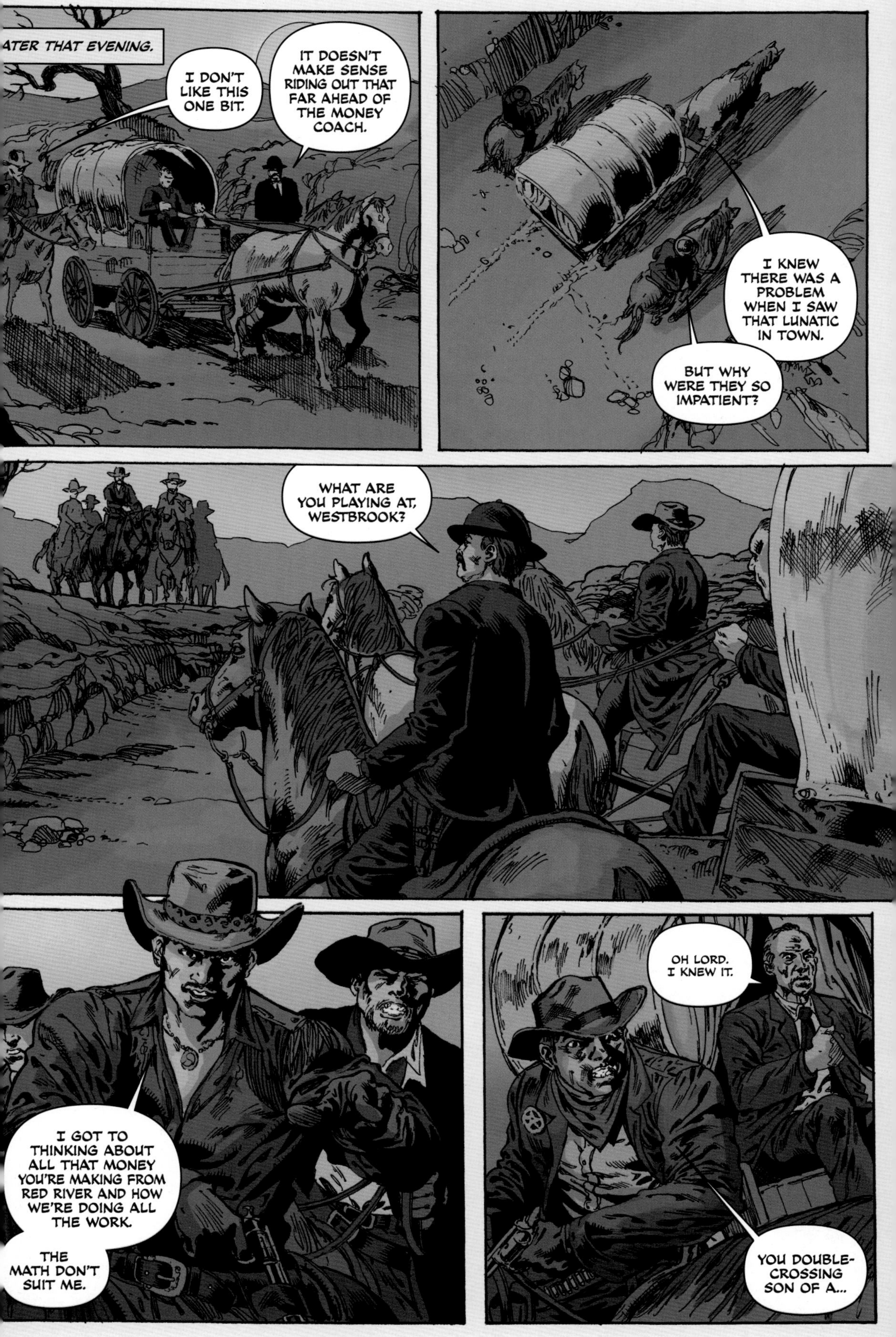
ATER THAT EVENING.
I DON'T LIKE THIS ONE BIT.
IT DOESN'T MAKE SENSE RIDING OUT THAT FAR AHEAD OF THE MONEY COACH.
I KNEW THERE WAS A PROBLEM WHEN I SAW THAT LUNATIC IN TOWN.
BUT WHY WERE THEY SO IMPATIENT?
WHAT ARE YOU PLAYING AT, WESTBROOK?
I GOT TO THINKING ABOUT ALL THAT MONEY YOU'RE MAKING FROM RED RIVER AND HOW WE'RE DOING ALL THE WORK.
THE MATH DON'T SUIT ME.
OH LORD. I KNEW IT.
YOU DOUBLE-CROSSING SON OF A...

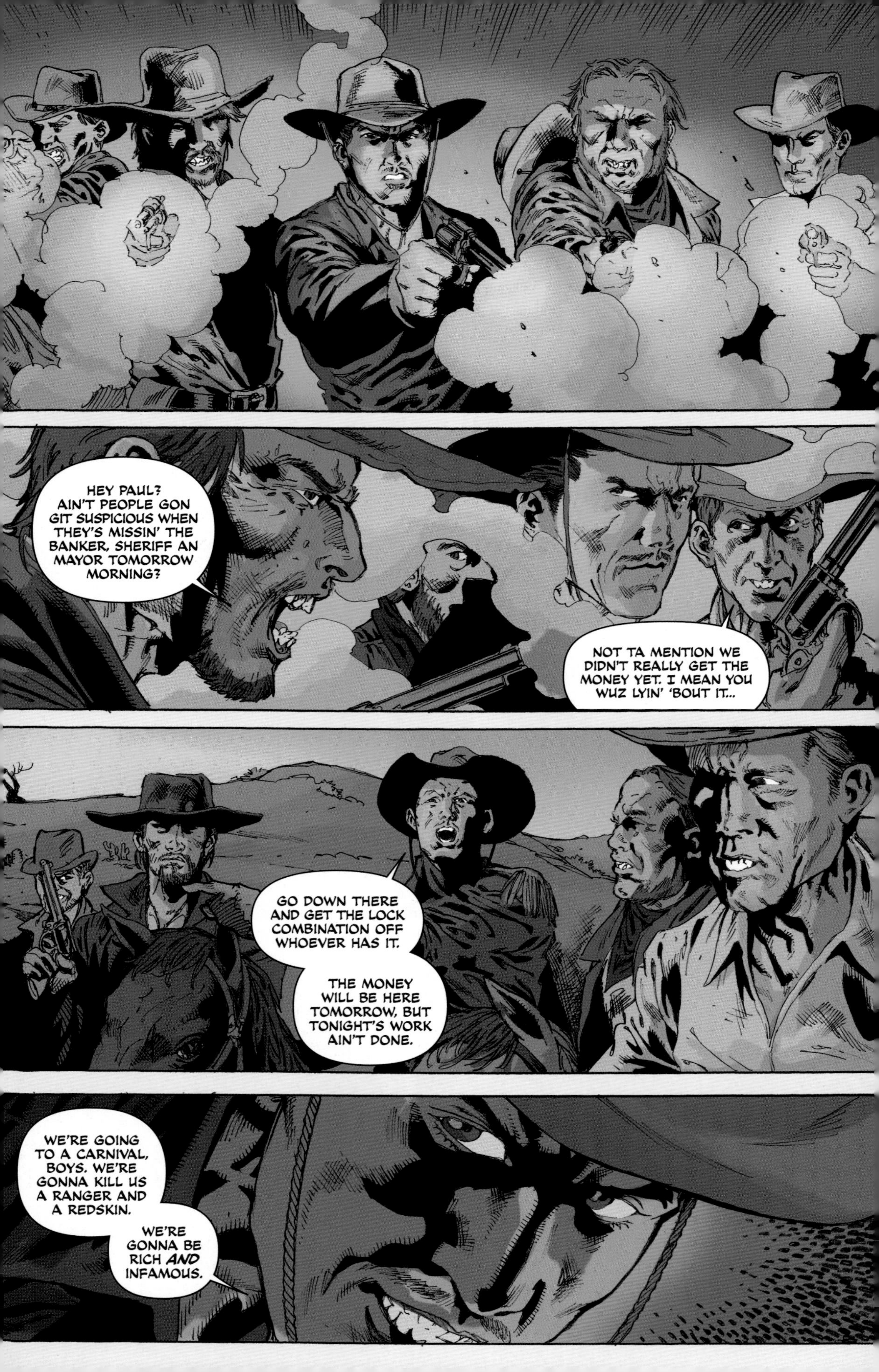
HEY PAUL? AIN'T PEOPLE GON GIT SUSPICIOUS WHEN THEY'S MISSIN' THE BANKER, SHERIFF AN MAYOR TOMORROW MORNING?
NOT TA MENTION WE DIDN'T REALLY GET THE MONEY YET. I MEAN YOU WUZ LYIN' 'BOUT IT...
GO DOWN THERE AND GET THE LOCK COMBINATION OFF WHOEVER HAS IT.
THE MONEY WILL BE HERE TOMORROW, BUT TONIGHT'S WORK AIN'T DONE.
WE'RE GOING TO A CARNIVAL, BOYS. WE'RE GONNA KILL US A RANGER AND A REDSKIN.
WE'RE GONNA BE RICH *AND* INFAMOUS.

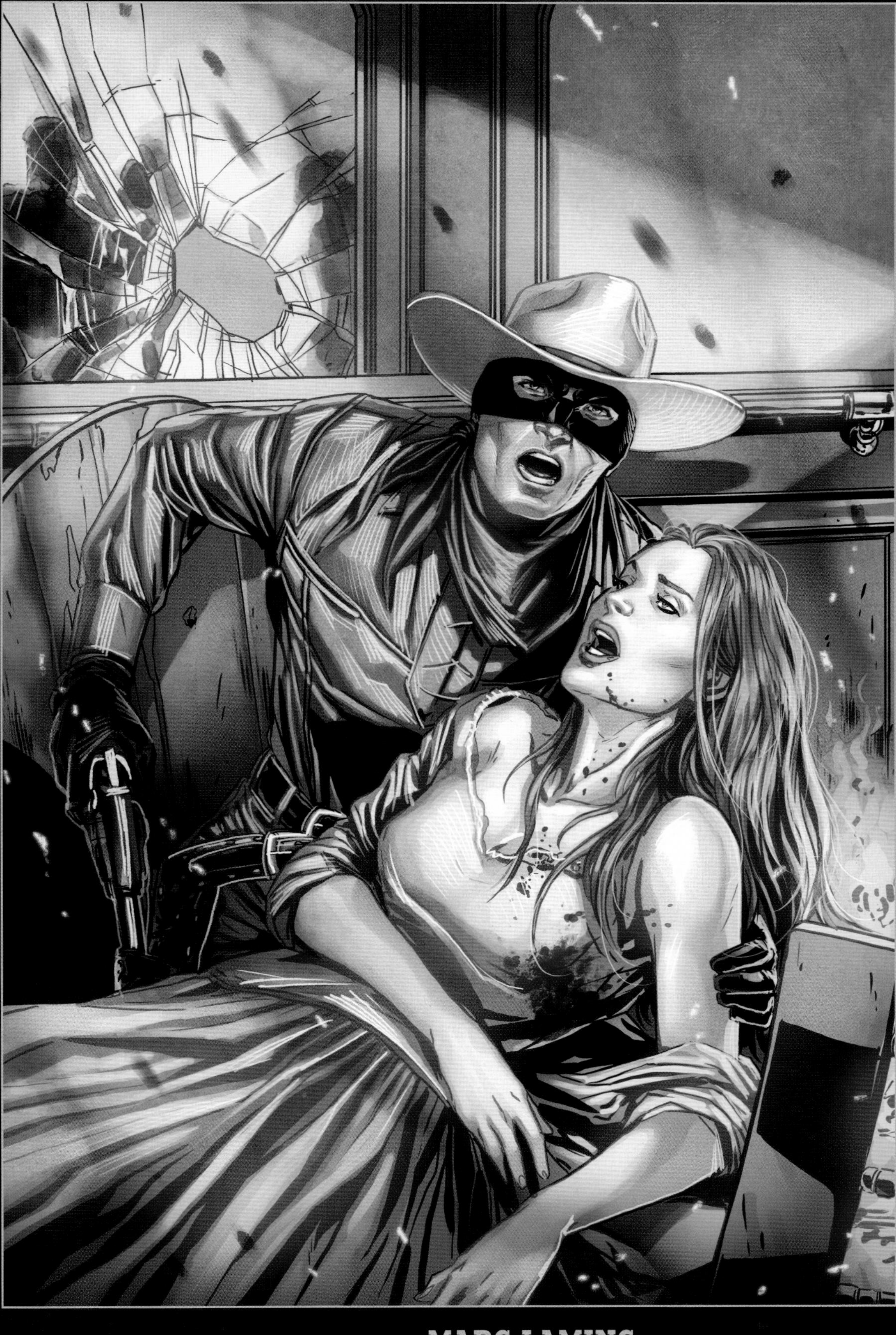

issue #4 cover by **MARC LAMING**
colors by **ELMER SANTOS**

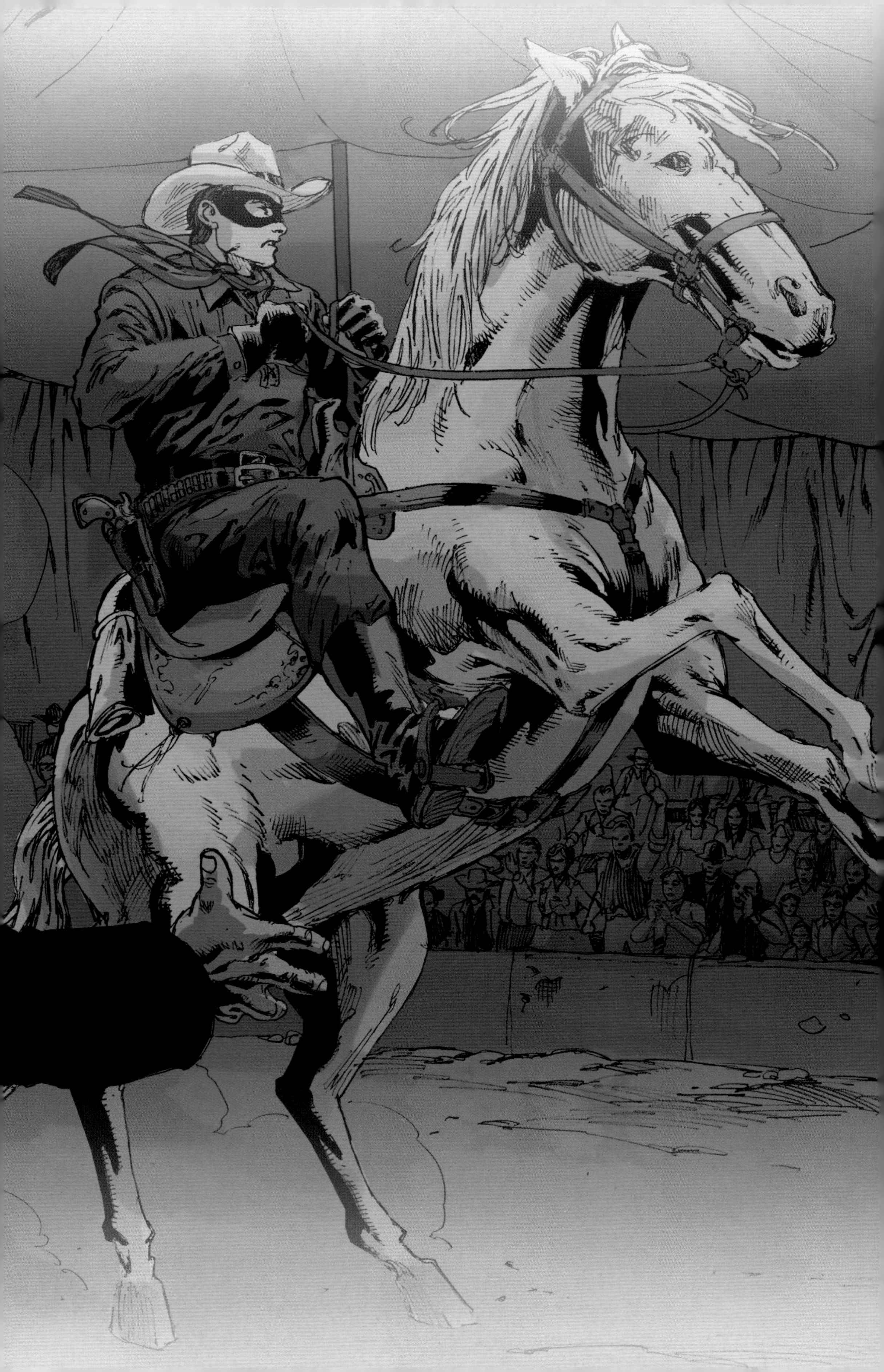

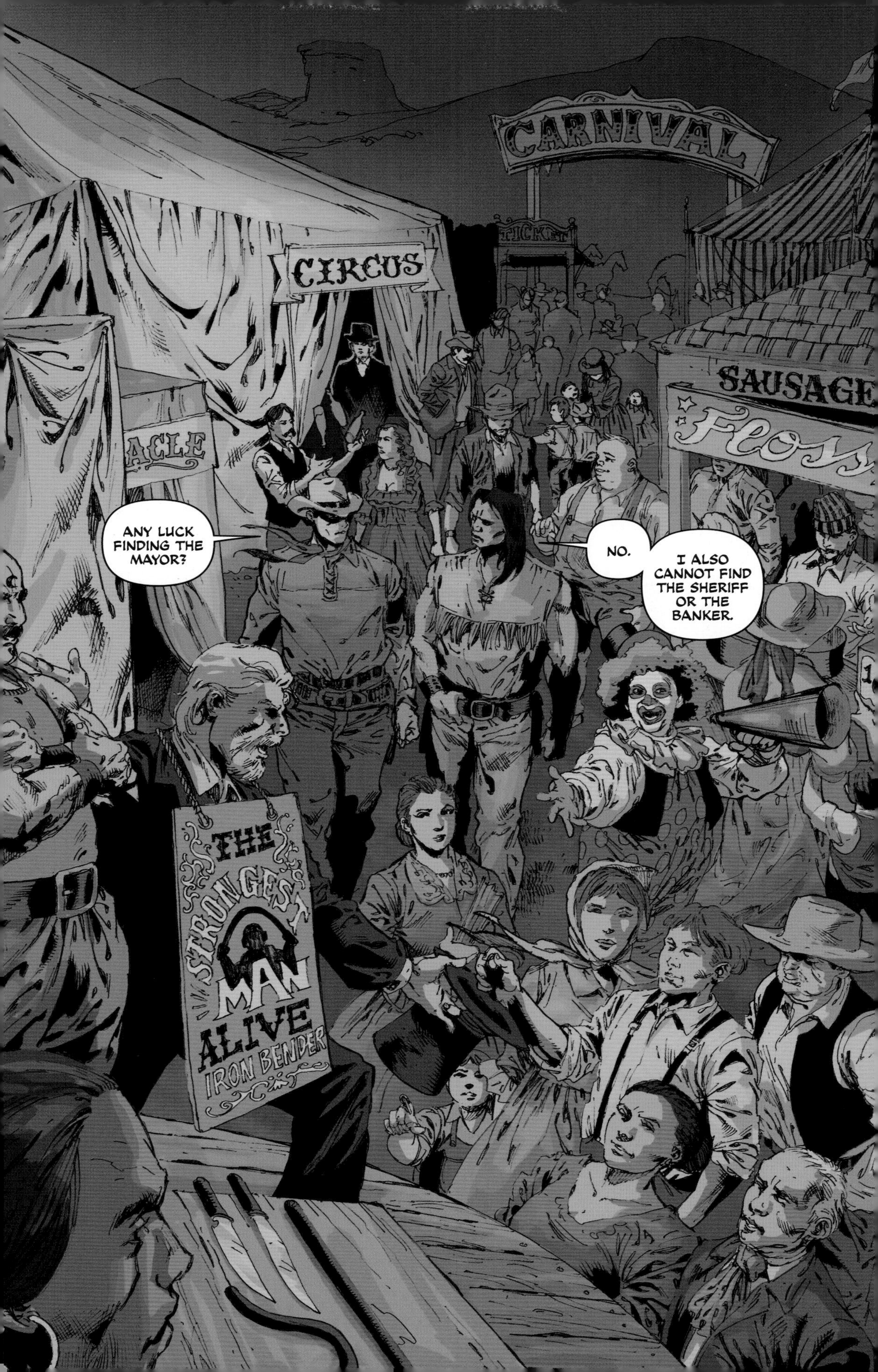
CARNIVAL
TICKET
CIRCUS
ACLE
SAUSAGE
Floss
ANY LUCK FINDING THE MAYOR?
NO.
I ALSO CANNOT FIND THE SHERIFF OR THE BANKER.
THE STRONGEST MAN ALIVE
IRON BENDER

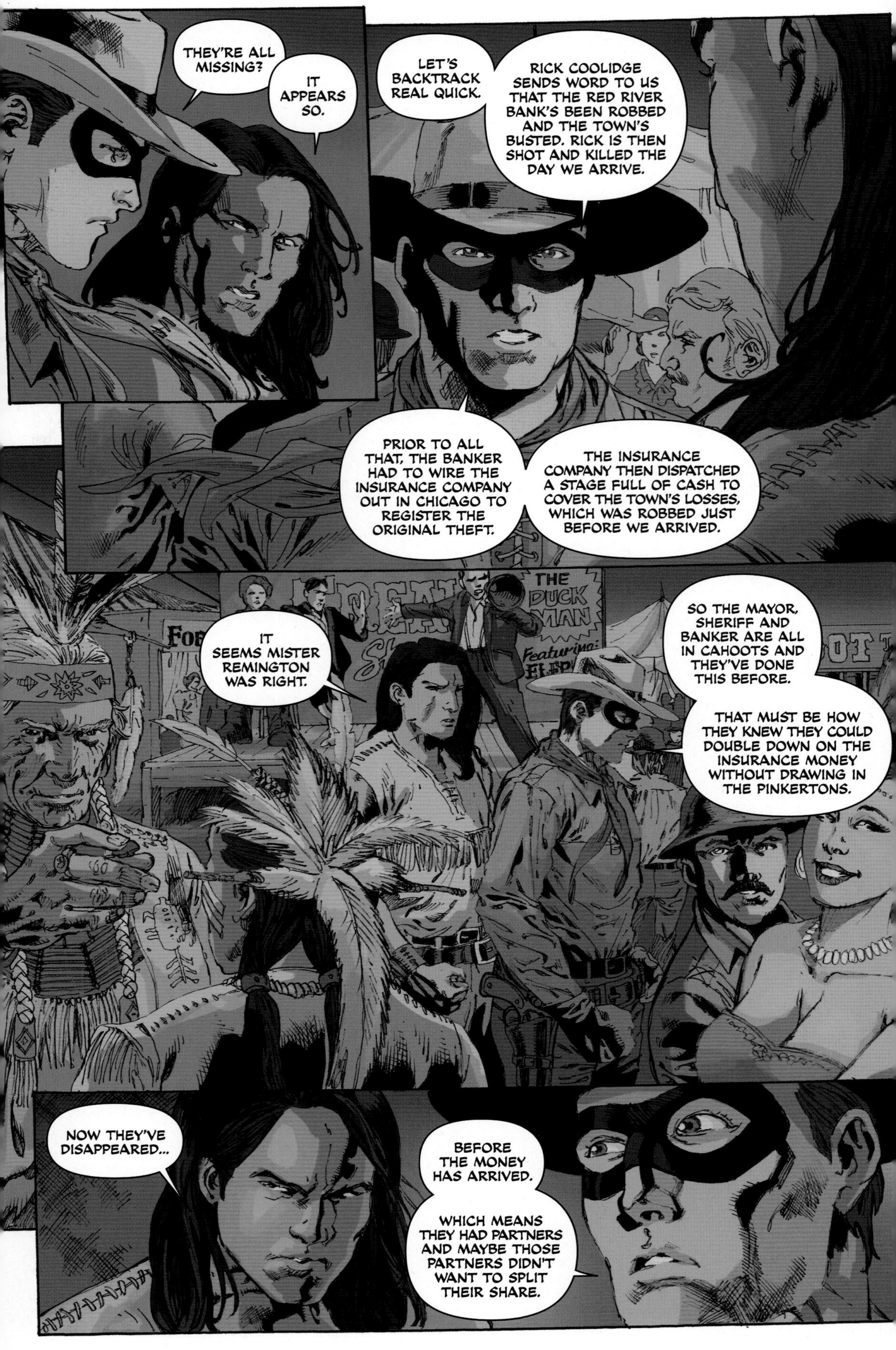
THEY'RE ALL MISSING?
IT APPEARS SO.
LET'S BACKTRACK REAL QUICK.
RICK COOLIDGE SENDS WORD TO US THAT THE RED RIVER BANK'S BEEN ROBBED AND THE TOWN'S BUSTED. RICK IS THEN SHOT AND KILLED THE DAY WE ARRIVE.
PRIOR TO ALL THAT, THE BANKER HAD TO WIRE THE INSURANCE COMPANY OUT IN CHICAGO TO REGISTER THE ORIGINAL THEFT.
THE INSURANCE COMPANY THEN DISPATCHED A STAGE FULL OF CASH TO COVER THE TOWN'S LOSSES, WHICH WAS ROBBED JUST BEFORE WE ARRIVED.
IT SEEMS MISTER REMINGTON WAS RIGHT.
SO THE MAYOR, SHERIFF AND BANKER ARE ALL IN CAHOOTS AND THEY'VE DONE THIS BEFORE.
THAT MUST BE HOW THEY KNEW THEY COULD DOUBLE DOWN ON THE INSURANCE MONEY WITHOUT DRAWING IN THE PINKERTONS.
NOW THEY'VE DISAPPEARED...
BEFORE THE MONEY HAS ARRIVED.
WHICH MEANS THEY HAD PARTNERS AND MAYBE THOSE PARTNERS DIDN'T WANT TO SPLIT THEIR SHARE.

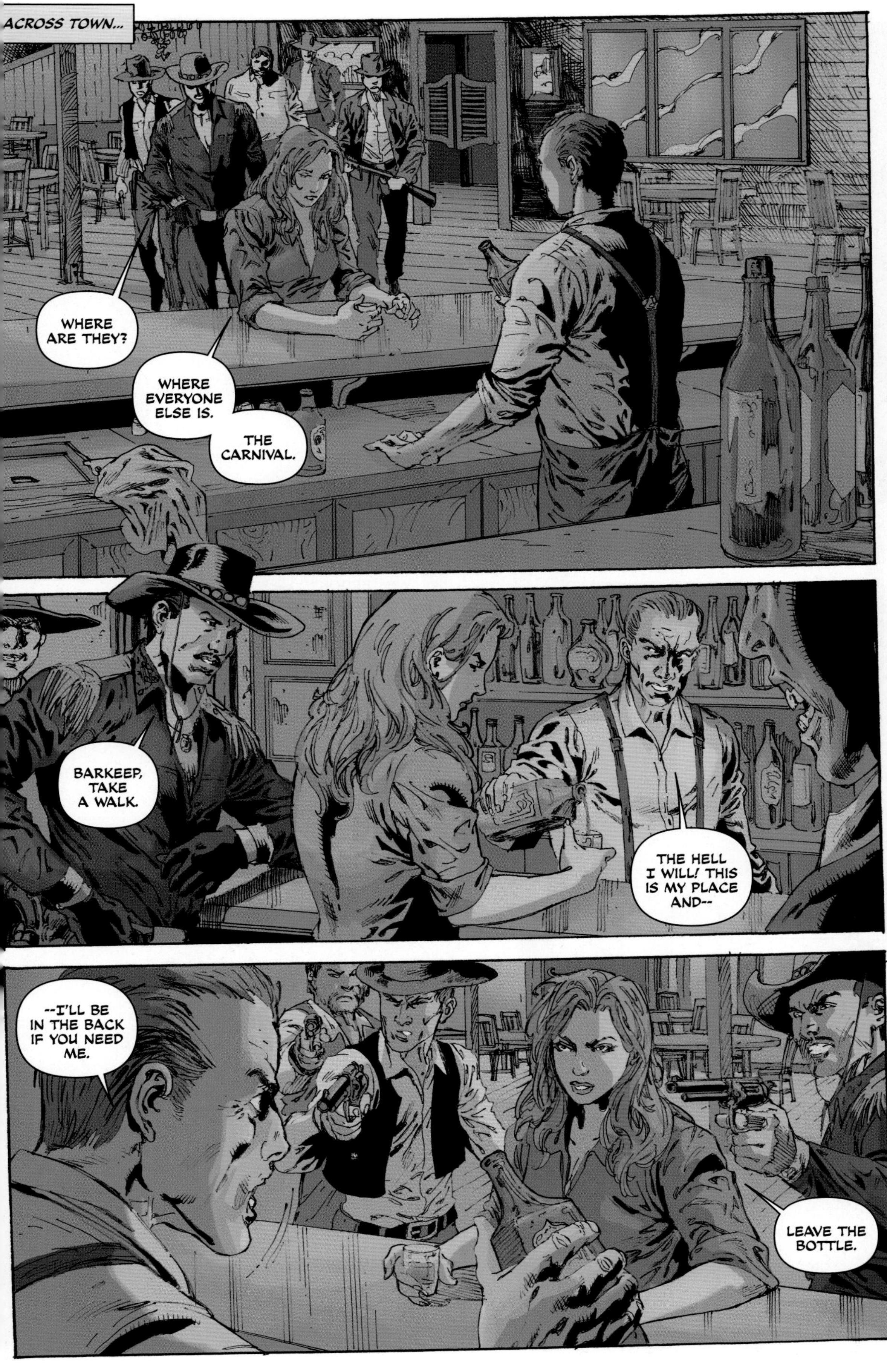
ACROSS TOWN...
WHERE ARE THEY?
WHERE EVERYONE ELSE IS.
THE CARNIVAL.
BARKEEP, TAKE A WALK.
THE HELL I WILL! THIS IS MY PLACE AND--
--I'LL BE IN THE BACK IF YOU NEED ME.
LEAVE THE BOTTLE.

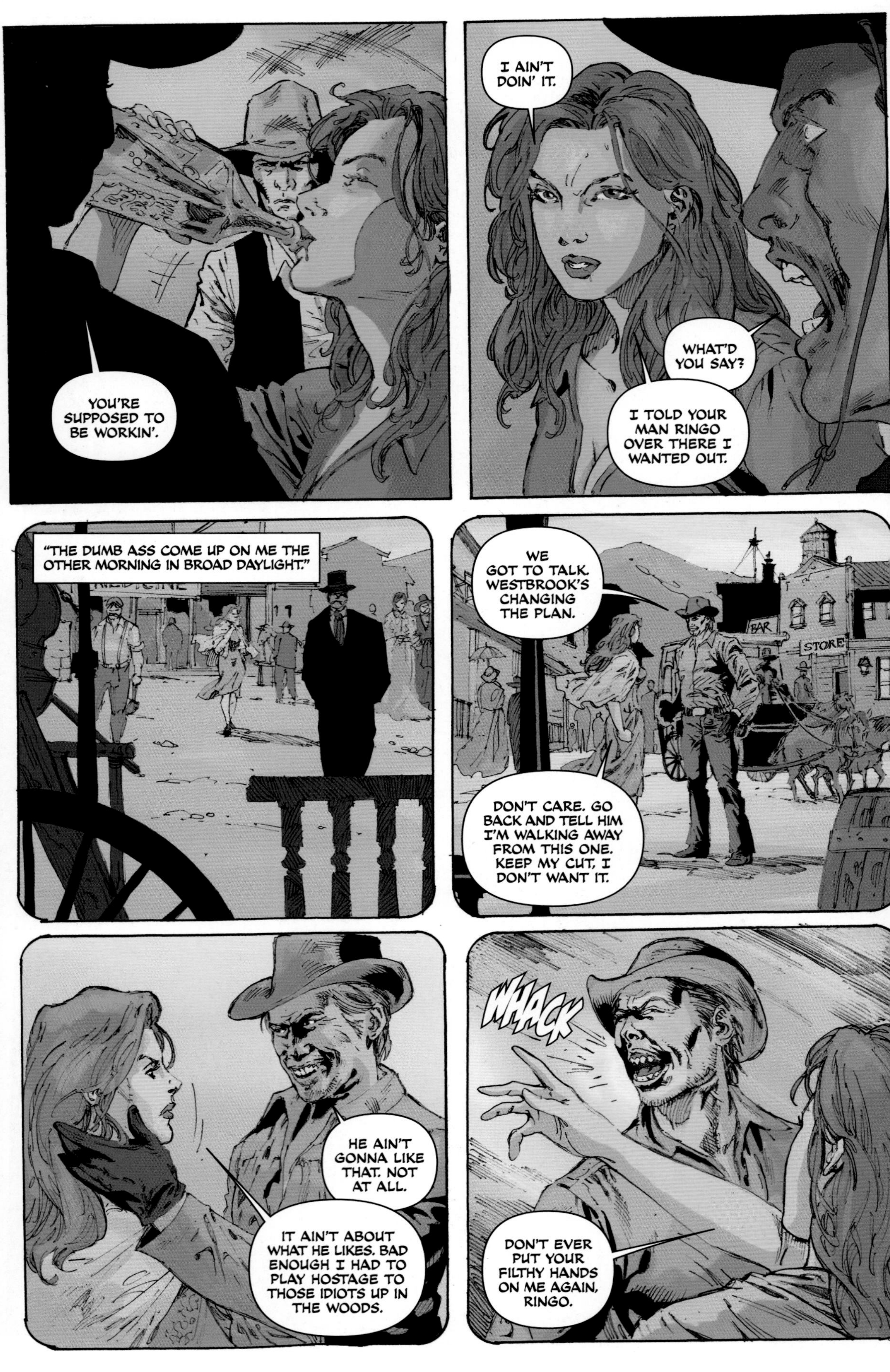
YOU'RE SUPPOSED TO BE WORKIN'.
I AIN'T DOIN' IT.
WHAT'D YOU SAY?
I TOLD YOUR MAN RINGO OVER THERE I WANTED OUT.
"THE DUMB ASS COME UP ON ME THE OTHER MORNING IN BROAD DAYLIGHT."
WE GOT TO TALK. WESTBROOK'S CHANGING THE PLAN.
BAR
STORE
DON'T CARE. GO BACK AND TELL HIM I'M WALKING AWAY FROM THIS ONE. KEEP MY CUT, I DON'T WANT IT.
HE AIN'T GONNA LIKE THAT. NOT AT ALL.
IT AIN'T ABOUT WHAT HE LIKES. BAD ENOUGH I HAD TO PLAY HOSTAGE TO THOSE IDIOTS UP IN THE WOODS.
WHACK
DON'T EVER PUT YOUR FILTHY HANDS ON ME AGAIN, RINGO.

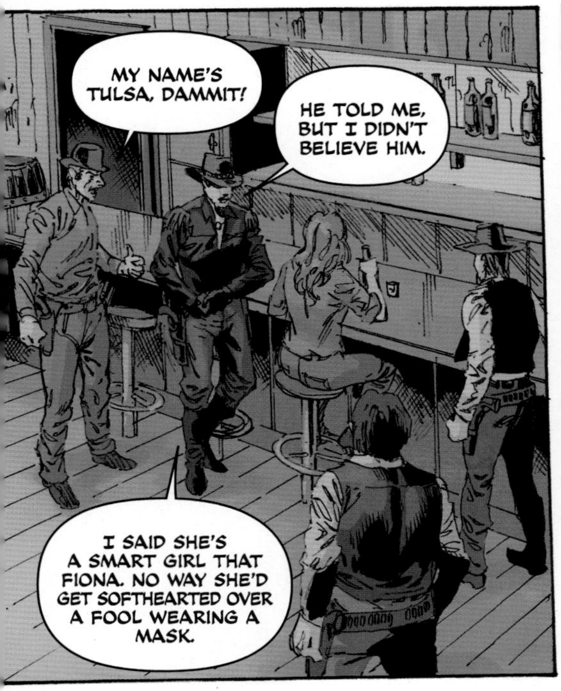
MY NAME'S TULSA, DAMMIT!
HE TOLD ME, BUT I DIDN'T BELIEVE HIM.
I SAID SHE'S A SMART GIRL THAT FIONA. NO WAY SHE'D GET SOFTHEARTED OVER A FOOL WEARING A MASK.

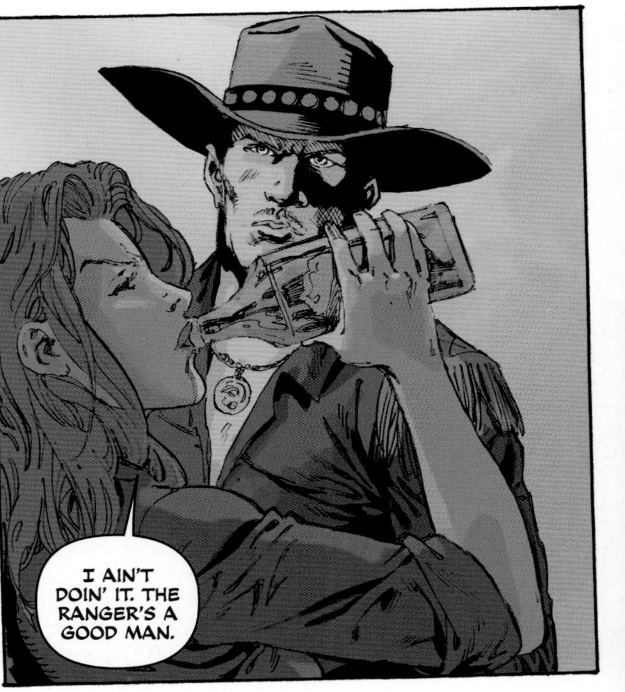
I AIN'T DOIN' IT. THE RANGER'S A GOOD MAN.

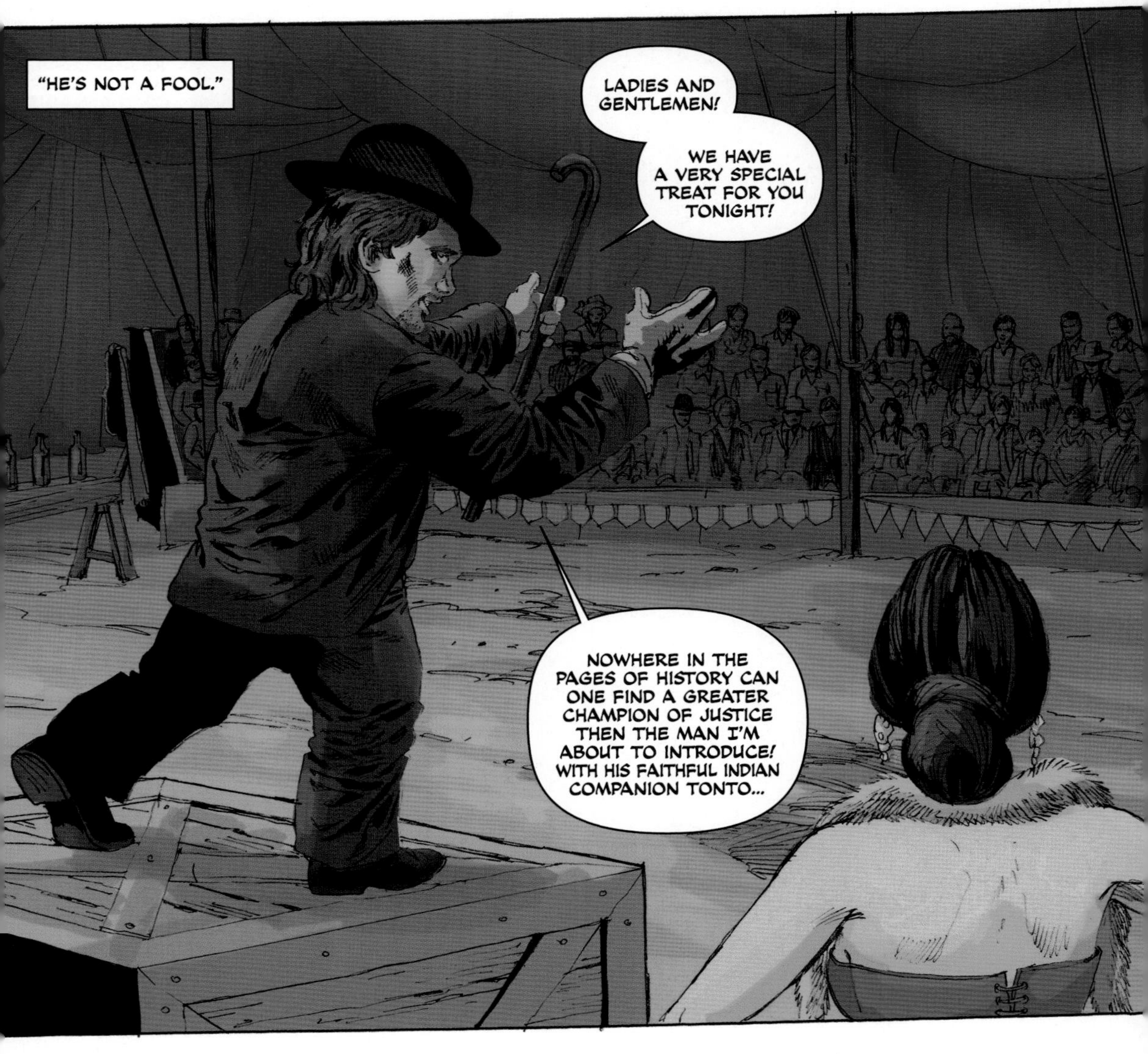
"HE'S NOT A FOOL."
LADIES AND GENTLEMEN!
WE HAVE A VERY SPECIAL TREAT FOR YOU TONIGHT!
NOWHERE IN THE PAGES OF HISTORY CAN ONE FIND A GREATER CHAMPION OF JUSTICE THEN THE MAN I'M ABOUT TO INTRODUCE! WITH HIS FAITHFUL INDIAN COMPANION TONTO...

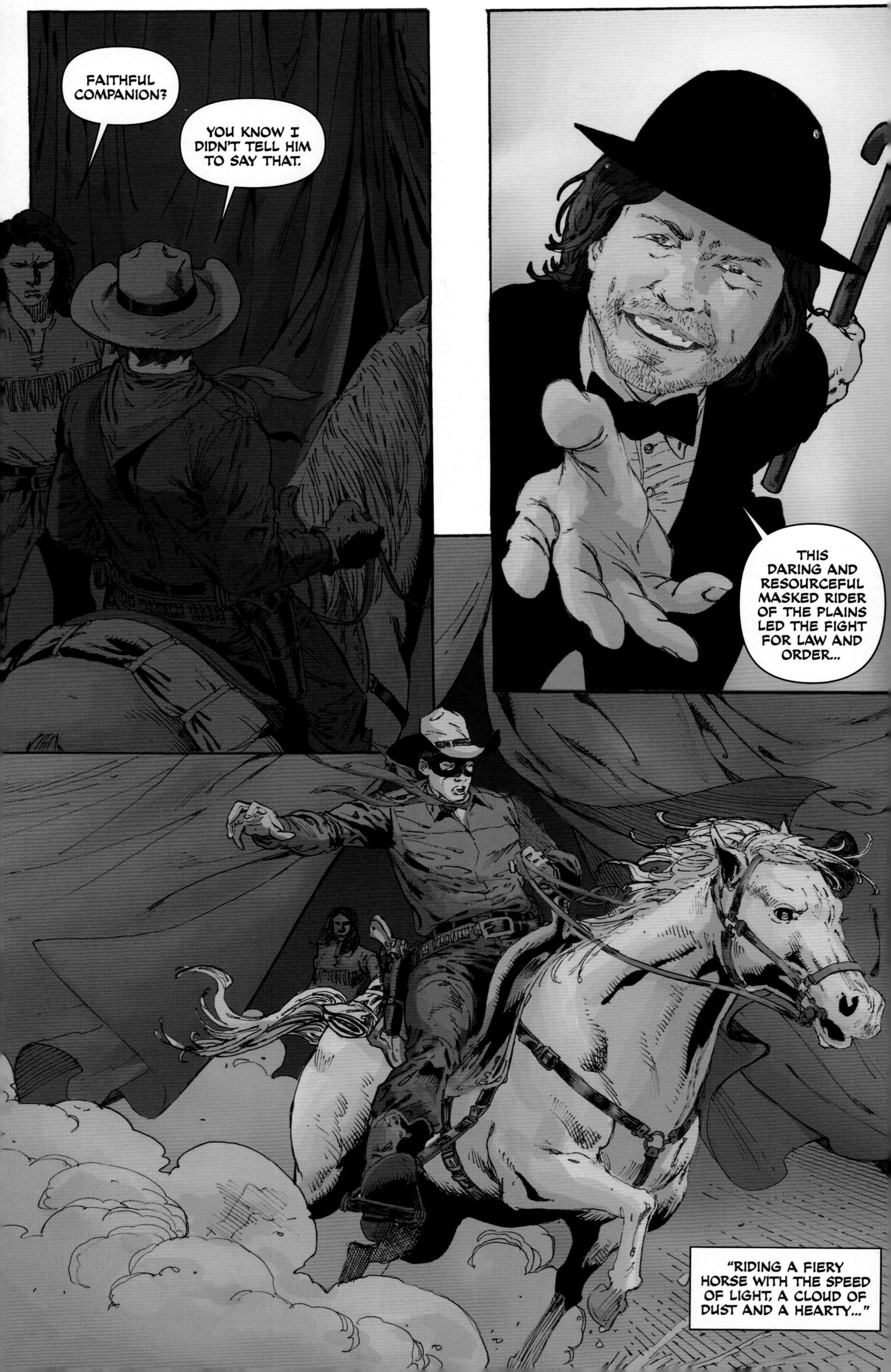
FAITHFUL COMPANION?
YOU KNOW I DIDN'T TELL HIM TO SAY THAT.
THIS DARING AND RESOURCEFUL MASKED RIDER OF THE PLAINS LED THE FIGHT FOR LAW AND ORDER...
"RIDING A FIERY HORSE WITH THE SPEED OF LIGHT, A CLOUD OF DUST AND A HEARTY..."

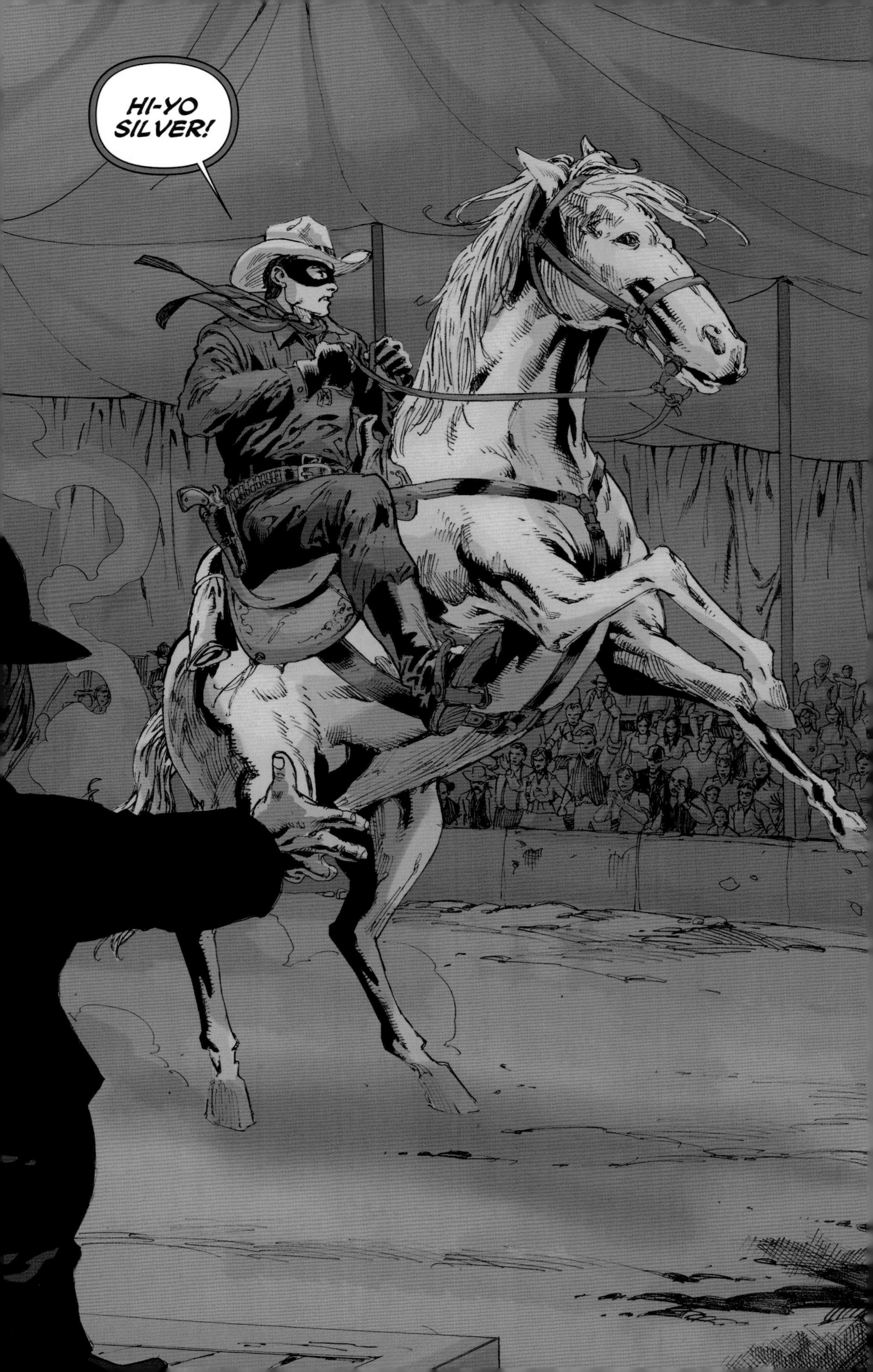
HI-YO SILVER!

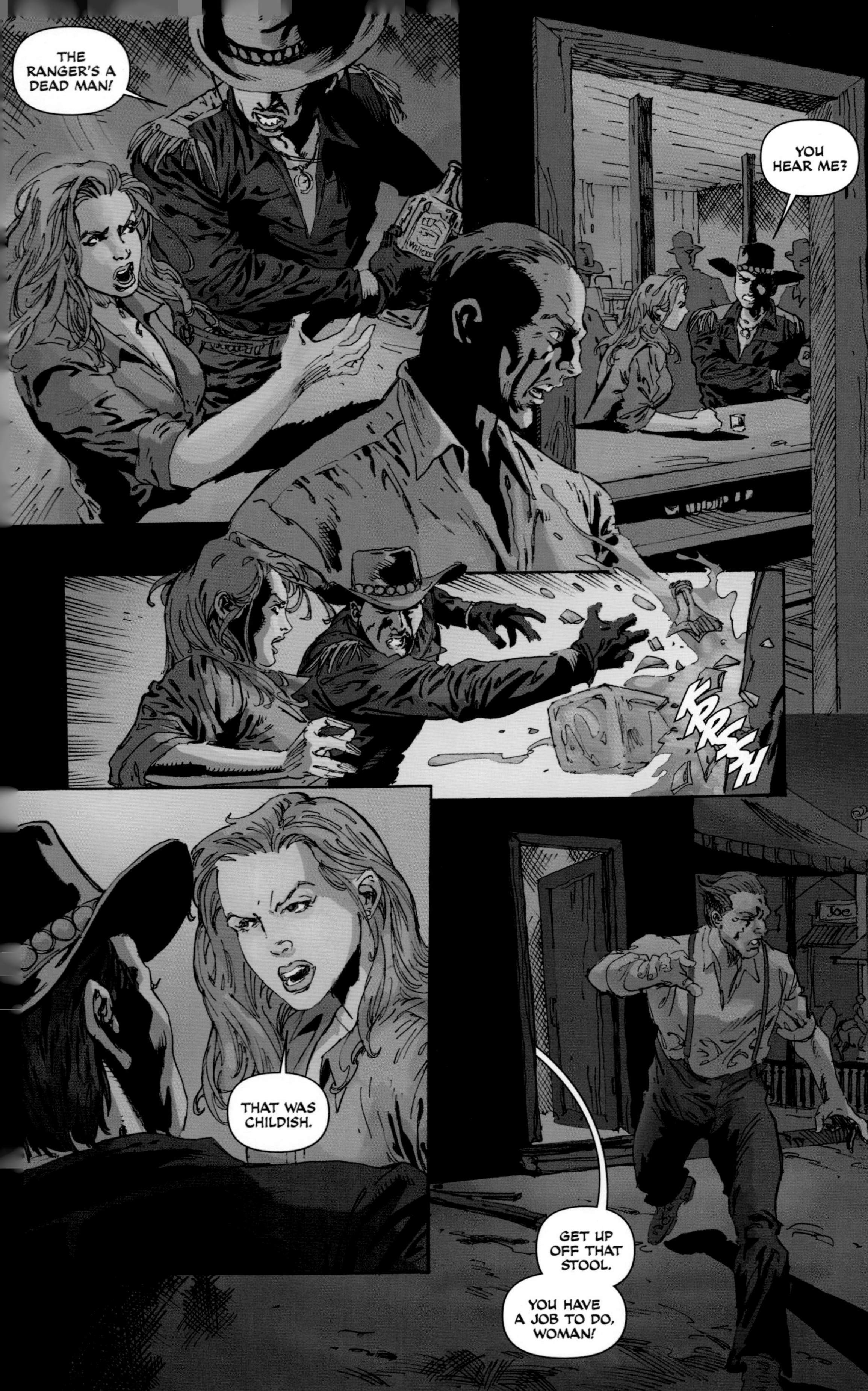
THE RANGER'S A DEAD MAN!
YOU HEAR ME?
KRRSSH
THAT WAS CHILDISH.
GET UP OFF THAT STOOL.
YOU HAVE A JOB TO DO, WOMAN!

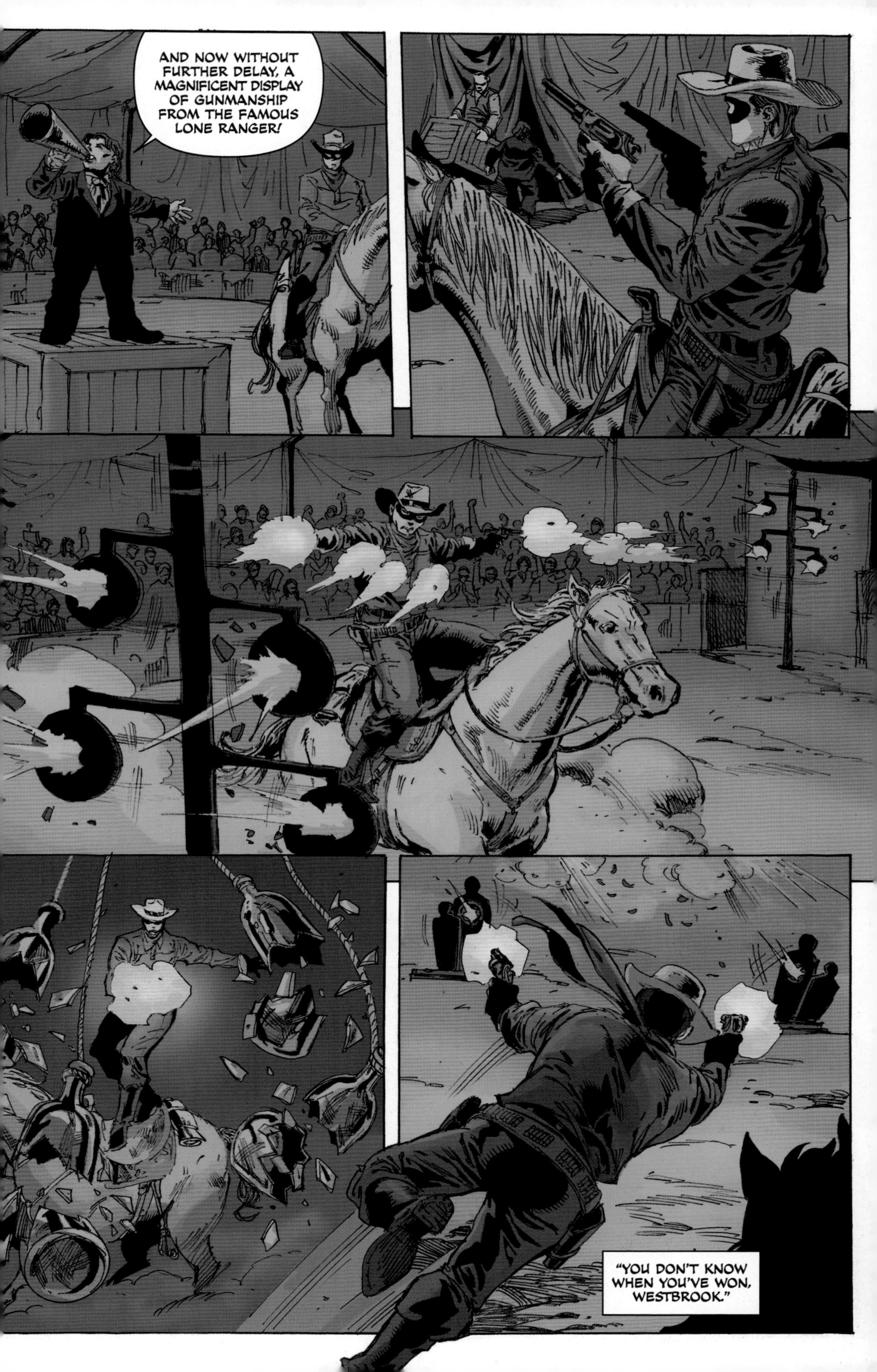
AND NOW WITHOUT FURTHER DELAY, A MAGNIFICENT DISPLAY OF GUNMANSHIP FROM THE FAMOUS LONE RANGER!
"YOU DON'T KNOW WHEN YOU'VE WON, WESTBROOK."

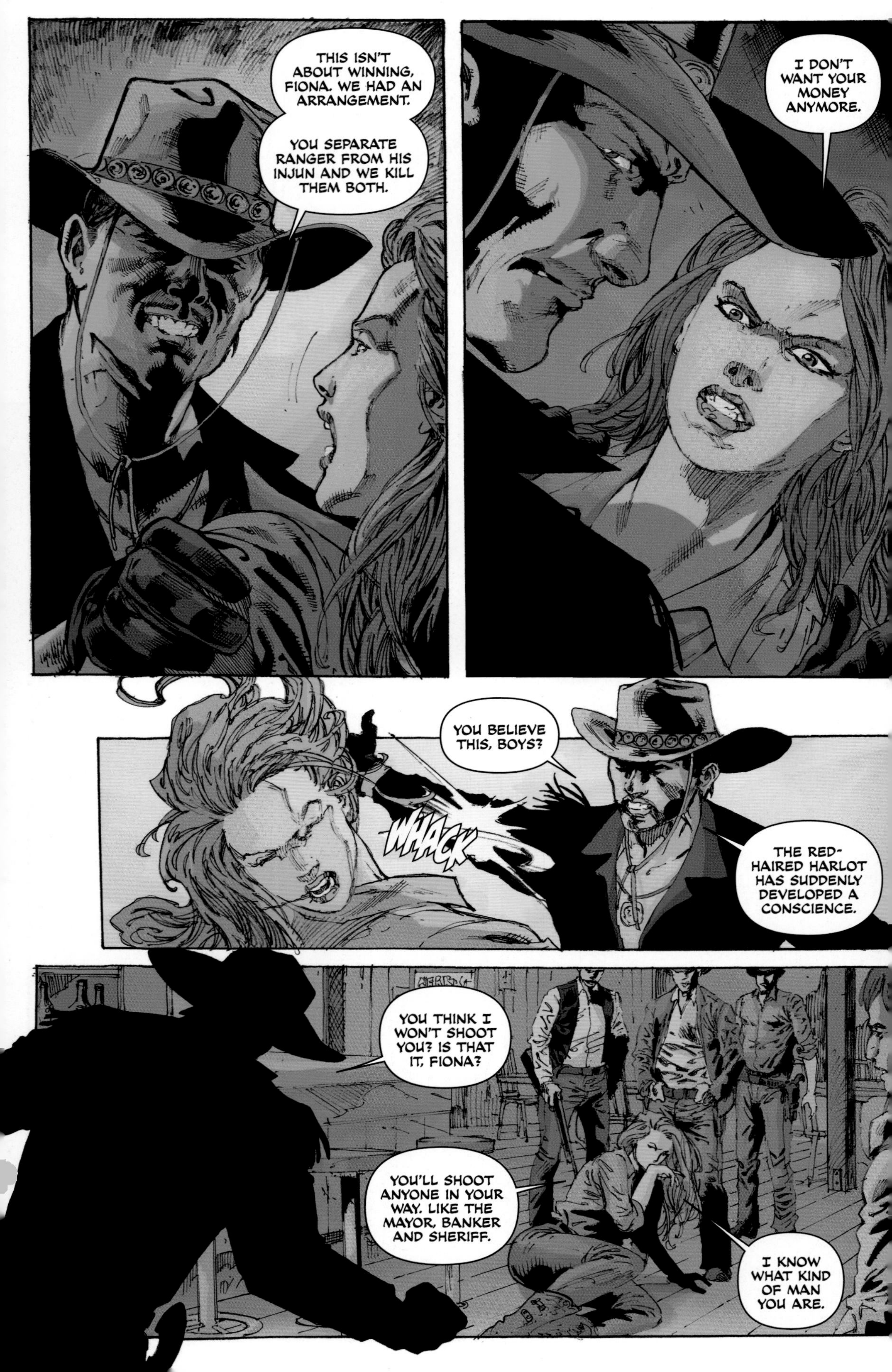
THIS ISN'T ABOUT WINNING, FIONA. WE HAD AN ARRANGEMENT.
YOU SEPARATE RANGER FROM HIS INJUN AND WE KILL THEM BOTH.
I DON'T WANT YOUR MONEY ANYMORE.
YOU BELIEVE THIS, BOYS?
WHACK
THE RED-HAIRED HARLOT HAS SUDDENLY DEVELOPED A CONSCIENCE.
YOU THINK I WON'T SHOOT YOU? IS THAT IT, FIONA?
YOU'LL SHOOT ANYONE IN YOUR WAY. LIKE THE MAYOR, BANKER AND SHERIFF.
I KNOW WHAT KIND OF MAN YOU ARE.

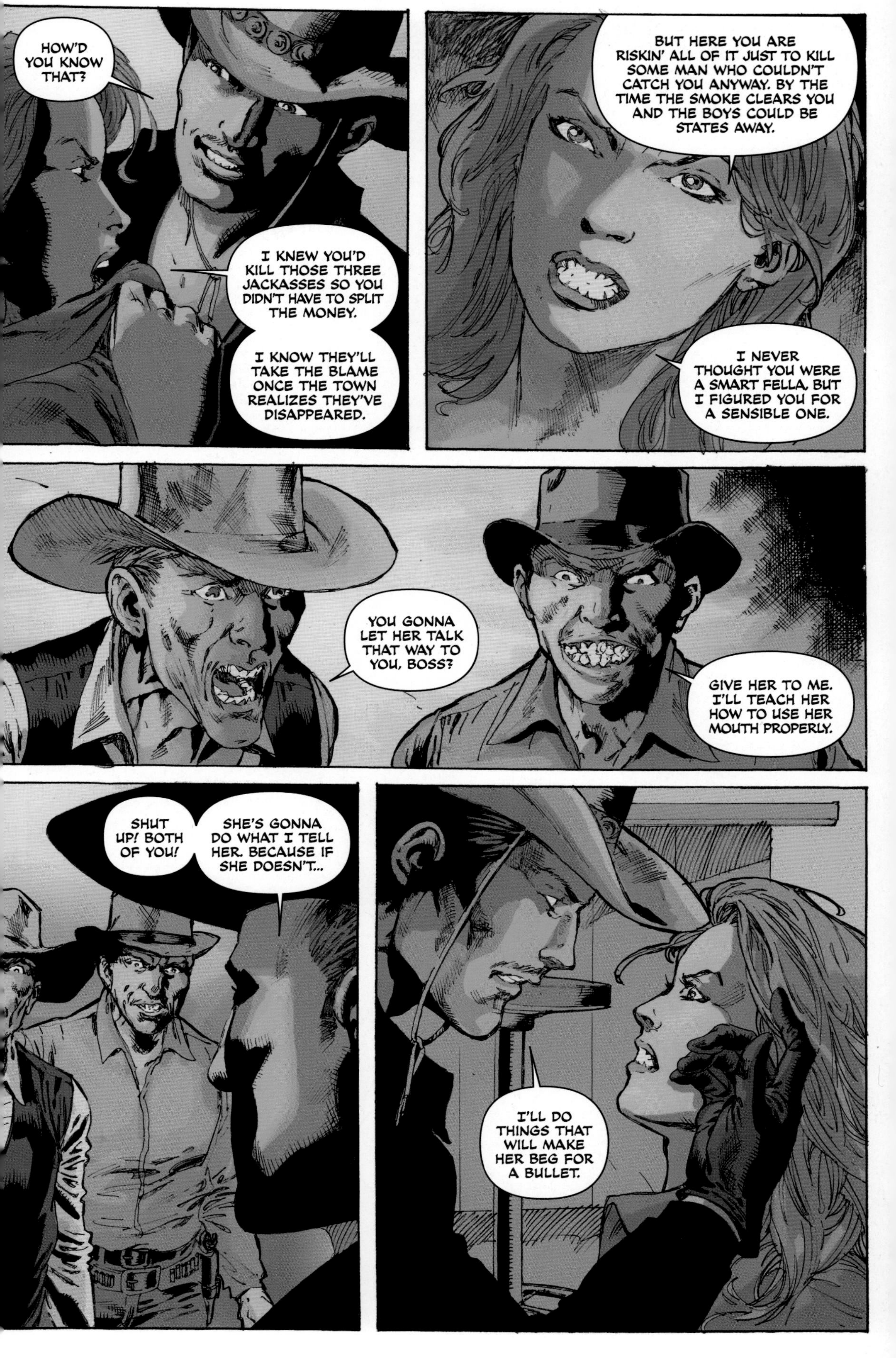
HOW'D YOU KNOW THAT?
I KNEW YOU'D KILL THOSE THREE JACKASSES SO YOU DIDN'T HAVE TO SPLIT THE MONEY.
I KNOW THEY'LL TAKE THE BLAME ONCE THE TOWN REALIZES THEY'VE DISAPPEARED.
BUT HERE YOU ARE RISKIN' ALL OF IT JUST TO KILL SOME MAN WHO COULDN'T CATCH YOU ANYWAY. BY THE TIME THE SMOKE CLEARS YOU AND THE BOYS COULD BE STATES AWAY.
I NEVER THOUGHT YOU WERE A SMART FELLA, BUT I FIGURED YOU FOR A SENSIBLE ONE.
YOU GONNA LET HER TALK THAT WAY TO YOU, BOSS?
GIVE HER TO ME. I'LL TEACH HER HOW TO USE HER MOUTH PROPERLY.
SHUT UP! BOTH OF YOU!
SHE'S GONNA DO WHAT I TELL HER. BECAUSE IF SHE DOESN'T...
I'LL DO THINGS THAT WILL MAKE HER BEG FOR A BULLET.

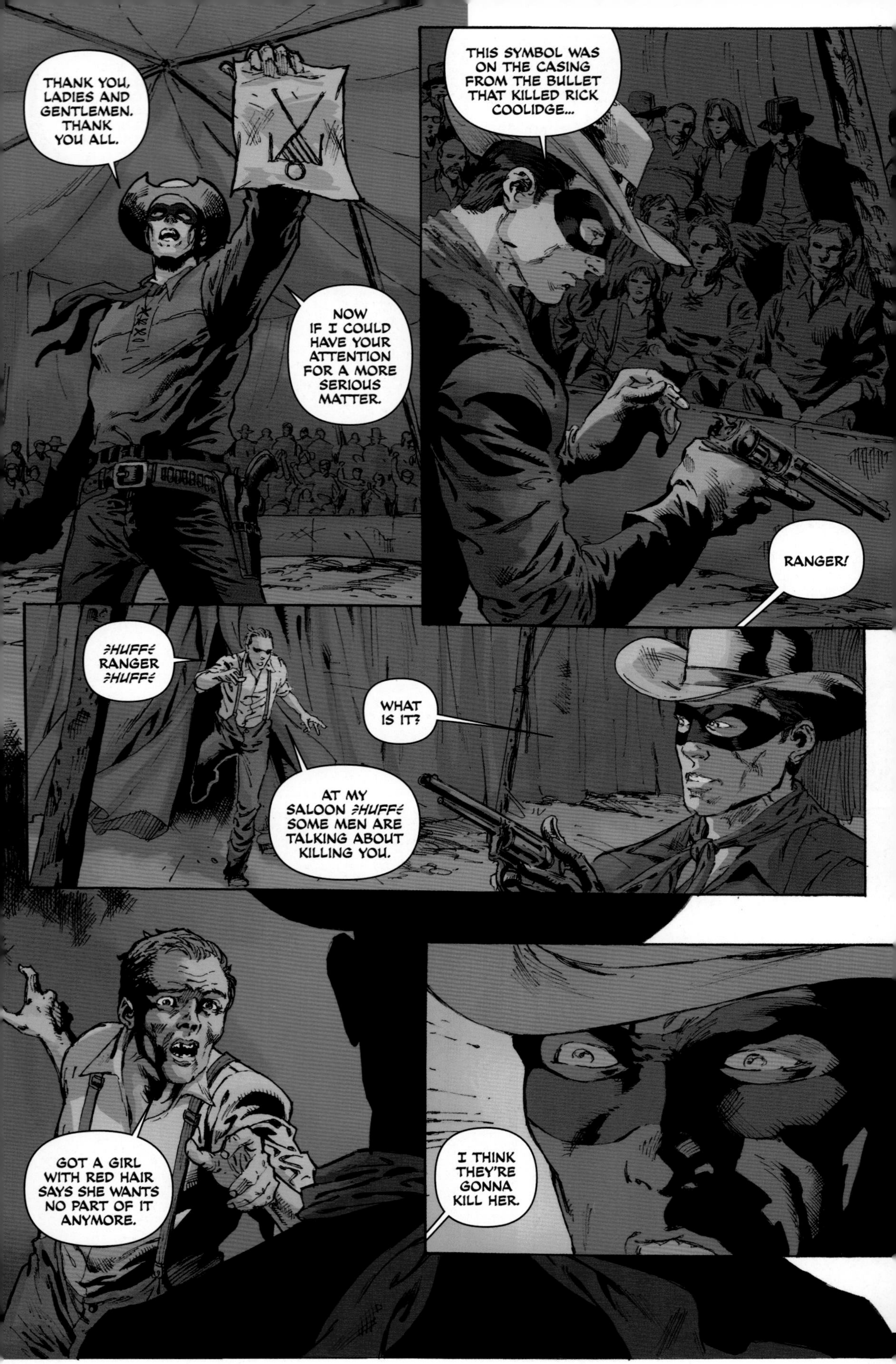
THANK YOU, LADIES AND GENTLEMEN. THANK YOU ALL.
NOW IF I COULD HAVE YOUR ATTENTION FOR A MORE SERIOUS MATTER.
THIS SYMBOL WAS ON THE CASING FROM THE BULLET THAT KILLED RICK COOLIDGE...
RANGER!
HUFF RANGER *HUFF*
WHAT IS IT?
AT MY SALOON *HUFF* SOME MEN ARE TALKING ABOUT KILLING YOU.
GOT A GIRL WITH RED HAIR SAYS SHE WANTS NO PART OF IT ANYMORE.
I THINK THEY'RE GONNA KILL HER.

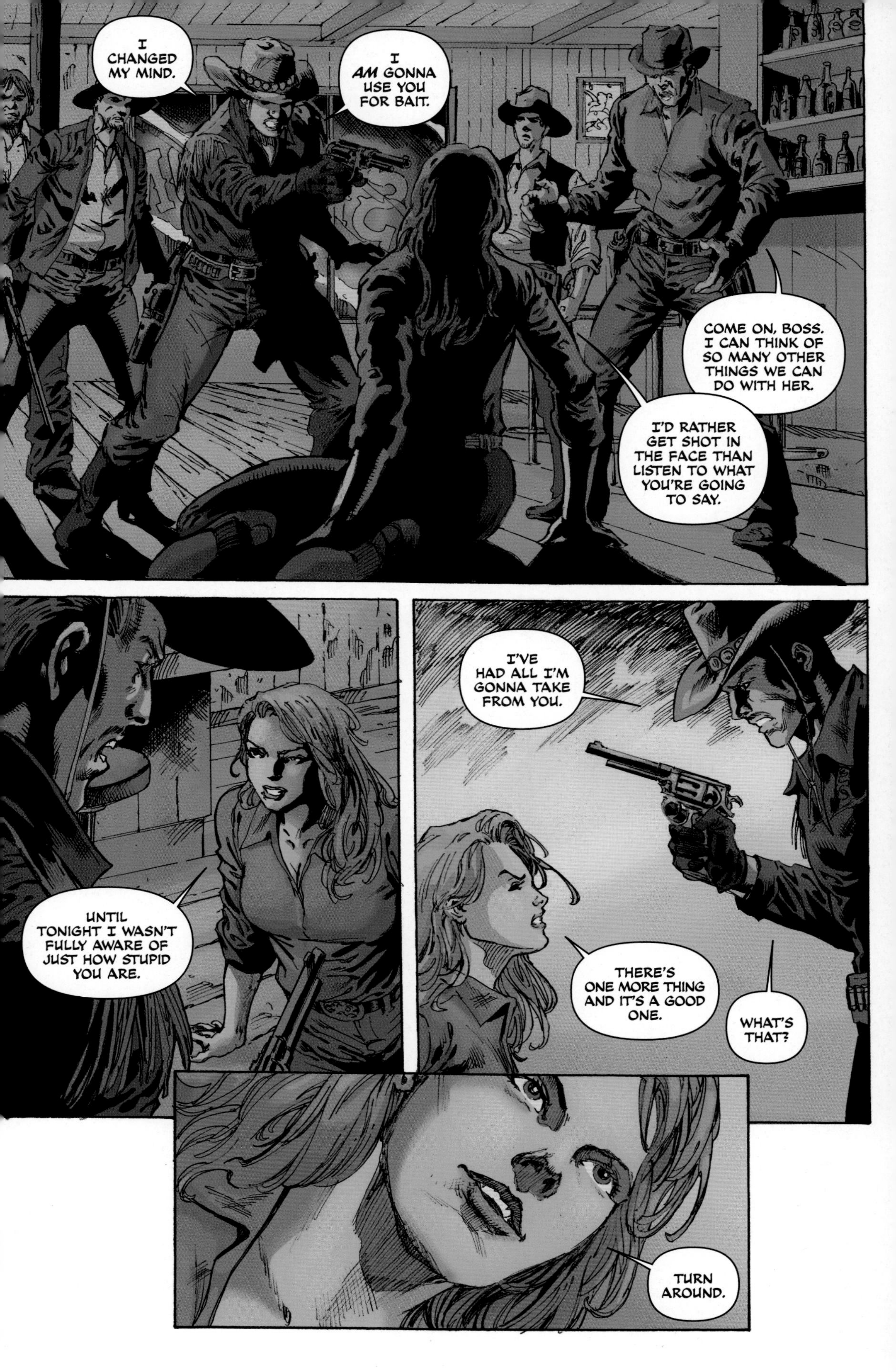
I CHANGED MY MIND.
I AM GONNA USE YOU FOR BAIT.
COME ON, BOSS. I CAN THINK OF SO MANY OTHER THINGS WE CAN DO WITH HER.
I'D RATHER GET SHOT IN THE FACE THAN LISTEN TO WHAT YOU'RE GOING TO SAY.
UNTIL TONIGHT I WASN'T FULLY AWARE OF JUST HOW STUPID YOU ARE.
I'VE HAD ALL I'M GONNA TAKE FROM YOU.
THERE'S ONE MORE THING AND IT'S A GOOD ONE.
WHAT'S THAT?
TURN AROUND.

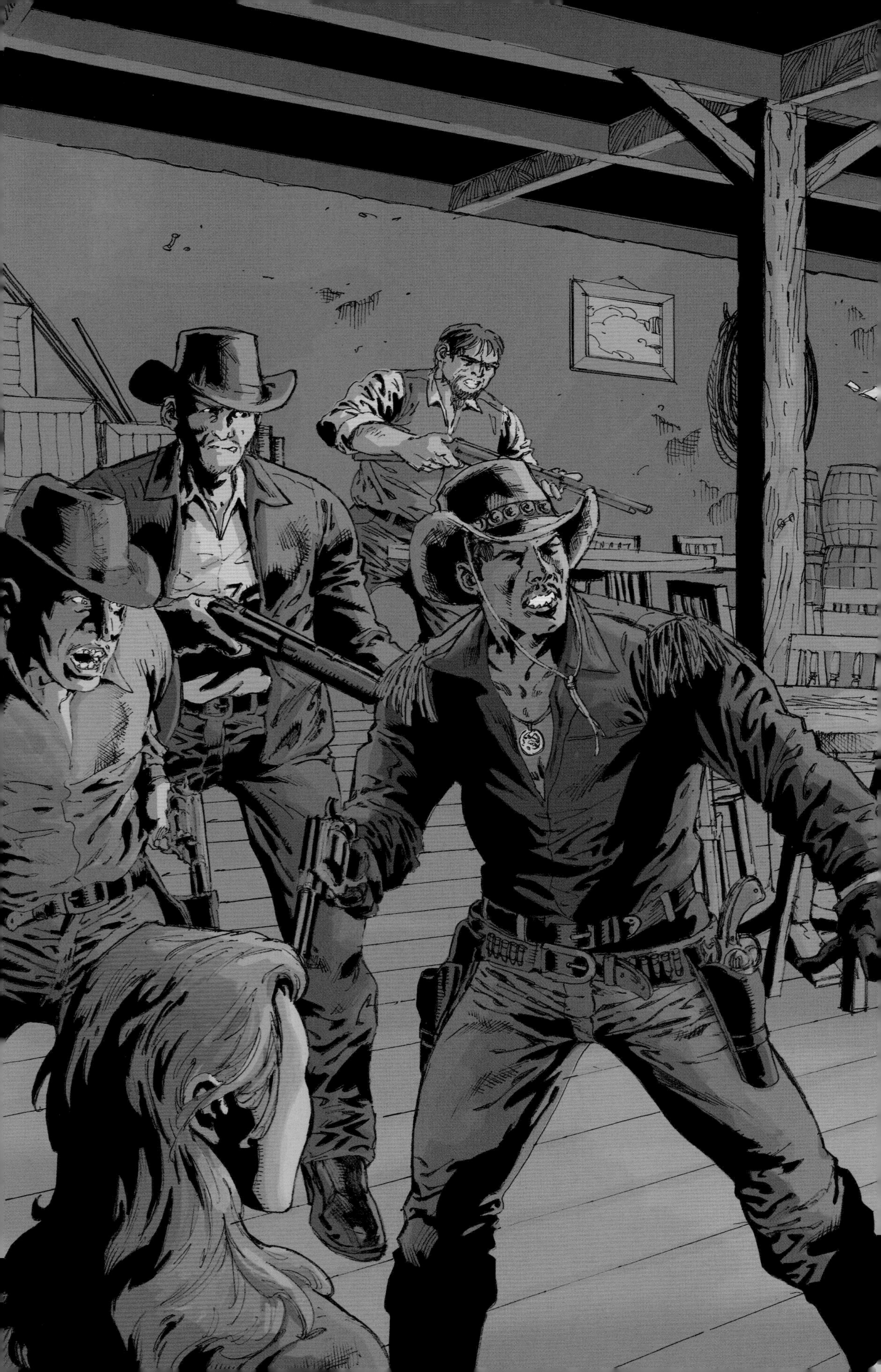

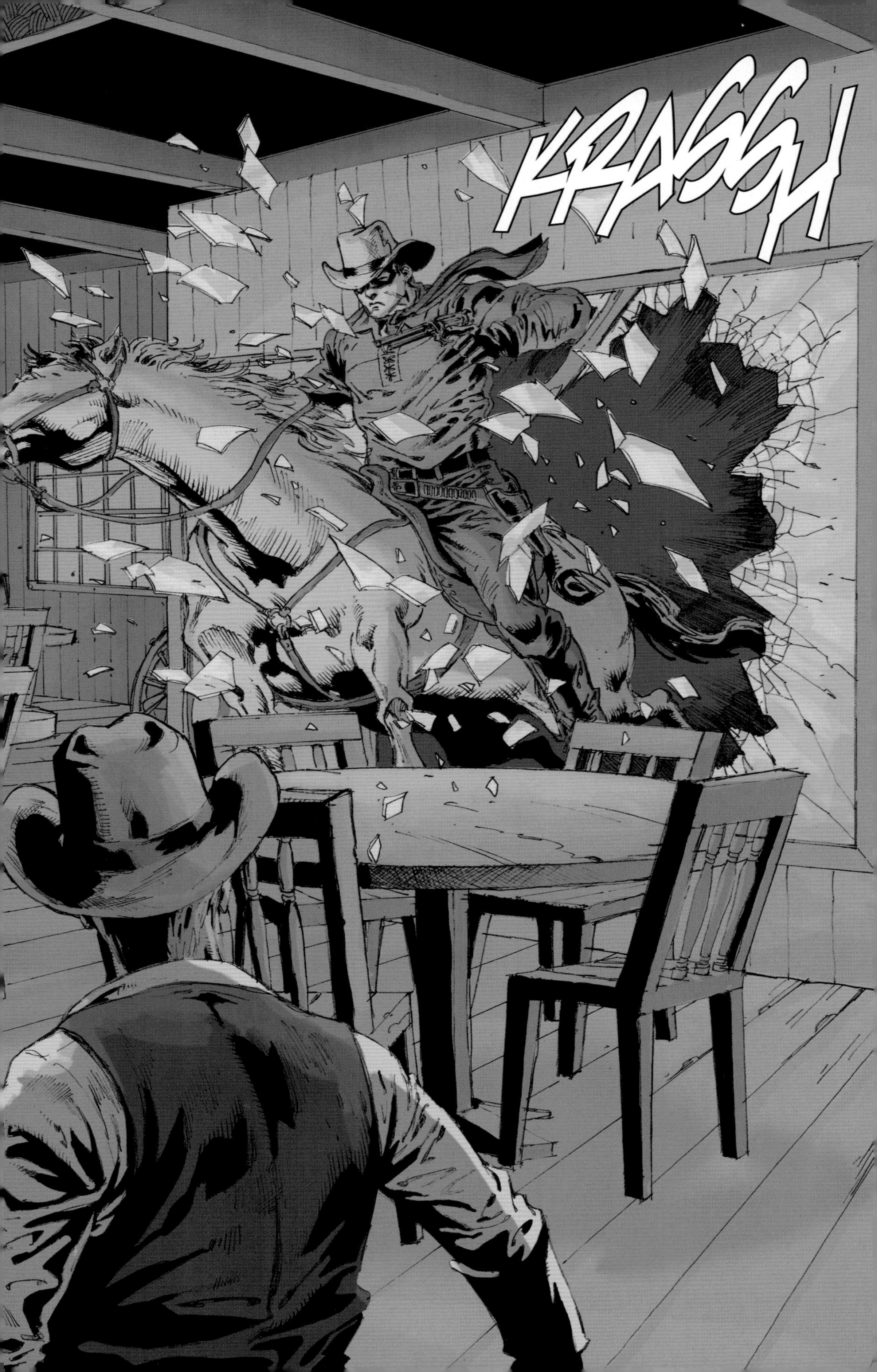
KRASSH

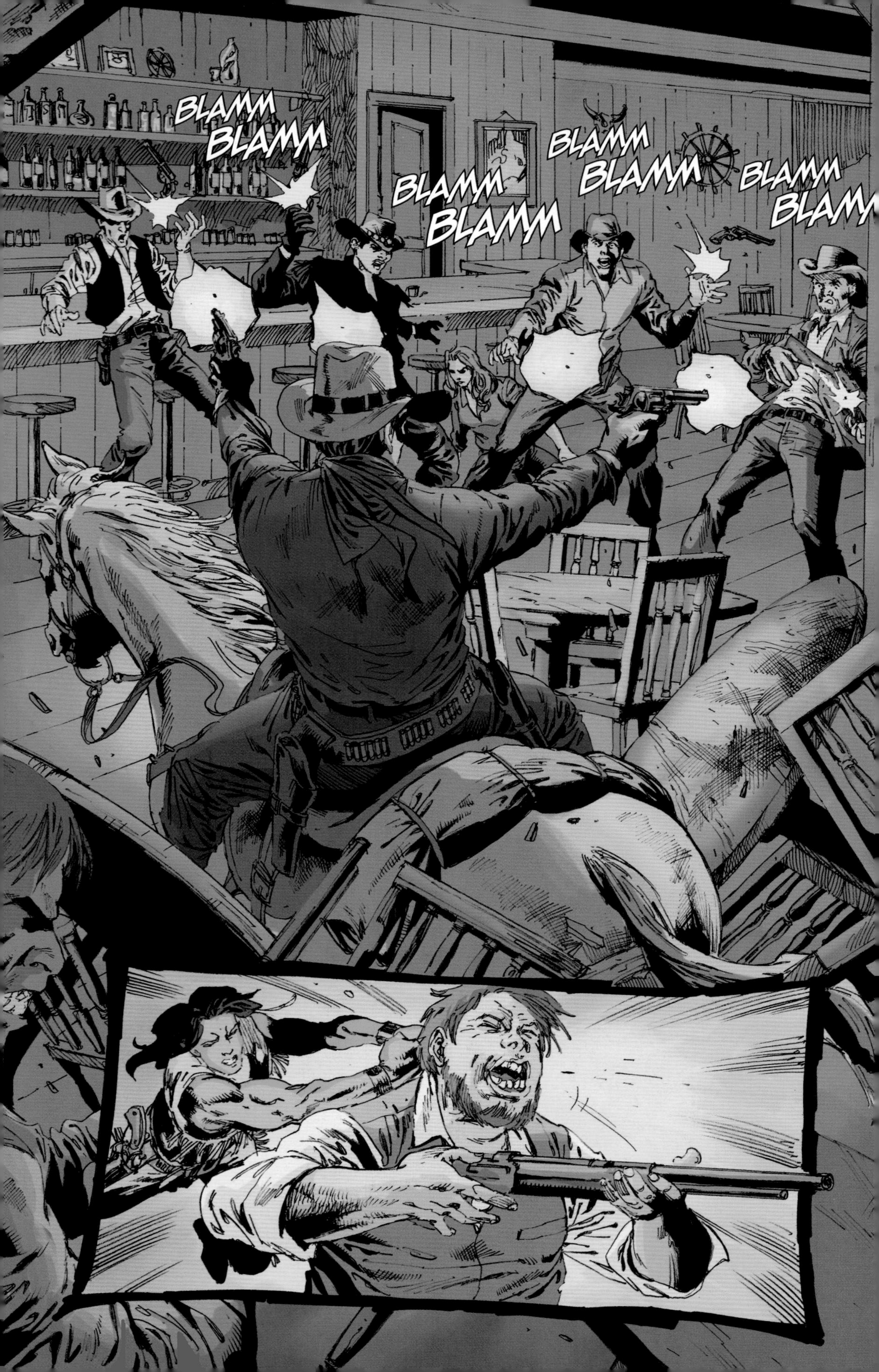
BLAMM BLAMM
BLAMM BLAMM
BLAMM BLAMM
BLAMM BLAMM

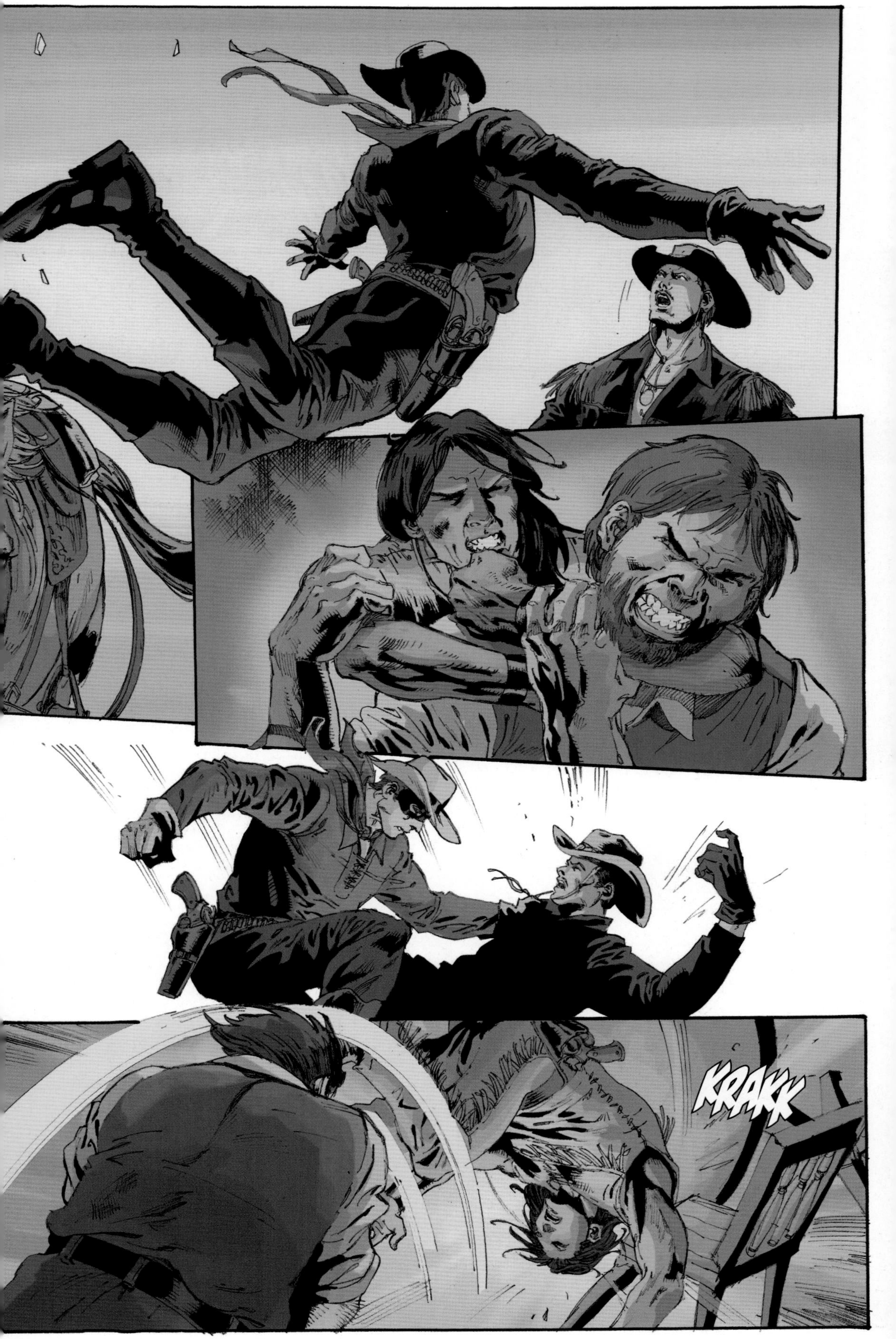
KRAKK

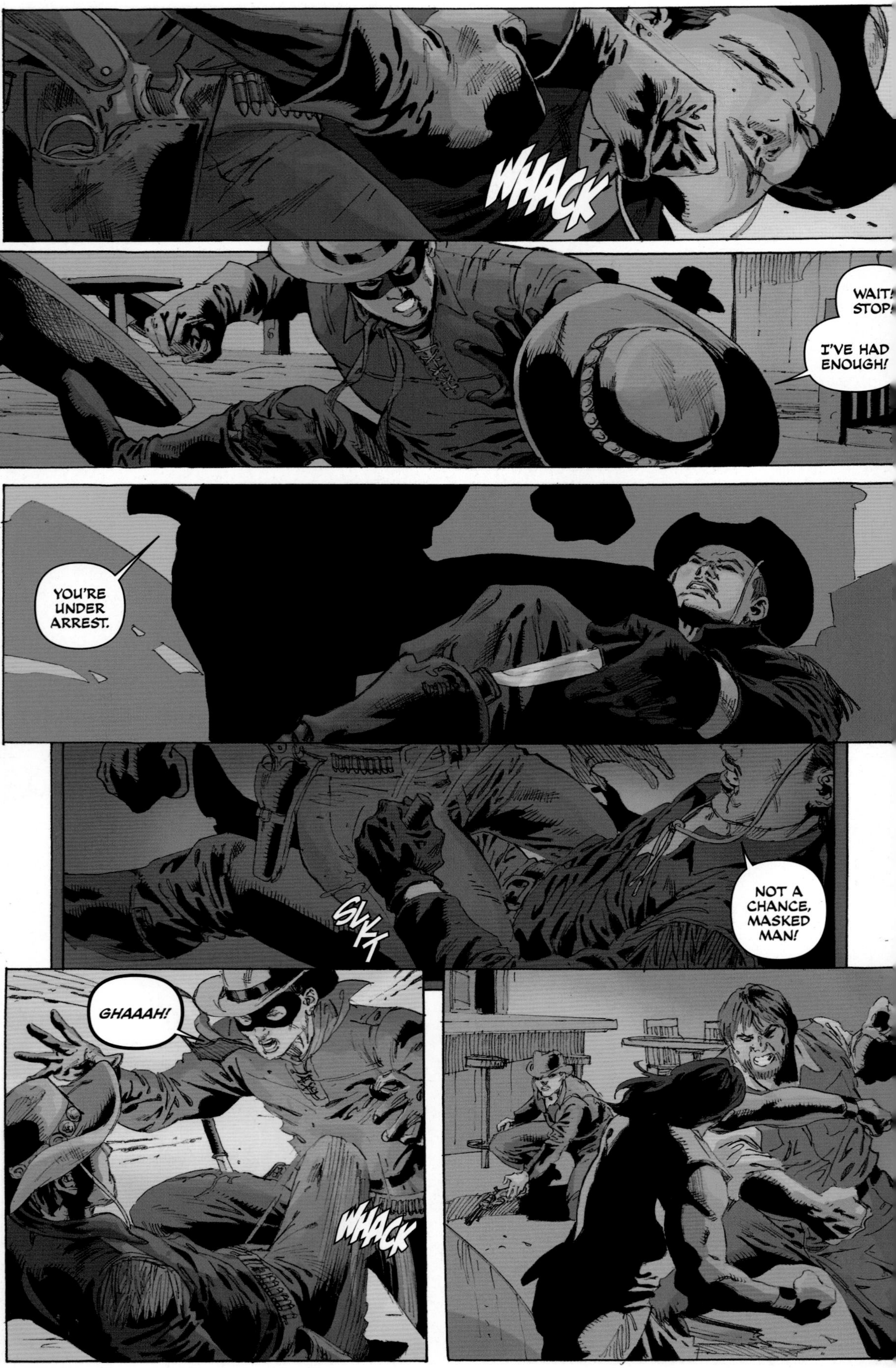
WHACK
WAIT! STOP!
I'VE HAD ENOUGH!
YOU'RE UNDER ARREST.
NOT A CHANCE, MASKED MAN!
SLIKK
GHAAAH!
WHACK

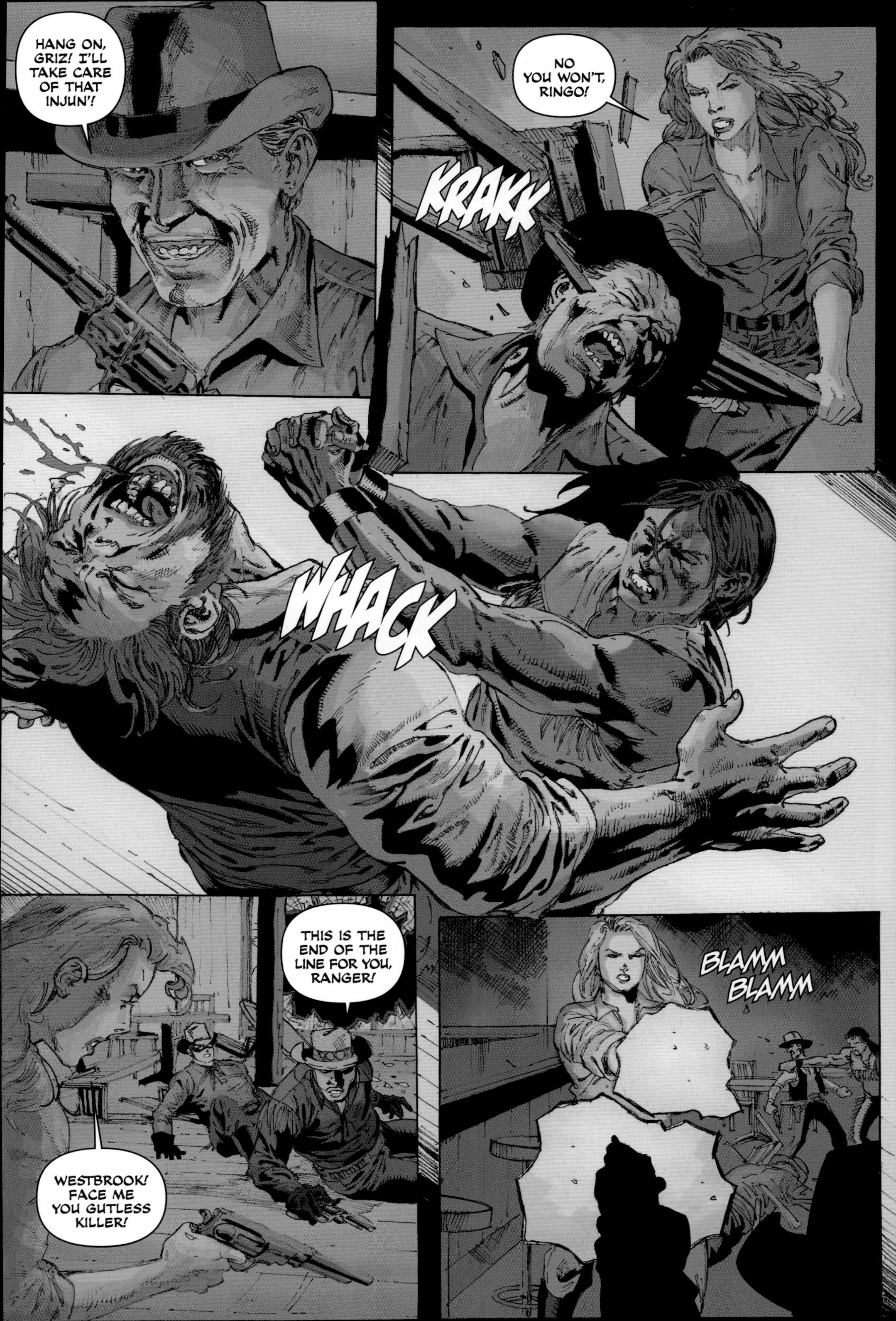
HANG ON, GRIZ! I'LL TAKE CARE OF THAT INJUN'!
NO YOU WON'T, RINGO!
KRAKK
WHACK
THIS IS THE END OF THE LINE FOR YOU, RANGER!
WESTBROOK! FACE ME YOU GUTLESS KILLER!
BLAMM BLAMM

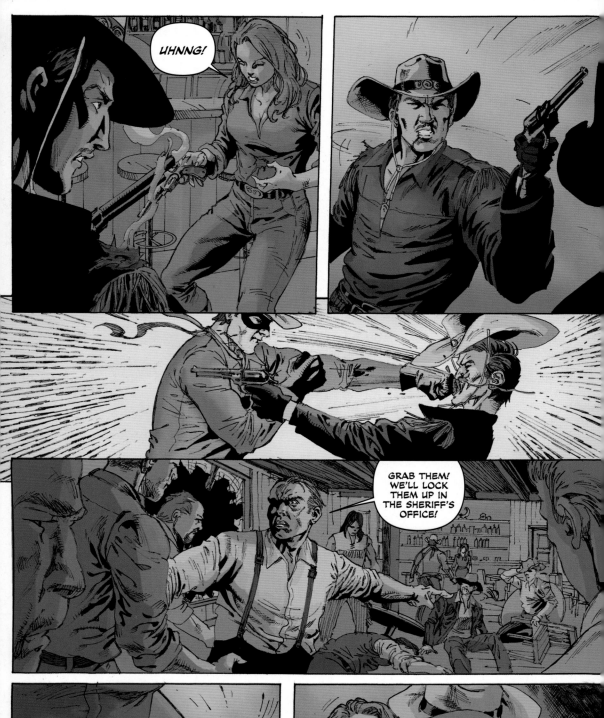

UHNNG!

GRAB THEM! WE'LL LOCK THEM UP IN THE SHERIFF'S OFFICE!

THIS IS NOT HOW I NORMALLY SPEND MY SATURDAY NIGHTS.

ITS OKAY, FIONA. WE'LL GET YOU TO THE DOCTOR.

I AIN'T GONNA MAKE IT.

WE WILL LET THE DOCTOR DECIDE.

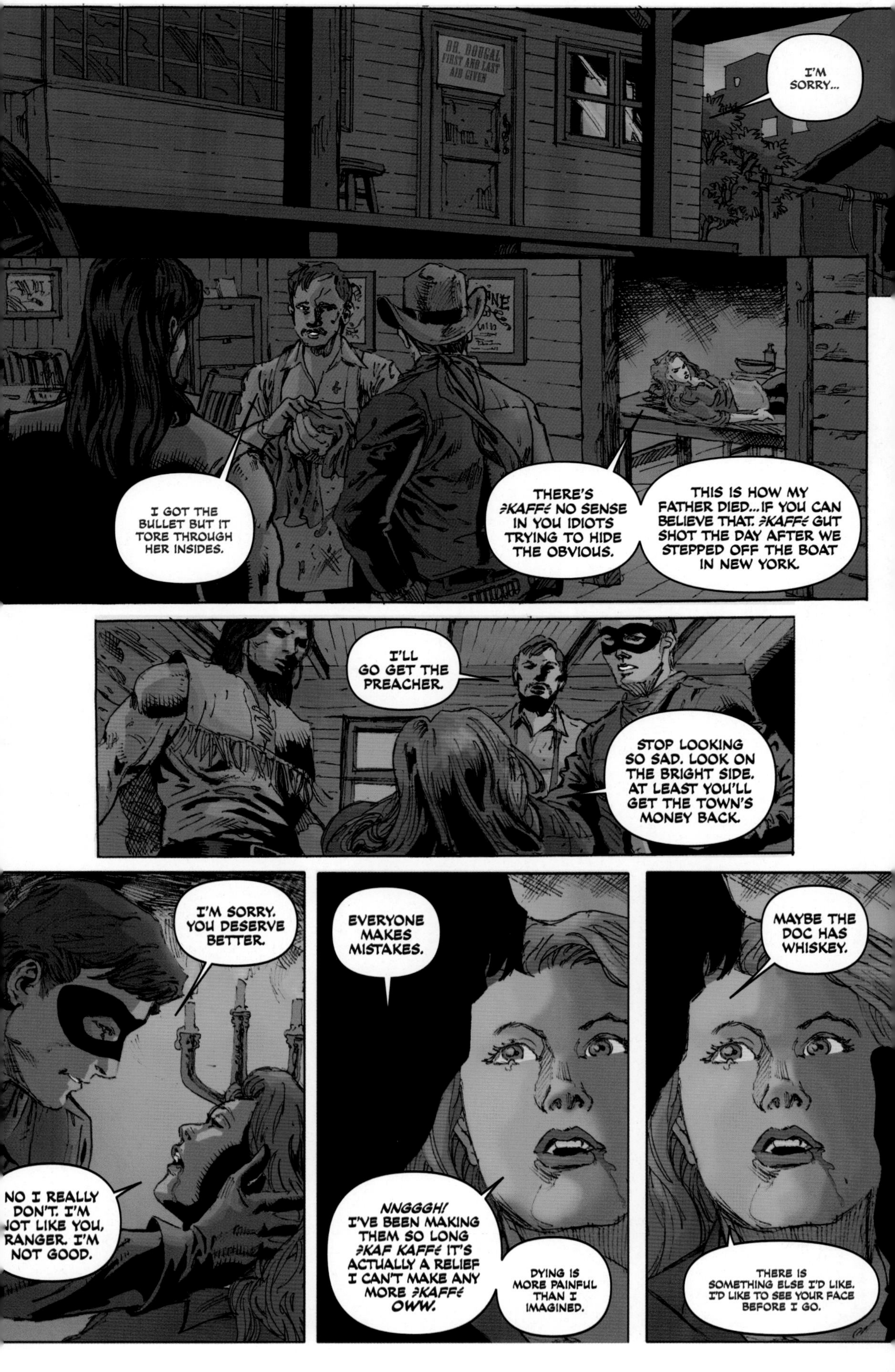
DR. DOUGAL
FIRST AND LAST AID GIVEN
I'M SORRY...
I GOT THE BULLET BUT IT TORE THROUGH HER INSIDES.
THERE'S ≈KAFF≈ NO SENSE IN YOU IDIOTS TRYING TO HIDE THE OBVIOUS.
THIS IS HOW MY FATHER DIED...IF YOU CAN BELIEVE THAT. ≈KAFF≈ GUT SHOT THE DAY AFTER WE STEPPED OFF THE BOAT IN NEW YORK.
I'LL GO GET THE PREACHER.
STOP LOOKING SO SAD. LOOK ON THE BRIGHT SIDE. AT LEAST YOU'LL GET THE TOWN'S MONEY BACK.
I'M SORRY. YOU DESERVE BETTER.
NO I REALLY DON'T. I'M NOT LIKE YOU, RANGER. I'M NOT GOOD.
EVERYONE MAKES MISTAKES.
NNGGGH! I'VE BEEN MAKING THEM SO LONG ≈KAF KAFF≈ IT'S ACTUALLY A RELIEF I CAN'T MAKE ANY MORE ≈KAFF≈ OWW.
DYING IS MORE PAINFUL THAN I IMAGINED.
MAYBE THE DOC HAS WHISKEY.
THERE IS SOMETHING ELSE I'D LIKE. I'D LIKE TO SEE YOUR FACE BEFORE I GO.

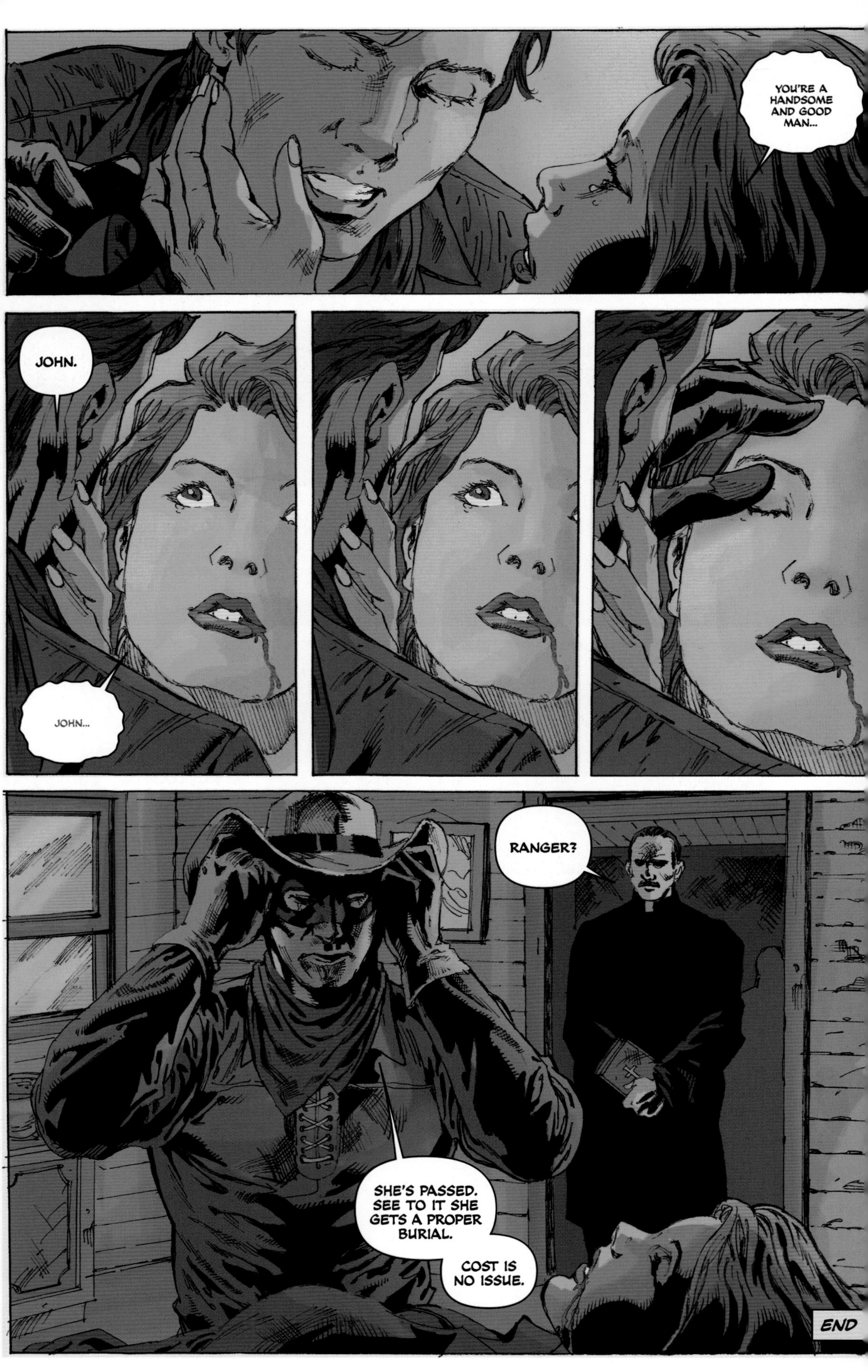
YOU'RE A HANDSOME AND GOOD MAN...
JOHN.
JOHN...
RANGER?
SHE'S PASSED. SEE TO IT SHE GETS A PROPER BURIAL.
COST IS NO ISSUE.
END

BONUS MATERIAL

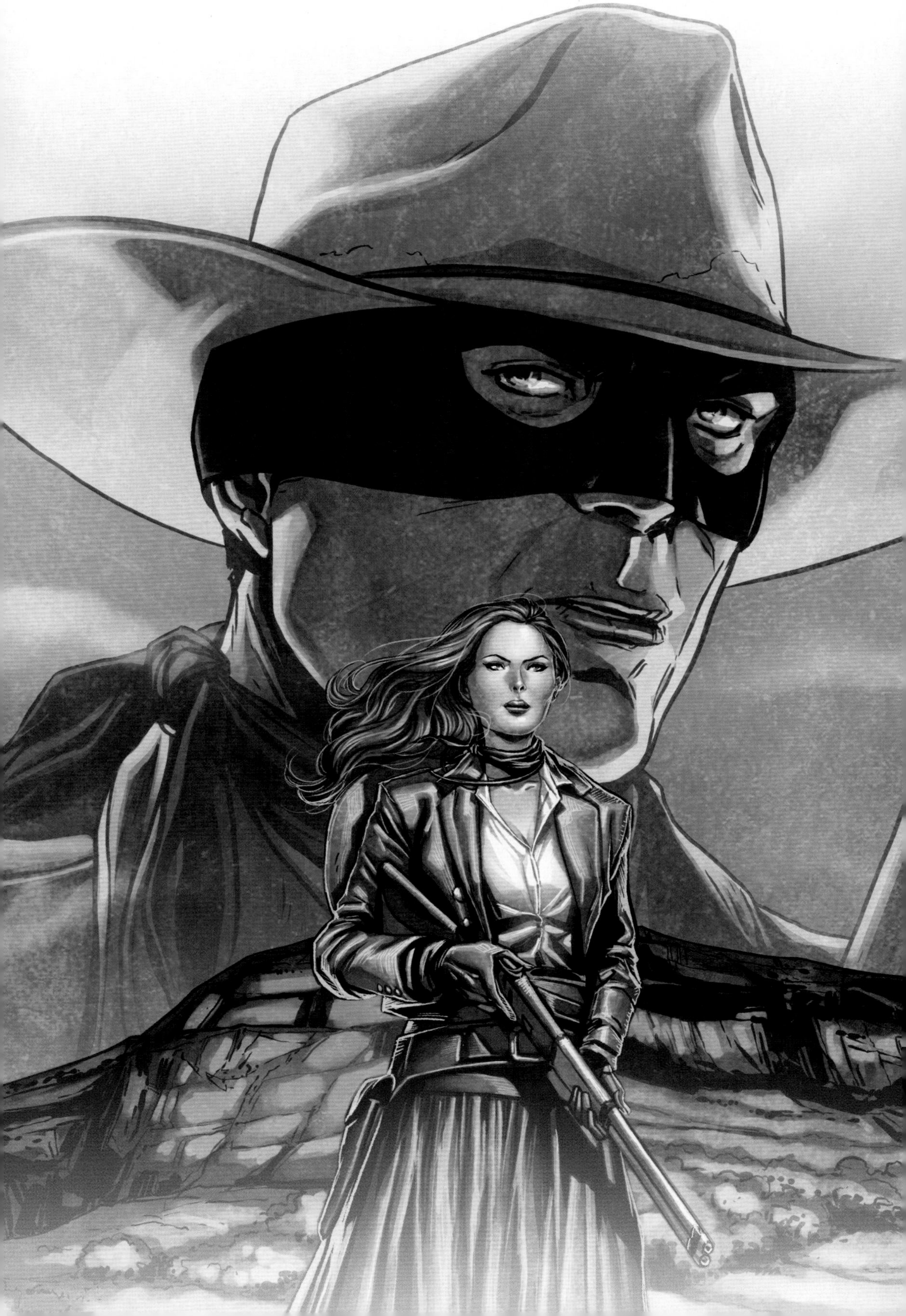

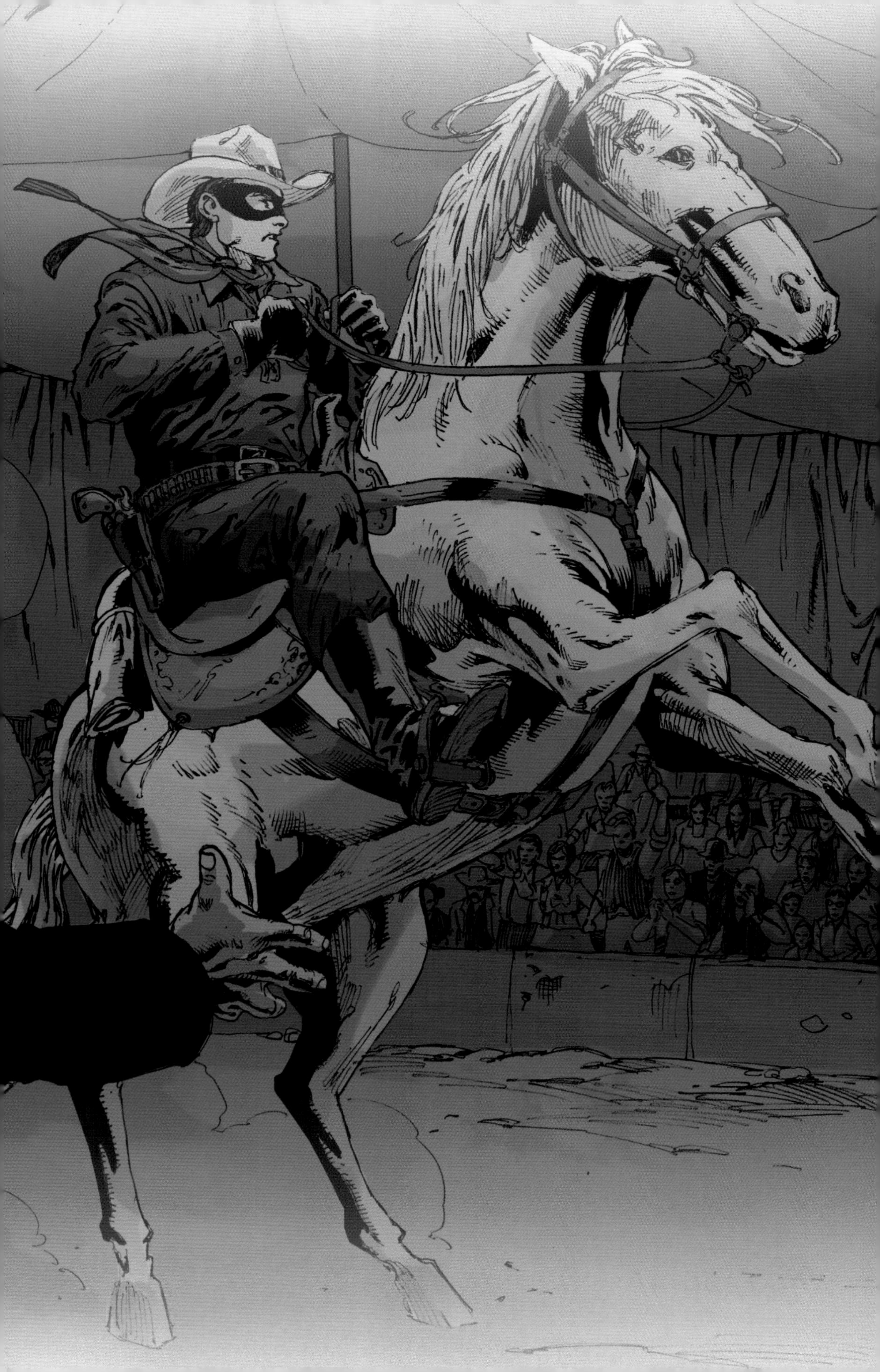

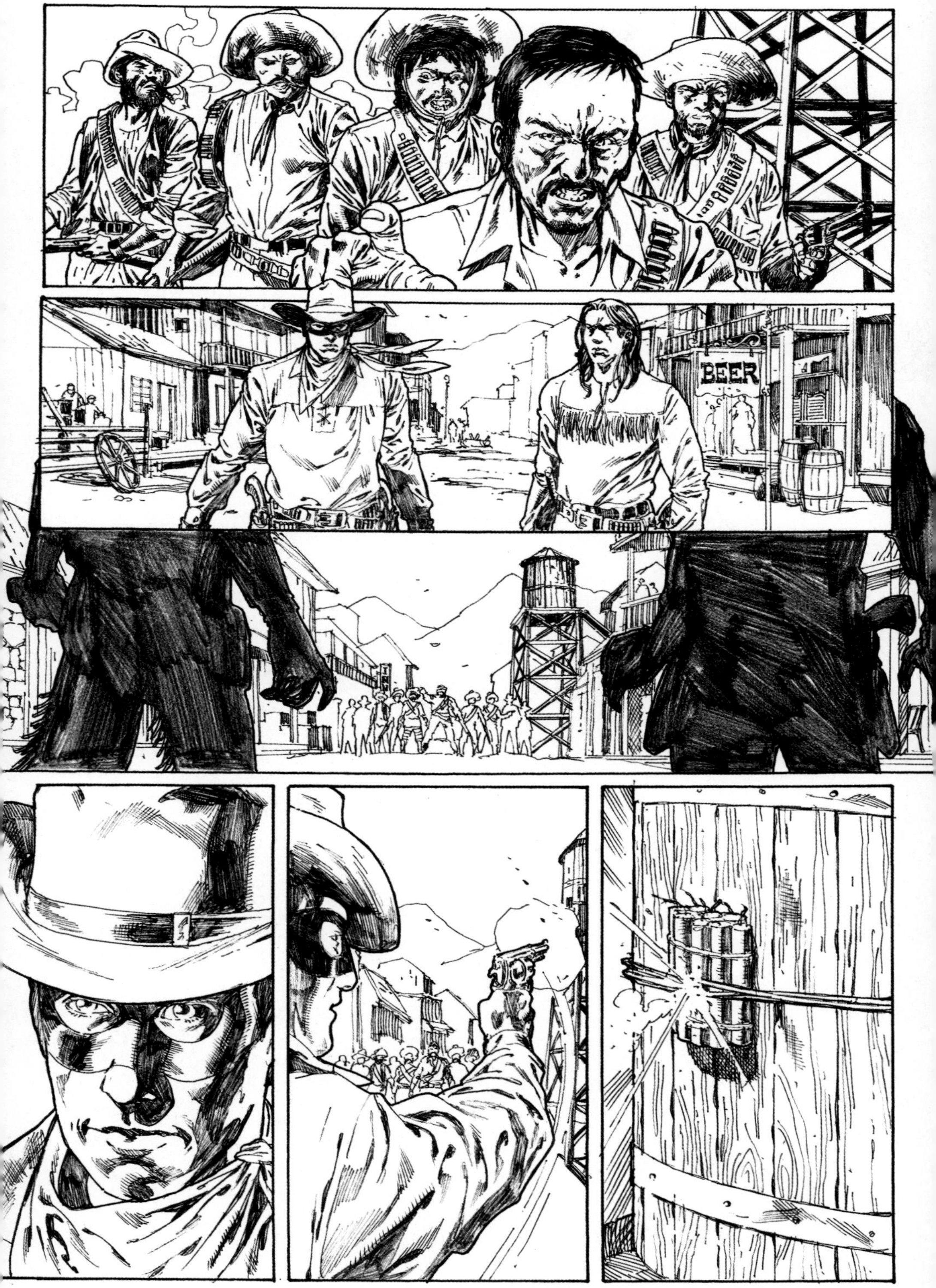
BEER

TLAWS:

ADER: Paul Westbrook, eerily cool under pressure, well groomed and charming.

THY GUY: Cletus

O TEETH GIANT: Grizzly because he's huge and hairy and kills bears.

NNY FELLA: Buck, is dumb as a stick.

EEPY FELLA: Tulsa, the guy is shady, unpredictable and psychotic – loves bladec apons.

w I'm writing this without knowledge of who is drawing it so forgive the lack of sonality directed at you, the artist, but know that I do love collaboration so if yc e ideas on how better to service the story then by all means speak up and lets rk it out. Likewise if you're up against something that seems like a bitch and a h draw lets work it out. With that said lets get to it.

PAG

NEL 1 EXT. TEXAS BORDERTOWN– DAY

e camera squarely focused on a line of men standing shoulder to shoulder in the in street. These are dangerous men, killers and swindlers and God knows what e. Banditos for sure as noted by the handlebar moustaches, sombreros, cigars ar doliers. With regard to color this scene should be bright, warm and exciting. Cl e sky, warm colors on the town.
o://www.pinterest.com/pin/77124212343836036/

NDITO LEADER: I think maybe you should be a mariachi.
NDITO LEADER: That pretty little blue suit needs a blue guitar.

NEL 2 EXT. TEXAS BORDERTOWN– DAY

shift the camera to Lone Ranger and Tonto – on foot, weapons still in their holst sheathes. Strong, determined heroes of legend. Silver and Scout are nowhere tc n.

NE RANGER: Esteban, it doesn't have to be this way. No one has been hurt yet.
NE RANGER: Surrender without a fight, give the town its silver back and I'm sur y'll give you and your men a fair trial.

NEL 3 EXT. TEXAS BORDERTOWN– DAY

der shot of the town and we can clearly see a water tower – this is important – v need the tower. The men are positioned close enough to the tower that when i s BOOM they'll be washed out.

EBAN: Hah! You are two men. We are ten. There will be no trial, amigo.
EBAN: I know you don't shoot to kill so do you really think you can disarm all c before we put bullets in you and your Indio?

NEL 4 TIGHT ON LONE RANGER SMILING

NE RANGER: Let's find out.

he Lone Ranger already has his gun in hand and is shooting not at the banditos but t the water tower.

PANEL 6 EXT. TEXAS BORDERTOWN– DAY

silver bullet hits a small bundle of dynamite strapped to the side of the water ower!

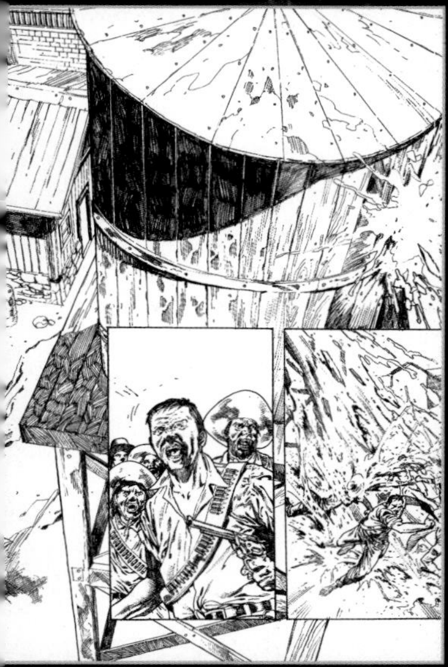

pg. 2

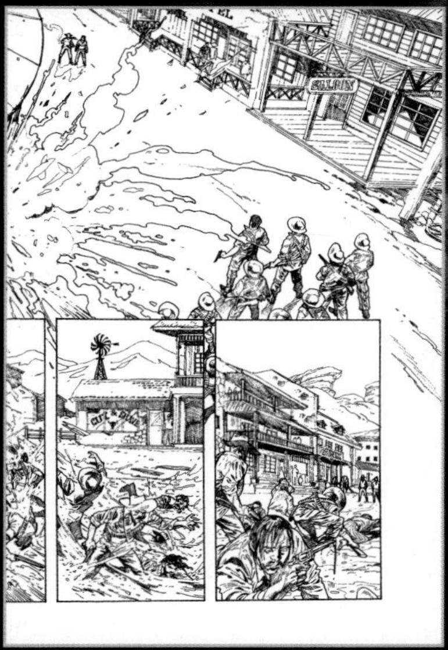

pg. 3

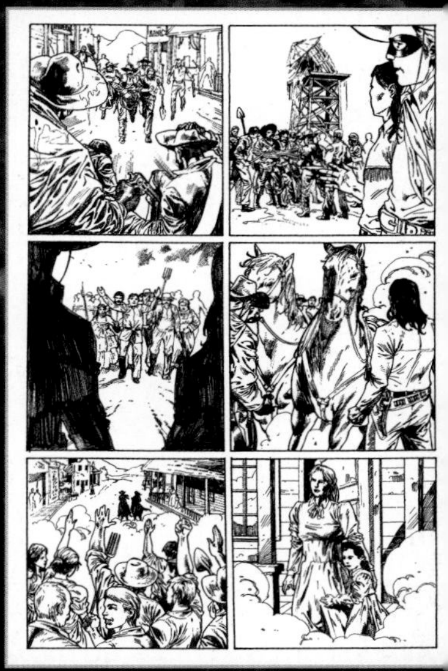

pg. 4

PAGE 2-3 SPREAD EXT. TEXAS BORDERTOWN– DA

ooking here at what Steranko did numerous times to great effect in the adaptation of Outlander, the upper portion and background of the spread gives us scope and cale – We see the explosion of the Water tower. With the inset panels we see the anditos first react to the surprising explosion to their right – the reader's left so the vater and motion sweeps them off the page the water subdues them. I knocks them round, soaks their guns making them useless and generally fucks up any plan they ad of killing our heroes. I'm going to be slightly more specific than I normally woulc e and that's largely for my own purposes. I've spent the better part of a decade resenting westerns that were filthy. What I'd like for us to do is embrace the lie that he old west was a romantic moment in American history in a strictly visual sense. 've set up a private Lone Ranger board on Pinterest with visual reference. We are in he real world but you don't have to concern yourself with pure logic with regard to cenery, just pure cinematography.

PAGE

PANEL 1 EXT. TEXAS BORDERTOWN– DAY

s the banditos struggle to gain their footing, rise to their feet and attack, the ownspeople rush from the surrounding buildings armed with rope and sticks or he townspeople are coming toward them with smiling faces at a decent distance up he street. Some are celebrating. Some in the background dragging banditos to their eet. Whatever you feel best conveys the moment here.

LONE RANGER: If works you can't call it foolish, Tonto.

PANEL 4 EXT. TEXAS BORDERTOWN– DAY

Before the happy townspeople can reach them, both Silver and Scout gallop into the rame between them and Lone Ranger.

TONTO: It would appear the good people of La Plata have regained control of their own.

LONE RANGER: In that case we best be on our way to Red River.

PANEL 5 EXT. TEXAS BORDERTOWN– DAY

Lone Ranger and Tonto riding away from town in the background. In the foreground he townspeople shouting and one man waving. In the shot a little girl and her mother have emerged from a building as Ranger and Tonto are passing.

PANEL 6 EXT. TEXAS BORDERTOWN– DAY

We're now with the mother and little girl looking up at her as our heroes race off under a cloud of dust.

LITTLE GIRL: Momma, who was that masked man?
MOTHER: I don't know, sweetheart.

PANEL 1 EXT. THE WEST – PRE-DAWN
WIDESCREEN SHOT of a stagecoach heading toward the horizon protected by a small troop of men riding behind in the pre dawn light. This is a radical shift in color and lighting from the last scene. The fog should be supernaturally dense – they can't see more than ten feet in front of them. Initially I'm thinking we play on the blue's, black's and milky whites for color and mood for this page and then when we move to page 6 we add violent splashes of red blood for further dramatic effect leading us to page 7 where the warmth of the sun comes up. Time of season might be fair to set it at early spring.

PANEL 2 EXT. THE WEST – PRE-DAWN
Move the camera in closer to the troop following the stage. These guys are all classical western imagery of dusters and Winchesters and red bandannas around their necks.

OLDER TROOPER: The war gave rise ta a restless, vagabond spirit in me. I had little heart to work and after reaching Missouri one of my damn wounds reopened.
YOUNGER TROOPER: Come on Gramp. We done heard this story already!

PANEL 3 EXT. THE WEST – PRED-DAWN
CUT TO: A band of 5 outlaws on horseback hide in a dense, fog enveloped wilderness set against a tremendous vista of mountains. Without their masks these man have faces of character, hardened by untold horrors and experiences, exposed to the elements, lacking in dental care, one is clearly opposed to bathing, but the leader, PAUL WESTBROOK, is a handsome and rugged individual as previously mentioned.
WESTBROOK: Get your masks on boys.

PANEL 4 EXT. THE WEST – PRE-DAWN
Now they are tying on black bandannas in a style that resembles Grifter except the eyes are just holes no pattern or design as they prepare to raid.

WESTBROOK: Remember what I said about the stage driver.

PANEL 5 EXT. THE WEST – DAWN
CUT BACK TO THE: Stage and troop guarding it.

TROOPER: You hear that?
TROOPER #2 (raising his rifle): Horses!

Break this down as you see fit. The basic elements are the outlaws riding in and gunning down the troopers amid dense fog in that combination of blue, black and milky white. Additional colors are now the orange flare of muzzle flashes and the spatter and tearing of violent red blood – as stylized as we can get away with but not gore for the sake of it. Our panels, as many as you like hold the fate of the troopers that are unable to escape their fate. The stage driver is also armed. However we need him alive to carry the message back to town about the robbery so he takes a bullet to the shoulder that not only causes him to drop his weapons, but also to fall from the stage.

PANEL 1 EXT. THE WEST – SUNRISE

WIDE SHOT – Everyone is dead with the exception of the stage driver who is on the ground clutching his bloody shoulder. We're full color golden dawn of our lord now like so: http://www.pinterest.com/pin/77124212343835706/

WESTBROOK: Cletus, will you and Buck be kind enough to retrieve what we came for?

PANEL 2 EXT. THE WEST – SUNRISE

WIDER SHOT – Cletus and Buck pulling a chest from the stage. The driver still on the ground.

WESTBROOK: Who hired these poor dead men to protect the bank's money?
DRIVER: It were Mayor Stamper, Sheriff Masterson and Mr. Hobbs. He's the fella whut runs the bank.

PANEL 3 EXT. THE WEST – SUNRISE

WIDER SHOT – Cletus and Buck stuffing the money into saddlebags

WESTBROOK: The three little pigs of Red River.

PANEL 4 EXT. THE WEST – SUNRISE

On Westbrook smiling charmingly. Cletus and Buck mounting their horses.

WESTBROOK: You head on back and tell them if they want to use this road they can pay us a levy.

PANEL 5 EXT. THE WEST – SUNRISE

Westbrook and the others turn their mounts to ride off. The Driver is on his feet still grabbing at his shoulder wound.

DRIVER: How much should I say the levy is?

PANEL 1 TIGHT ON THE MAYOR

The man is outraged. He cannot believe it.

MAYOR STAMPER: Half, Jesus Christ!
MAYOR STAMPER: *Half?*
SHERIFF: Gentlemen, need I *remind* you we're about to have a *riot* on our hands.

PANEL 2 INT. BANK – DAY

The Sheriff, Mayor and bank owner are there with the stage driver from the last scene.

BANK MANAGER HOBBS: They'll be calling for *my* neck if we don't sort this out, Sheriff!

MAYOR STAMPER: Settle down, Hobbs. The people of Red River are reasonable folk.
SHOUTING OVER PANEL: We want our money!

PANEL 3 EXT RED RIVER – DAY

Establishing shot of the town. This page has some great reference
http://www.pinterest.com/lbuxton25/western-towns/ I'd like to model the town
after Ouray, Colorado. I've been there it is amazing.
http://www.sanjuansilverstage.com/06travel/colorado/ouray/ouray_history.html

SOUTING OVER PANEL: Come out here and face us, Hobbs!
SHOUTING OVER PANEL: We've come fer whut's ours!

PANEL 4 EXT. BANK – DAY

We're in town now where we clearly see the RED RIVER TRUST and there is a mob of
angry people out front confronting the aforementioned three pigs – the Mayor, Sheriff
and bank man Hobbs. These guys should all look well groomed and respectable. The
sheriff is Gary Cooper or John Wayne clean and inspiring. There should be no hint that
these men are criminals and con men. We also need to see Rick Coolidge who I
imagine is inspired by Viggo Mortenson from Appaloosa. We cut to the town of Red
River where an angry mob of ranchers and farmers has gathered. They're demanding
their money from the bank. The Sheriff, Mayor and Bank owner are trying to calm the
crowd – telling them they'll get their money when the insurance company reimburses
them for the robberies.

MAYOR STAMPER: Everyone please calm down!
RICK: The hell with calm, Stamper! Something's got to be done!
MAN #1: Rick's right! It's our damn money and we were fools to give it to you!
SHERIFF: Now hold on a minute! You'll all get your money once the insurance comes
through.

PANEL 5 EXT. BANK – DAY

We have a lot going on here obviously, but the general idea is that Rick is whipping the
crowd into a frenzy. They're all in favor as he takes the lead voice in their argument.

RICK: For half a year we've heard you sing that tune, Henry! We're fed up and ready
to go after them ourselves!
MAYOR: That would be an ill-advised course of action and you know it!
MAYOR: They took down hired guns like they were nothing!

PANEL 1 EXT. BANK – DAY

On an impassioned Rick.

RICK: Hired guns _we_ paid for!

PANEL 2 EXT. BANK – DAY

On the sheriff with his two cohorts.

SHERIFF: Now before ya'll go off half cocked looking for a fight. Just give us a little more time and we'll have it sorted.
SHERIFF MASTERSON: You'll get what's owed.

PANEL 3 EXT. BANK – DAY
Rick has turned to the crowd. He has them eating out of his hand.

RICK: You bet we will, sheriff! I've already sent word to the men I think can truly help us in our hour of need.
RICK: Men who get results. Men that don't take hard earned money from folks because they believe in justice over personal gain.

PANEL 4 EXT. BANK – DAY
The mayor's turn to speak up.

MAYOR: What are you talking about, Coolidge? Who ***are*** these men?
RICK: I've sent word to the Lone Ranger. He and his companion have agreed to take up our cause.

PANEL 5 EXT. BANK – DAY
The three pigs have lost control of the crowd and the situation.

SHERIFF: Now you hold on a damned minute, Rick Coolidge! This is a town matter and no place for some masked man and his pet injun!

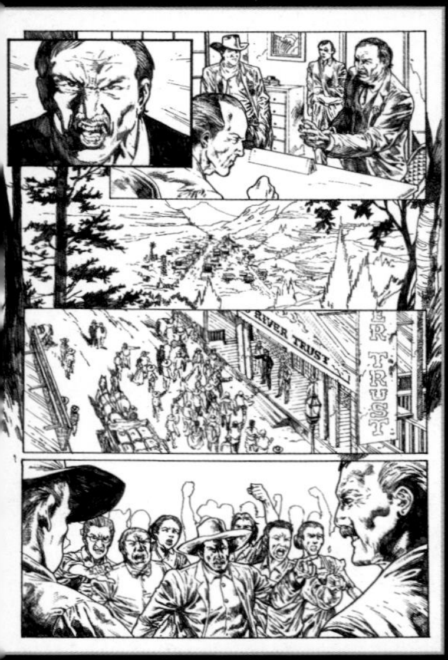
pg. 8

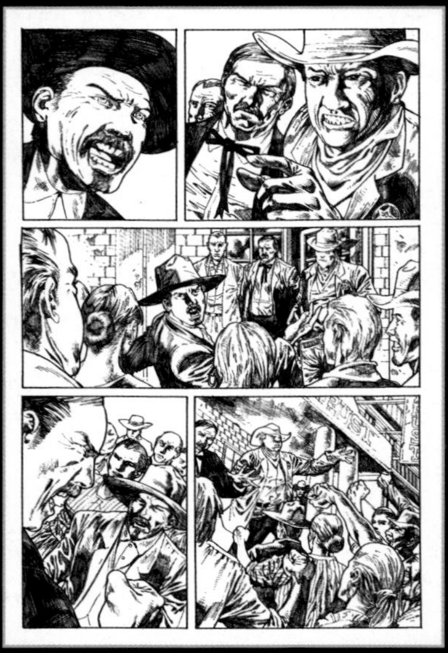
pg. 9

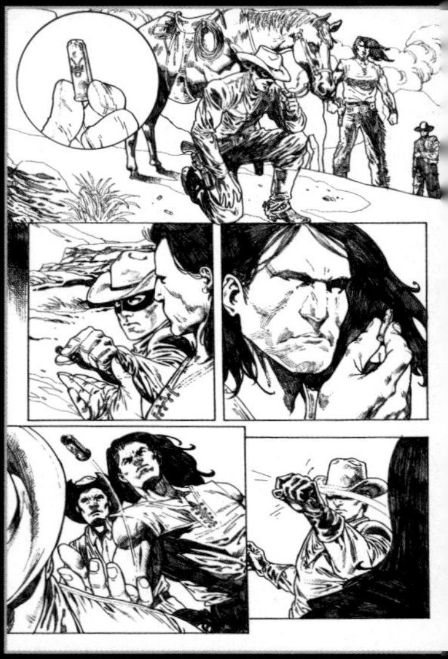
pg. 10

PAGE 10

PANEL 1 EXT. THE WEST – DAY
Lone Ranger's gloved hand reaches for a brass bullet casing on the ground. The casing has a symbol etched into it.

PANEL 2 EXT. THE WEST – DAY

one Ranger and Tonto with the stage driver who has shown them where he was
mbushed. The bodies have been removed but the shell casings from the bullets that
vere fired remain. Lone Ranger examines the brass casing.
RIVER: This here's the spot, Ranger. We wuz slowed to a crawl on account of the
norning's weather.
RIVER: Ya couldn't see the hand in front of your face by golly, but they came right
ut of the fog like it were a sunny day.
ONE RANGER: This is hand rolled casing. Quality work too.

ANEL 3 EXT. THE WEST – DAY
one Ranger handing the casing to Tonto.

ONE RANGER: Tonto, do you recognize that symbol?

ANEL 4 EXT. THE WEST – DAY
n Tonto examining the casing.

ONTO: The upside down man means death. Apache sometimes use it.

ANEL 5 EXT. THE WEST – DAY
onto tossing the casing back to Lone Ranger – it tumbles through the air.

ONE RANGER: The men that attacked you...
RIVER: They wore masks, but I don't think they were Apache.

ANEL 6 EXT. THE WEST – DAY
one Ranger snatches the casing out of the air.

ONE RANGER: You said they had no trouble with the fog.
ONTO: They know the land well. Might even be hiding in Red River.
ONE RANGER: The sheriff will want to see this.

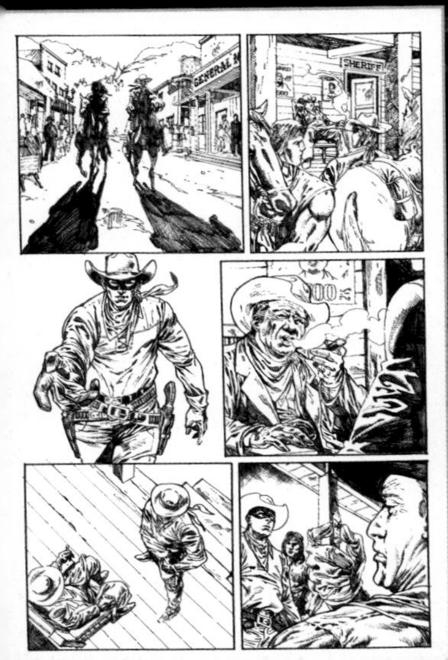
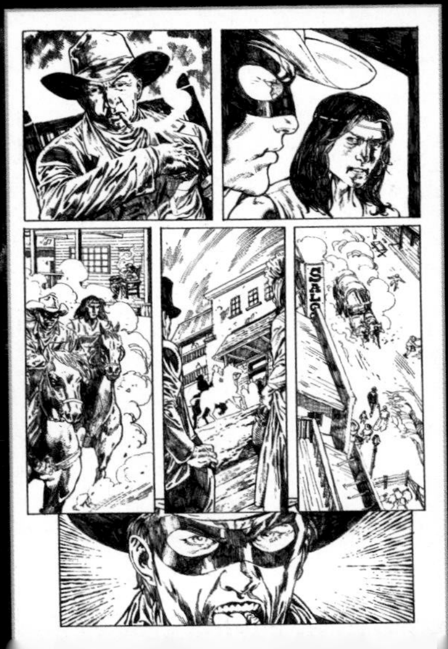
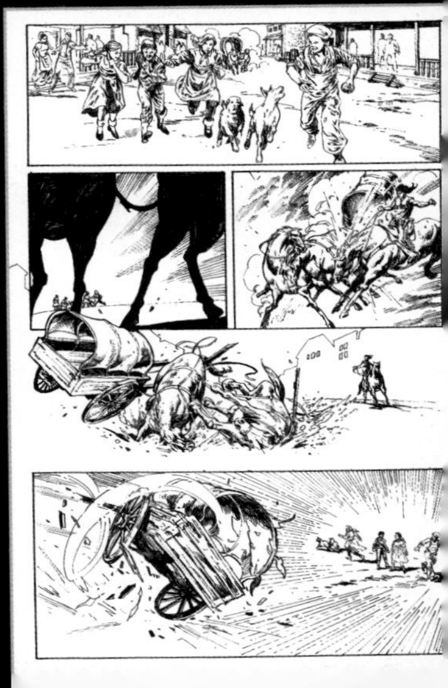

PANEL 1 EXT. RED RIVER – LATE AFTERNOON
Lone Ranger and Tonto riding into Red River during the late afternoon. Curious onlookers watch the strange duo but do not approach them. Long shadows for dramatic effect.

PANEL 2 EXT. RED RIVER – LATE AFTERNOON
Ranger and Tonto dismount in front of the SHERIFF'S OFFICE. Wanted posters paper litter the outside wall. The sheriff is seated in a chair outside the open door of the office. Nonplussed, he smokes a hand rolled cigarette taking in the impending sunset

PANEL 3 EXT. RED RIVER – LATE AFTERNOON
Sheriff's POV looking up from chair level at Lone Ranger who has his gloved hand extended – light pouring in behind him.

LONE RANGER: Hello Sheriff, I'm...

PANEL 4 EXT. RED RIVER – LATE AFTERNOON
The sheriff exhales smoke and doesn't shake his hand.

SHERIFF MASTERSON: I know who the hell you are.
LONE RANGER: We're here to help not step on your toes, Sheriff.

PANEL 5 EXT. RED RIVER – LATE AFTERNOON
Lone Ranger fishing in his pocket for the bullet casing.

SHERIFF MASTERSON: I'll tell you how you can help. Climb back on them horses ride back the way you came.
LONE RANGER: I have something you might want to see.

PANEL 6 EXT. RED RIVER – LATE AFTERNOON
The sheriff holds the casing and examines it.

LONE RANGER: I found it in the woods where the stage was robbed. You'll notice it as hand rolled and the symbol...

PANEL 1 EXT. RED RIVER – LATE AFTERNOON
Looking blankly at Lone Ranger and Tonto, the sheriff deposits the casing into the breast pocket of his shirt – cigarette dangling from his lip – an expression of indifference on his face.

PANEL 2 EXT. RED RIVER – LATE AFTERNOON
Lone Ranger and Tonto exchange a look.

PANEL 3 EXT. RED RIVER – LATE AFTERNOON
Lone Ranger and Tonto ride toward the camera – in the background the sheriff is still there in the chair outside the office.

TONTO: The sheriff is not pleased.
LONE RANGER: You can't blame him. He's the law in this town and we're unwelcome strangers.
TONTO: He places his pride above the needs of the town.

PANEL 4 EXT. RED RIVER – LATE AFTERNOON
They continue to ride through town.

LONE RANGER: We'll tread lightly where the sheriff's concerned. We should head out to Coolidge's...
FROM OFF PANEL: Oh my God! Someone stop that wagon!

PANEL 5 EXT. RED RIVER – LATE AFTERNOON
A wagon without a driver comes around a corner at the far end of town moving at breakneck speed. People are reacting – anyone in the street has the potential to be run down.

PANEL 6 TIGHT ON LONE RANGER

LONE RANGER: KIAA SILVER! GO!

PANEL 1 EXT. TOWN – LATE AFTERNOON
There are kids playing in the dusty street chasing after mangy stray dogs and they don't see the runaway wagon hurtling toward them. Happy smiling faces. Laughter fills the air.

PANEL 2 EXT. TOWN – LATE AFTERNOON
Clearly the children are doomed. Time is running out as the wagon draws closer.

PANEL 3 EXT. TOWN – LATE AFTERNOON
A dusty, thundering trick shot with the camera where the legs of the horses seem much closer to the oblivious children than they really are.

PANEL 4 EXT. TOWN – LATE AFTERNOON
TONTO selflessly urges SCOUT into one of the two horses pulling the runaway wagon. The impact is tremendous forcing one horse to collide with the other.

PANEL 5 EXT. TOWN – LATE AFTERNOON
The wagon horses are collapsing at an awkward angle as the wagon starts to turn and outpace them.

PANEL 6 EXT. TOWN – LATE AFTERNOON
The leads between the fallen horses and the wagon snap, but the wagon continues its forward motion at a broadside angle that will cause it to roll like an overturned car in an action movie. The rolling of the car will directly threaten the children in the street.

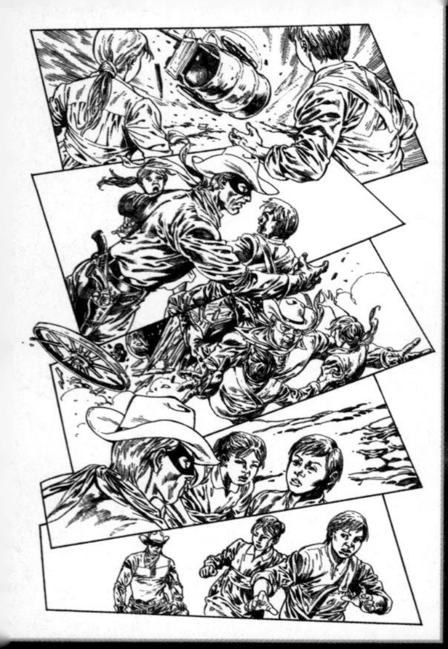
pg. 14

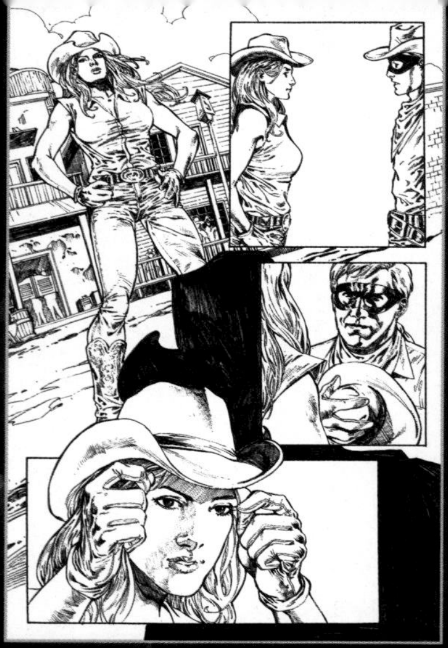
pg. 15

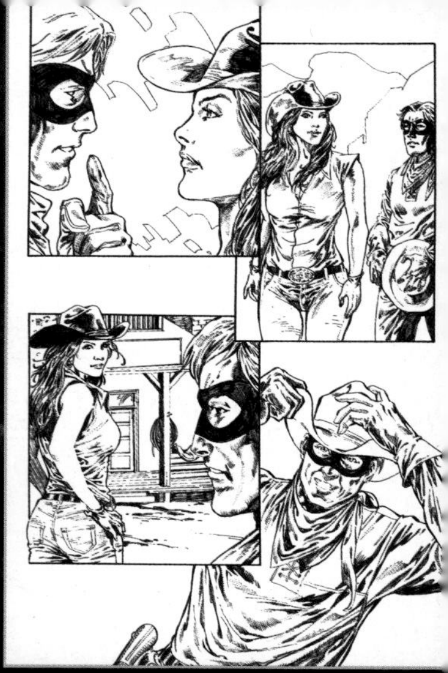
pg. 16

PAGE 14

PANEL 1 EXT. TOWN – LATE AFTERNOON

Two children are in the foreground with their backs to the camera as the wagon rolls over and over coming apart in chunks and hurtling uncontrollably toward them. The other kids and dogs have bolted to safety.

PANEL 2 EXT. TOWN – LATE AFTERNOON

Lone Ranger cutting through the panel – grabbing the kids – one in each arm – that wagon seemingly inches from impacting them.

PANEL 3 EXT. TOWN – LATE AFTERNOON

Lone Ranger dives! The wagon narrowly misses his feet as it rips and splinters through the street.

PANEL 4 EXT. TOWN – LATE AFTERNOON

Lone Ranger lies on the ground with the kids – everyone is safe.

LONE RANGER: Everyone okay?

PANEL 5 EXT. TOWN – LATE AFTERNOON

The kids running away from him like the kid in groundhog day after Bill Murray catches him falling out of the tree. Lone Ranger standing and brushing the dust from his pants. Tonto is there on horseback.

LONE RANGER: You're welcome.
FROM OFF PANEL: I would have thanked you...

PAGE 15

PANEL 1 EXT. TOWN – LATE AFTERNOON –BIG PANEL

Here she is FIONA DOYLE looking more like a cowboy than a flower in the desert. She has the hat, she has the jeans, chaps and button down shirt. The boots and the sex appeal without having to be all curves – modest proportions. She looks like she's been working. There's sassiness to her body language. She stands outside a LIVERY and STABLE, one boot on a bail of hay. Here's the thing about Fiona as well, she's just as tall as the Ranger. Keep Tonto out of the scene until Panel 4 on the next page. This should feel like Lone Ranger and Fiona are the only people in the world.

FIONA: That was the bravest thing I've ever seen.

PANEL 2 EXT. TOWN – LATE AFTERNOON
Fiona stands across from Lone Ranger. He is awestruck. Silent.

FIONA: You act like you've never seen a woman before.

PANEL 3 EXT. TOWN – LATE AFTERNOON
Lone Ranger has his hat in hand, realizing of course that he's speaking to a lady. She's torturing him.

LONE RANGER: I...I have...plenty of times. Seen women. I mean.
FIONA: My name's Fiona Doyle. Don't worry I won't ask yours.
LONE RANGER: Why not?

PANEL 4 ON FIONA
Using her hands she mimics wearing a mask.

PANEL 1 EXT. TOWN – LATE AFTERNOON
Lone Ranger is awkward. Smiling uncomfortably hat in his hands.

LONE RANGER: Right. The mask.
FIONA: You know I thought you'd be taller?
LONE RANGER: Why would you think that?

PANEL 2 EXT. TOWN – LATE AFTERNOON

FIONA: There's so **many** tall tales circulating about the mysterious **Lone Ranger**.
FIONA: A person might think you could look in a second story window without use of a ladder.
LONE RANGER: You have a funny way of talking, Miss Doyle.

PANEL 3 EXT. TOWN – LATE AFTERNOON
Fiona slyly walking away. She peers back over her shoulder. She's got him hooked.

FIONA: The burden of being over educated.
FIONA: Well I imagine you've got enough trouble to deal with so I won't contribute.

PANEL 4 EXT. TOWN – LATE AFTERNOON
Lone Ranger awkwardly putting his hat on backward with both hands.

LONE RANGER: Its no trouble, Miss Doyle. No trouble at all.

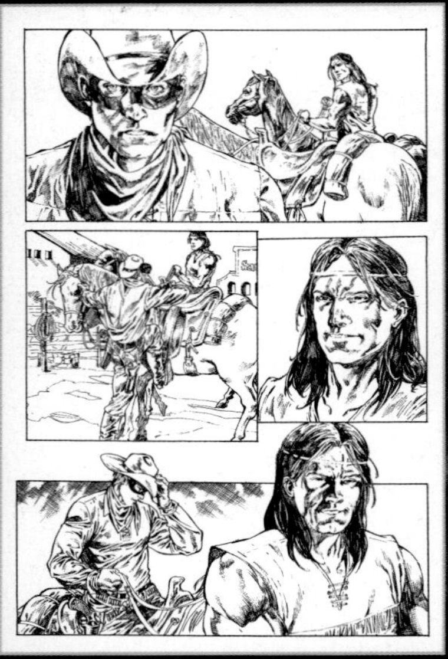
pg. 17

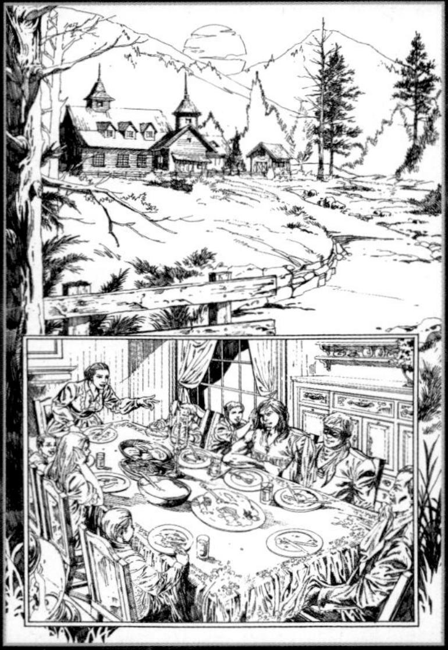
pg. 18

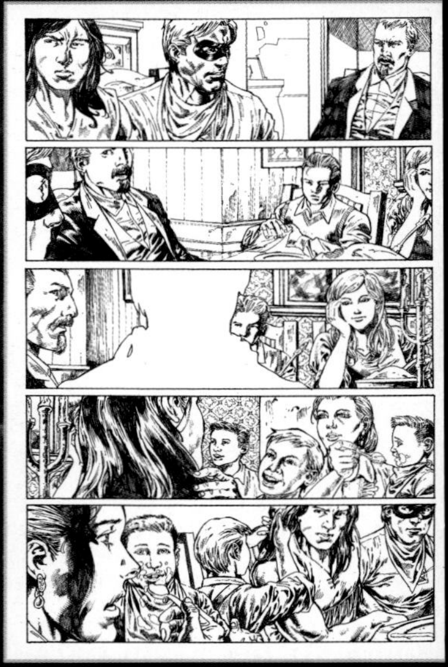
pg. 19

PAGE 17

PANEL 1 EXT. TOWN – LATE AFTERNOON

Pull the camera back so that Tonto is now in the shot sitting on Scout and holding the lead for Silver. Lone Ranger oblivious to the fact that his hat is on backward.

TONTO: I don't think she meant she was troubling you.
TONTO: She meant that she ***is*** trouble.
LONE RANGER: Really? I didn't hear it that way.

PANEL 2 EXT. TOWN – LATE AFTERNOON

Lone Ranger mounting Silver.

TONTO: That's because you were looking more than you were than listening.
LONE RANGER: That's not what happened at all.

PANEL 3 EXT. TOWN – LATE AFTERNOON

On Tonto with the faintest Mona Lisa smile.

TONTO: Then why's your hat on backward?

PANEL 4 EXT. TOWN – LATE AFTERNOON

Ranger reaching up to touch his hat in the background realizing it is true and being embarrassed. Tonto in the foreground with that smile.

LONE RANGER (whisper): Dammit!

PAGE 18

PANEL 1 EXT. COOLIDGE RANCH – EVENING – BIG

An establishing shot of the large ranch house. Lets continue giving the reader lavish set pieces.

PANEL 2 INT. HOUSE – EVENING

A rustic wooden dinner table for the ages covered in lace and topped with bowls of potatoes, vegetables, corn, platters of meat, a turkey, chickens, steaks. The Coolidge family is large with five children from 16 (the only girl who happens to be staring dreamily at Ranger) down to a 3-yr old with a face full of food. Both the panels on this page can be big and encompassing. Lone Ranger (still wearing the mask) and Tonto seated at the table and are a major point of focus for the children. Mom chastises the kids.

MRS. MARTHA COOLIDGE: William you stop your staring! Bart I will not say it again leave Mr. Tonto's hair alone!
MRS. COOLIDGE: I am ever so sorry. My boys are an excitable lot.
LONE RANGER: Not at all. This chicken is delicious, Mrs. Coolidge.
RICK: I sure am grateful to you men for coming all the way up here.

PANEL 1 INT. HOUSE – NIGHT

Pan the camera around the table as the dialogue unfolds. It might be fun to play on elements of Tonto being so stoic in the face of obnoxious young boys and the sort of "dreamy stare" from the daughter ala Raiders of the Lost Ark. They're eating through the panels until the next page where Mrs. Coolidge and the kids start cleaning up and pulling plates from the table.

LONE RANGER: It's our pleasure, Mr. Coolidge.
LONE RANGER: The sheriff is none to happy, but we'll do our best to help catch the men responsible.

PANEL 2 INT. HOUSE – NIGHT

RICK: Masterson tends to rub people the wrong way but he's a good man.
LONE RANGER: You know anyone around here that rolls his own ammunition?

PANEL 3

RICK: A handful maybe.
TONTO: Any of them of mixed blood or have an apache wife?

PANEL 4

RICK: I don't think so...
MRS. COOLIDGE: What about that fella that lives out on Elk ridge, Rick? He looks like he could be...

PANEL 5

RICK: Preston Chavez? Nah, he's half Mexican.
MRS. COOLIDGE (looking at Tonto): I'm sorry, did I offend you?
TONTO: No. I'm Potawatomi. We don't offend easily.

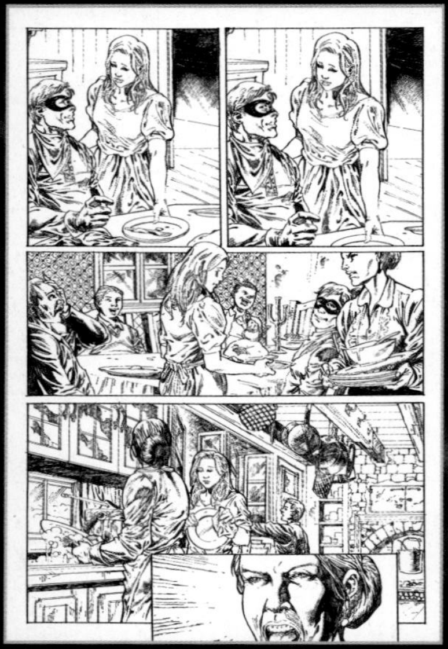

pg. 20

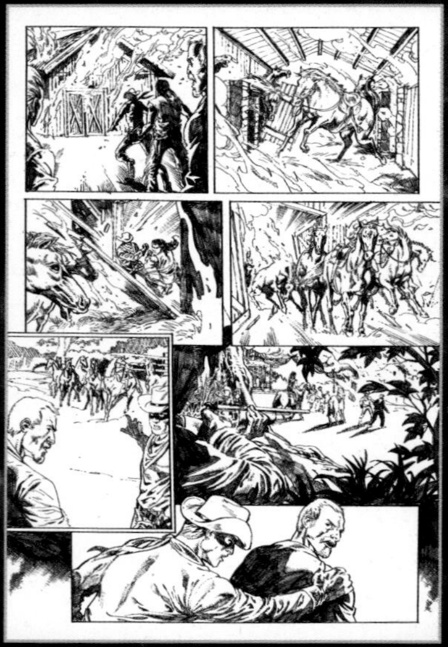

pg. 21

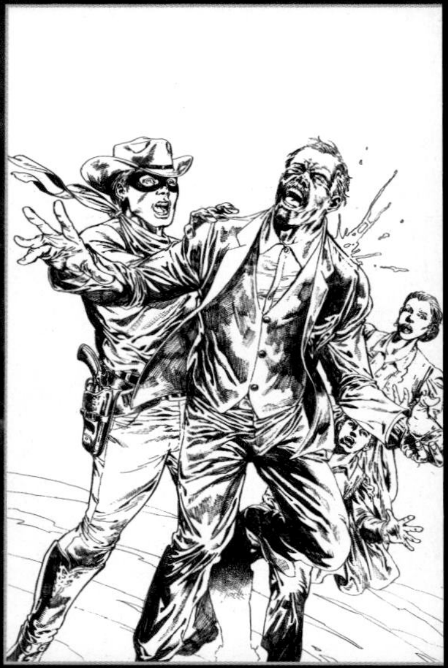

pg. 22

PAGE 20

PANEL 1 INT. HOUSE – EVENING

The meal is over. Mom and the kids are helping to clear the table. The daughter is taking Lone Ranger's plate.

DAUGHTER: Mister Ranger, sir, are you finished?
LONE RANGER: yes, thank you.

PANEL 2

Same shot only the girl hasn't moved. She's smiling blankly at the Lone Ranger who looks uncomfortable.

PANEL 3

Rick rolls his eyes. Mrs. Coolidge comes in raging. Her brothers LAUGHING.

MRS. COOLIDGE: Maybelle Marie Coolidge, quit staring at that man! There's dishes to be done!

PANEL 4 INT. KITCHEN – EVENING

A spacious country kitchen with lots of windows – imperfect glass. Warm and inviting Mother is reprimanding her daughter. There is an unnatural orange light that grows brighter from this panel to the next.

MRS. COOLIDGE: Maybelle you might be sixteen, but there are ways to behave on front of guests and...
BROTHER POINTING AT THE WINDOW: Ma! Loook...!

PANEL 5 ON MRS. COOLIDGE

Orange light reflecting on her face.

MOTHER: RIIIICCCKKK!!!

ANEL 1 EXT. RANCH – NIGHT

he stables are on FIRE! As everyone is coming out of the house.

ANEL 2 INT. SABLE – NIGHT

he walls are on fire and among the horses are SILVER and SCOUT! Silver rears up
n hind legs.

ANEL 3 INT. SABLE – NIGHT

one Ranger, Tonto and Rick come crashing through the front door of the stables.
re everywhere!

ONE RANGER: Get as many as you can!

ANEL 3 EXT. SABLE – NIGHT

orses come charging out of the barn, some on fire.

ANEL 4 EXT. SABLE – NIGHT

he horse appear to be clear of the raging fire. Lone Ranger has Silver's lead – Rick is
the shot.

ONE RANGER: A few were lost but most of the made it out!
CK: Who would do this?

ANEL 5 EXT. SABLE – NIGHT

the foreground at a distance there's a gunman on his belly with an exceptionally
ng rifle. In the background the fire rages. Tonto swinging up onto Scout's back. Rick
d Ranger are close together.

ONTO: Whoever it is might be in the area!
ONE RANGER: Be careful! Rick, get your family back inside.
CK: I have to look in the stable again!

ANEL 6 EXT. STABLE – NIGHT

one Ranger grabs Rick positioning the man between him self and the oncoming
llet that no one see's.

ONE RANGER: Its too late! The fire's too big and...

PAGE 22 SPLASH

one Ranger is holding onto Rick as the Bullet Mean for him slams into Rick's back.
ife and family in the background or somewhere so they can witness it. Maybe an
xplosion of blood to drive home what has happened.

ICK: Uhngghh!!
AUGHTER: Daddyyyyyy!!!
OTHER: Riiickk!!!

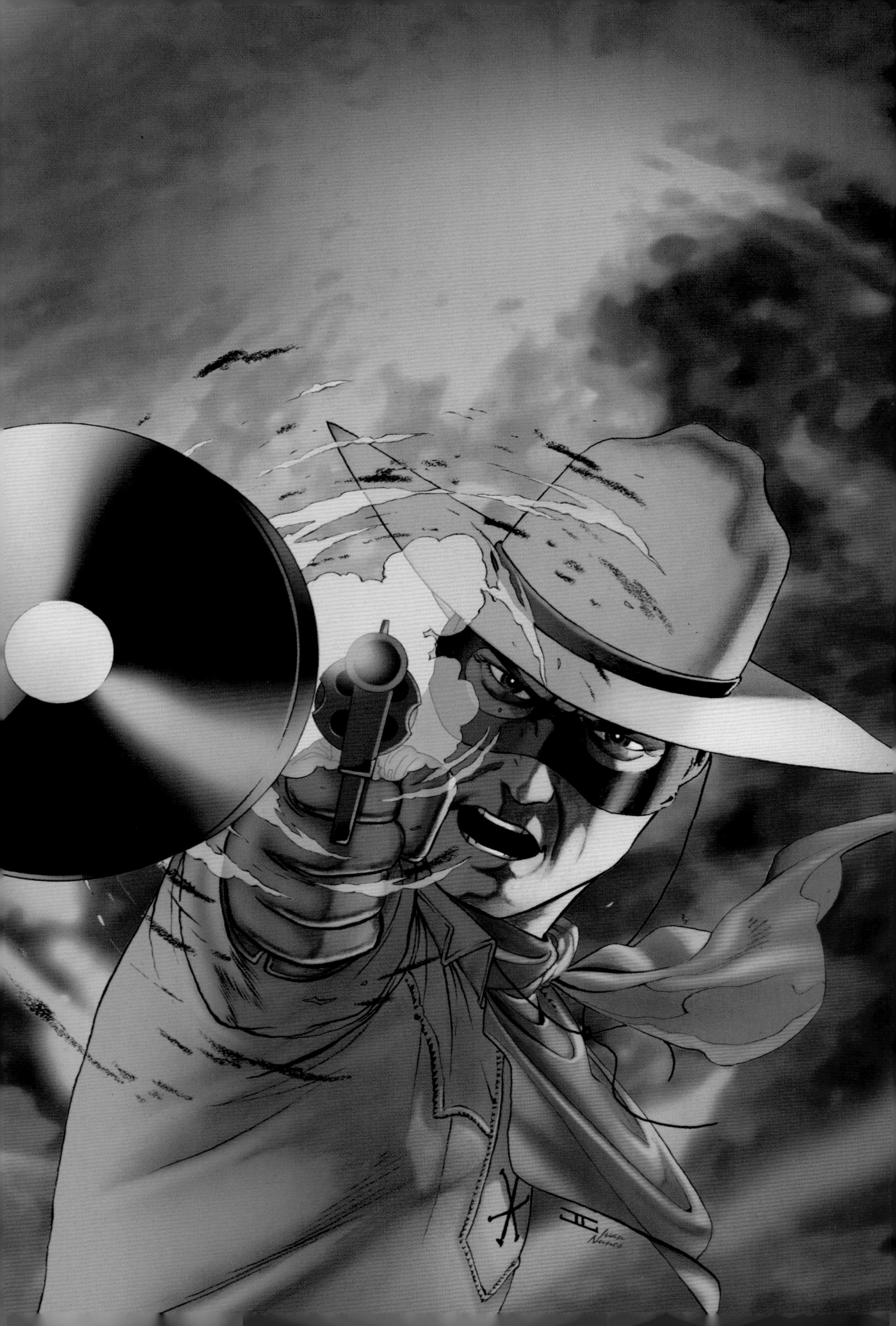

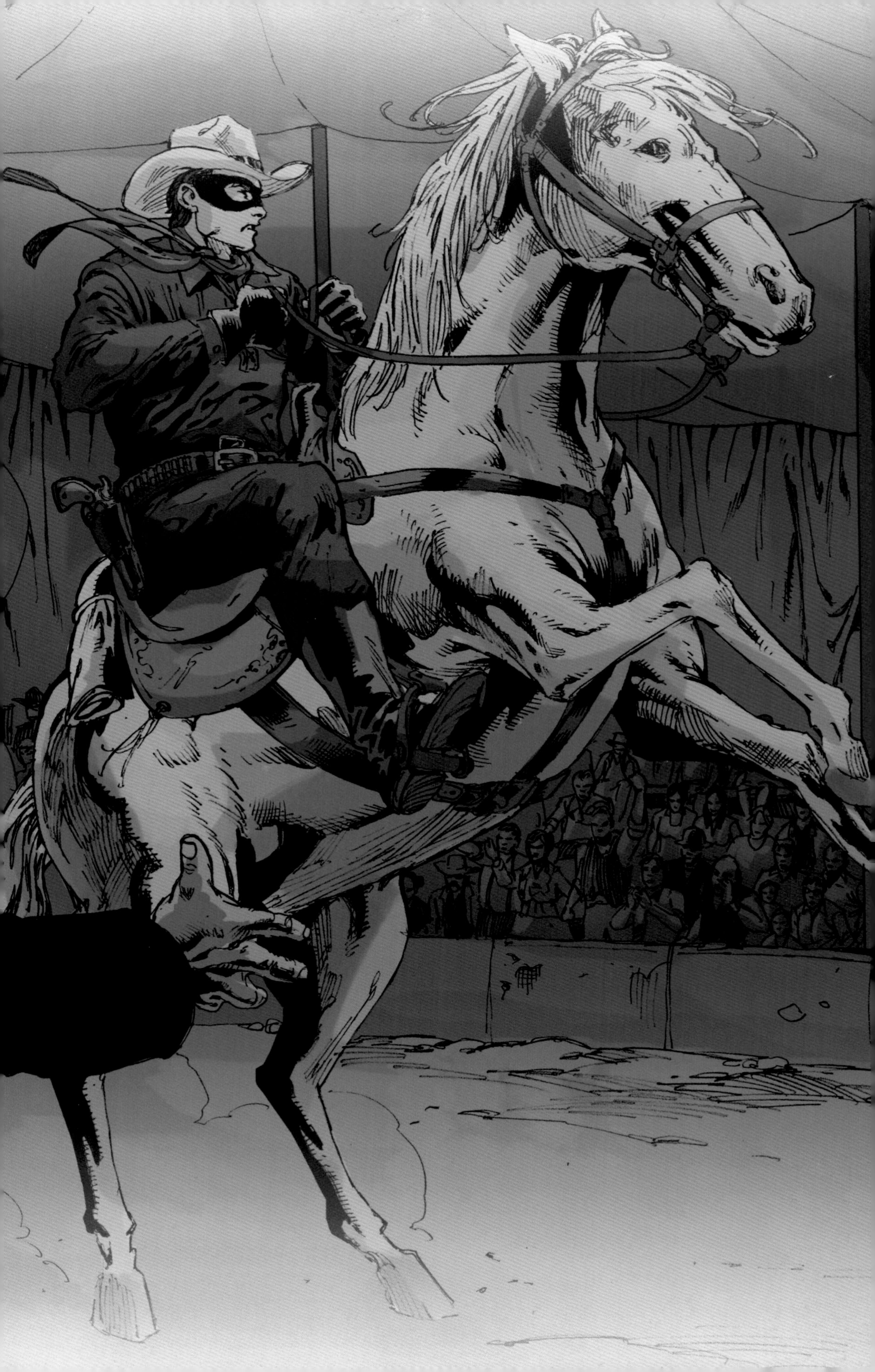

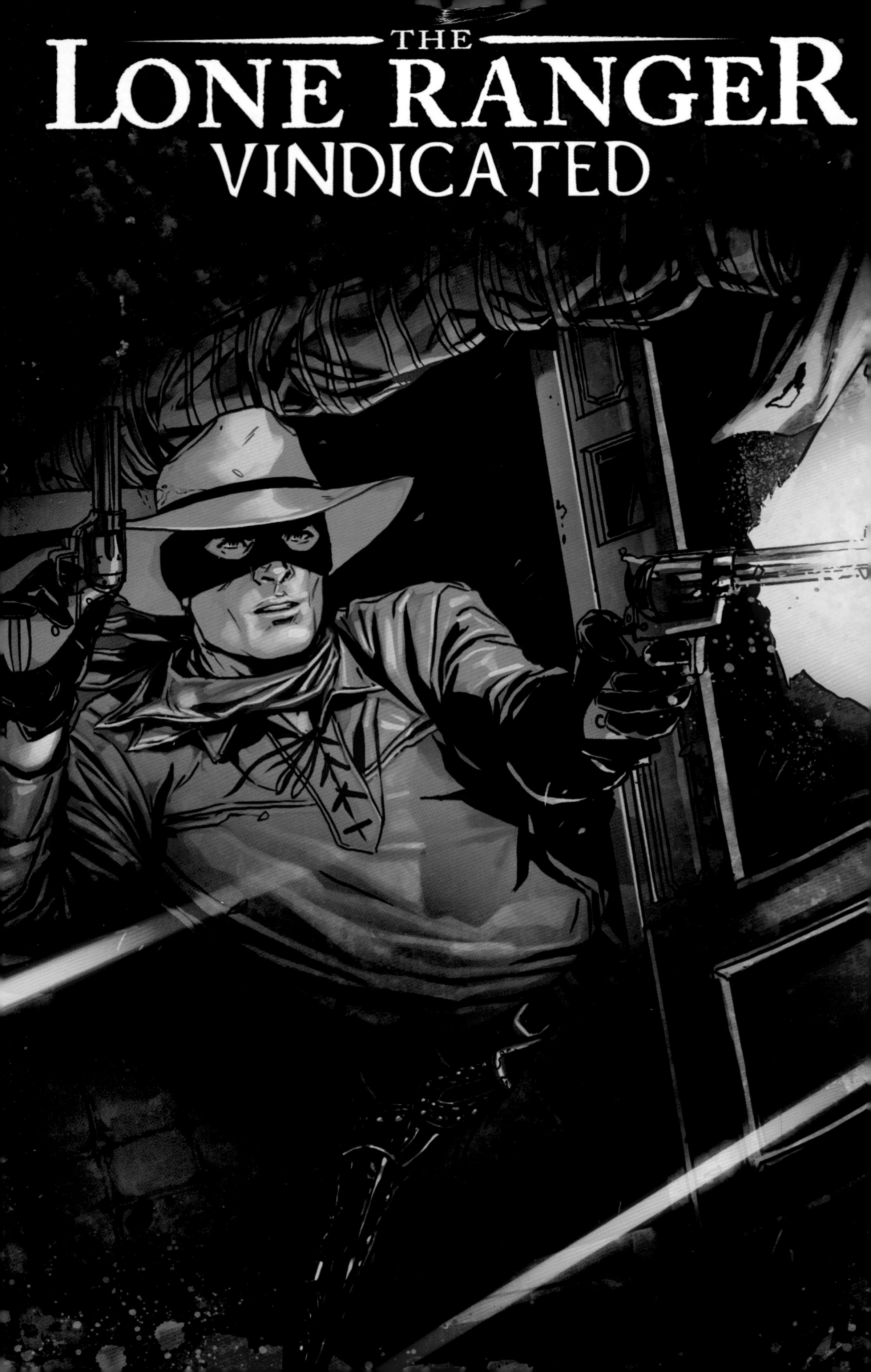
THE
LONE RANGER®
VINDICATED